Portuguese Trade and Socio-Economic Changes On the Western Coast of India (1600-1663)

Afzal Ahmad

Originals
Delhi-110052

Distributed By:
D K Publishers Distributors P Ltd.
4834/24, Ansari Road, Darya Ganj,
New Delhi-110002
Phones: 3278368, 3261465
Fax : 3264368
visit us at: www.dkpd.com
e-mail: dkpd@del3.vsnl.net.in

First Published 2000

ISBN 81-7536-197-2

Published By:
ORIGINALS
(an imprint of Low Price Publications)
A-6, Nimri Commercial Centre,
Near Ashok Vihar Phase-IV,
Delhi-110052
Phone: 7401672, 7452453
visit us at: www.lppindia.com
e-mail: lpp@nde.vsnl.net.in

Printed At:
D K Fine Art Press P Ltd.
Delhi-110052

PRINTED IN INDIA

CONTENTS

List of Abbreviations

ACE	Assentos do Conselho do Estado.
ACF	Assentos do Conselho da Fazenda.
AHU	Arquivo Histórico Ultramarino, Lisbon.
ANTT	Arquivo Nacional da Torre do Tombo, Lisbon.
APO-BP	Arquivo Português Oriental, (ed) A.B. de Bragança Pereira.
APO-CR	Arquivo Português Oriental, (ed) J.H. da Cunha Rivara.
B. Aj.	Biblioteca da Ajuda, Lisbon.
BIVG	Boletim do Instituto Vasco da Gama, Goa.
BSGL	Biblioteca Sociedade de Geografia de Lisboa.
CARTAS	Cartas de Affonso de Albuquerque.
COD	Códices / Codex.
CX.	Caixas da India, AHU.
DHM	Documentação para a História do Padroado Português do Oriente, (ed) A. da Silva Rego.
DOC(S).	Documento(s) / Document(s).
DUP	Documentação Ultramarina Portuguesa, (ed) A. da Silva Rego.
E.F.	The English Factory Records, 1618-1669, (ed) W. Foster.
HAG	Historical Archives of Goa, Panaji.
IHR	Indian History Review, ICHR., New Delhi.
INDIA	Documentos Soltos Relativos à India, caixas, AHU.
JBHS	Journal of the Bombay History Society, Bombay.
LMG	Livro das Monções, ou Monções do Reino, Goa.
LML	Livro das Monções, ou Documentos Remettidos da Índia, Lisbon, ANTT. Res. Reservado Section at BSGL and AHU.
SPHI	Subsidios para a História da India Portuguesa,
SPHMMI	Subsidios para a História Militar Marítima da Índia.
Xs.	Xerafins / Ashrafis.

Plates

Acknowledgements

This study was made possible with a University Grants Commission Fellowship granted to me through the efforts of Prof. (Late) S.C. Misra, our head of the Department. I wish to place on record my gratitude and indebtedness to him and the department of History. Dr. José Blanco, through the International Section of the Gulbenkian Foundation, Portugal, was kind enough to award me a one year research fellowship. Without this fellowship, my work would have never been completed. I extend my heartfelt gratitude to him. Drª Maria Clara Farinha, and other staff members of the Foundation have been of particular help to me during my stay in Lisbon. I wish to thank all of them.

I wish to place on record the unflinching help I received from my supervisor, Prof. K. S. Mathew. He was a constant source of inspiration to me. his love, care and affection inspired me throughout the period of my research work. I shall always cherish with profound gratitude my period of work under his guidance.

Before I started my research, I had the privilege of learning Portuguese from a distinguished teacher, Prof. J. L. Ferreira (Jr.)., at J.N. University, New Delhi. Prof. Ferreira not only taught me the language but also encouraged me for this research in every possible way. I do not have adequate words to describe my indebtedness to him.

I am grateful to Dr. H. K. Naqvi, who initiated the idea of working on the Indo-Portuguese History.

Dr. George D. Winius of Lieden University, Lieden, Netherlands, had been kind enough to do all the possible editing and corrections along with his comments and suggestions in the manuscript. I gratefully thank him for his pains taking work.

I am highly indebted to Dr. Geoffrey Parker whose valuable

suggestions and encouragement during the period of my research forced me to complete this work.

The material for this work was primarily collected from the National Archives of India, Goa Historical Archives, *Arquivo Nacional da Torre do Tombo*, Lisbon, Arquivo Histórico Ultramarino, Lisbon, Archives of the Kings' College, London, I wish to thank all the Directors and staff members who rendered their help during my research.

My gratitude is also due to all the Librarians and staff members of Dr. Z.H. Library, Jamia Millia Islamia, New Delhi, Smt. Hansa Mehta Library, the M.S. University of Baroda, Bombay University Library, Bombay, Post Graduate College Library, Panjim, Central Library, Panjim, Xavier Centre for Historical Research, Panjim, Goa. While in Portugal, Biblioteca Nacional, Biblioteca Ajuda, Biblioteca Sociedade de Geografia de Lisboa, and Biblioteca Academia das Ciências de Lisboa, have been of great source of information for the present study. I extend my indebtedness to the respective Directors and Library staffs of these institutions for their help.

My sincere thanks are due to Dr. B.S. Shastry, who always spared his valuable time in discussing with me the various nuances of the subject during my stay at Panjim, Goa.

Prof. (late) Moonis Raza, Prof. M.A. Ansari, Mr. Shahabuddin Ansari, Mr. Mehfooz Khan, Mr. S.A. Raheem, Mr. A. A. Farooqui, Dr. R.W. Bauss, Dona Maria Benedita, Dr. (Mrs.) Indira Saxena, Mr. Iftekhar Khan, Mr. Bharat Ram, Mr. Ram Kumar, Mr. Pradeep Singh Choondawat, Mrs. Helena M. Alegre and Mr. Ismail G. Doodhwala, not only helped me in possible ways, but also encouraged me from time to time during my period of anguish and trouble. I wish to record my thanks to all of them.

Afzal Ahmad

Preface

Present work was initially submitted as a Ph. D. dissertation to the Department of History, M.S. University of Baroda in 1984; I was awarded the degree in 1985.

During the recent years, there have been quite a few attempts to reconstruct the history of the Portuguese maritime trade in the East in general, and with India in particular. More important of them dealing with the socio-economic relation during the sixteenth and the seventeenth centuries are by K. M. Panikkar, J. Lúcio Azevedo, V. M. Godinho, M. N. Pearson, A.R. Disney and K.S. Mathew, While contributing to our knowledge of the Portuguese commercial activities in the East, especially in the western coastal regions of India, it has been found that these studies have overlooked the trade in several commodities such as textiles, diamonds, precious stones, saltpetre and rice among numerous others of considerable economic value. It has been held by some scholars that 'the second half of the sixteenth century witnessed the decline of the Portuguese maritime powers and their commercial activities in India', but I find it quite difficult to accept after going through the seventeenth century Portuguese documents.

In this context the seventeenth century that witnessed the interference of various European powers in western India presents itself as a subject of absorbing interest for historians, economists and sociologists. Indian economy was brought into the network of world economy during this period. The Dutch and the English crossed swords with the Portuguese and dealt a fatal blow to the Portuguese hegemony over maritime trade with India.

The present work attempts to make some contribution to the study of international trade on the western coast of India in the seventeenth century (1600-1663), keeping in view several points mentioned above, making use mostly of primary sources in Portuguese in the form of cargo diaries, factory records, reports of the Vice-Roy, Governors, letter between the king of Portugal and the officials of the Portuguese *Estado da India*, collected both from India and Europe.

This study focuses on the Portuguese trade on the western coast of India in the seventeenth century and the area covered is the region from Diu in the territory of Gujarat in the north, to Cape Camorin in south. Spices, textiles and various other profitable commodities were available in abundance in these areas and the Portuguese concentrated their attention mainly on this coast.

The period covered in this study is 1600 to 1663 which is chosen in the light of a number of factors. It may be argued why 1600? This year and soon after, turned out to be reasonably important at least for the Indian ocean and the Arabian sea where the Portuguese possessed their major strong holds and shipping, appeared two strong European commercial companies with firm determinations of sharing the above mentioned goods specifically the pepper and textiles which had far reaching impact on the Portuguese politico-commercial relations in this region. Though the English and the Dutch had already appeared in the Asian waters towards the end of the sixteenth century, they interfered actively in the Indian Ocean politics and commerce only after the foundations of their East India Companies (The English in 1600 and the Dutch in 1602). I found it quite interesting that at the end of the sixteenth century, the resistance from the Indian rulers and the merchants had almost weakened if not completely over. As it shall be seen in the chapter on the trade diplomacy, the international rivalries right from the beginning of the seventeenth century continued unabated until 1663 when the Portuguese lost almost all the major strongholds on the south-western coast of India, especially Cochin where they first set their footholds in the early sixteenth century, the major spice producing centre, to the Dutch. Nevertheless, they, even in such a political and economical crisis all around, tried to maintain their supremacy of trade but their efforts proved fruitless. These form the subject of discussion in nine chapters of this work. The appendices and select bibliography indicate the source of research.

The first chapter studies the existing Indo-Portuguese trade at the dawn of the seventeenth century and the briefing the political developments in the sixteenth century, so as to examine the changes that took place with the passage of time during the period already mentioned.

In the second chapter, Portuguese diplomatic relation with Indian states and the international rivalries for eastern goods have been studied. The Dutch and the English wars which affected the Portuguese shipping and commerce have been given due attention.

Pepper was the major item of the Portuguese trade throughout the sixteenth century, which fetched the maximum profit for the Portuguese crown. During the first half of the seventeenth century, however, Portuguese trade in this profitable and monopoly commodity gradually declined. In the late sixteenth century the average export of pepper per year was around 12,000 quintals. But during the first three decades of the seventeenth century it declined by ten to thirty percent. During the fourth, fifth and the sixth decades it further declined by fifty to eighty percent. The entire picture of trade is illustrated on the accompanying tables in chapter three.

Throughout the sixteenth century the Portuguese traded mainly in pepper, ginger, cinnamon and various other spices and marginally in textiles. But during the period under review, a new change has been noticed. Amidst all-round decline in other commodities, textile trade increased at least for the first four decades. The reason seems to be the international conflict with the Dutch and the English. Throughout the sixteenth century the Dutch who in return purchased Indian spices and other wares from them met the Portuguese demand for textile. But the closure of Iberian ports to Dutch commerce by the king Philip II of Spain, towards the late sixteenth century, stopped the flow of the goods from both Portugal and Netherlands. The Dutch could now get their supply from India directly. On the other hand, the Portuguese, in order to get their demand of textiles fulfilled, concentrated their attention on the Indian textiles and carried shiploads to their homeland. Another reason seems to be that during war numerous slaves were needed on the ships both as soldiers and as porters. To get the slaves from Africa, textiles and food grains were required in abundance. Thus, when the demand for soldiers increased, the consumption of textiles increased considerably. Therefore, it can very well be assumed that the international turbulence increased the volume of the textile trade during the seventeenth century. If it declined during the late period, it was only due to the weak financial resources. However, the Portuguese traded in more than ninety varieties of textiles. Its quantitative details have been shown in various tables in chapter four.

Chapter five has been devoted to study cinnamon, rice and tobacco trade. Cinnamon had been a prohibited item of trade for the non-Portuguese merchants throughout the sixteenth century, and was declared to be the commodity of the royal monopoly in the early seventeenth century due to its growing demand and profit. The trade in this commodity also declined during the fourth and fifth decades of the seventeenth century. Rice was never traded on such a large scale before 1628. It was needed for the provisions of soldiers and the people residing in the war-affected areas. Thus, as long as the war continued the volume of this commodity went on increasing. Tobacco was not really an item of regular export but the Portuguese did drive much rent on its cultivation.

In chapter six, trade in saltpetre and sundry items has been studied. Volume of export of saltpetre, an item of exclusive use in producing gunpowder, also increased to a higher level, to a certain extent, due to the wars. There were more than fifty other items of merchandise in which the Portuguese traded during this period.

The Portuguese imported a number of commodities from various regions to the western coast of India. Some of the commodities were brought from the Portuguese settlements in Asia and Africa to exchange for the Indian goods as well as for the minting of coins. Among the imported items, metals like copper, bronze, quicksilver, besides gold and silver occupied considerable importance. Among the other goods, slaves, ivory, horses, elephants, musk, amber, precious stones of various value, and leather bags were included. All these commodities were used for the exchange of Indian products like spices and textiles. This is discussed in chapter seven.

During the sixteenth century, mainly the German and the Italian merchant financiers, who through their agents supplied the Indian goods to the other European countries, financed the Portuguese trade. But due to the international turbulence, these aforesaid merchants kept away from the Portuguese ports. Consequently, a new set of merchant bankers in India both the Portuguese and the Indian, emerged to finance the trade. However, it is to be mentioned that during the sixteenth century, these merchants were entirely at the mercy of the local rulers of the western coast as well as of the Portuguese authorities and they earned marginal profit on their goods. But, as they found several buyers and war weakened the rulers in both power and wealth, they became very rich and at times dictated terms to the Portuguese as well as the Indian rulers. Thus, the international rivalry and the Portuguese trade led to the fast emergence of merchant capital in India. This theme has been discussed in the chapter eight.

Chapter nine focuses on the impact of the Portuguese trade in India. The Portuguese trade during this period had multi-faced impact on the western coast of India. It had vast economic impact on the Portuguese settlers in India. The wealth of the local merchants and contractors increased substantially. The production of commodities went up in proportion to the increasing demands and presumably new areas were brought under cultivation. The flow of the Portuguese wealth for the purchase of the Indian commodities accelerated the growth of Indian economy. Colonies of the Portuguese as well as Eurasians took root in India and developed day by day in size. Urban life and flow of more people from villages to the coastal towns were boosted up by the Portuguese trade. Shipping and shipbuilding on the Portuguese strongholds gave employment to the workers.

Thus it has been concluded that the Portuguese trade in spices on the whole declined considerably due to the rivalries, but the production and trade of certain commodities like textiles, saltpetre, rice and so on increased. The emergence of merchant capitalism and monetisation of economy are two main features of this period.

There are altogether thirteen appendices, one is a specimen of a *Cartaz* issued to the ruler of Ahmadnagar, and other one is a map of a ship showing places reserved for pepper. Number three and four show the export of pepper in its geographical setting and a glance at the volume of export. Tables of equivalence of coins, weight and measures have been provided in appendices five and six respectively. A detailed list of textiles exported by the Portuguese has been provided in appendix seven, its volume and textiles trade at a glance and its prices have been furnished in appendices eight, nine and ten. Rice trade at a glance has been given in appendix eleven. A list of commodities sent for exchange for saltpetre is found in appendix twelve. Appendix thirteen furnishes a table of saltpetre export.

Bibliography has been divided into three parts. Part first gives the details of primary sources in manuscript form. Second provides information about the primary sources, which are printed. Travel accounts too are discussed here in this section. In the third part a list of published works consulted by me is provided.

Afzal Ahmad

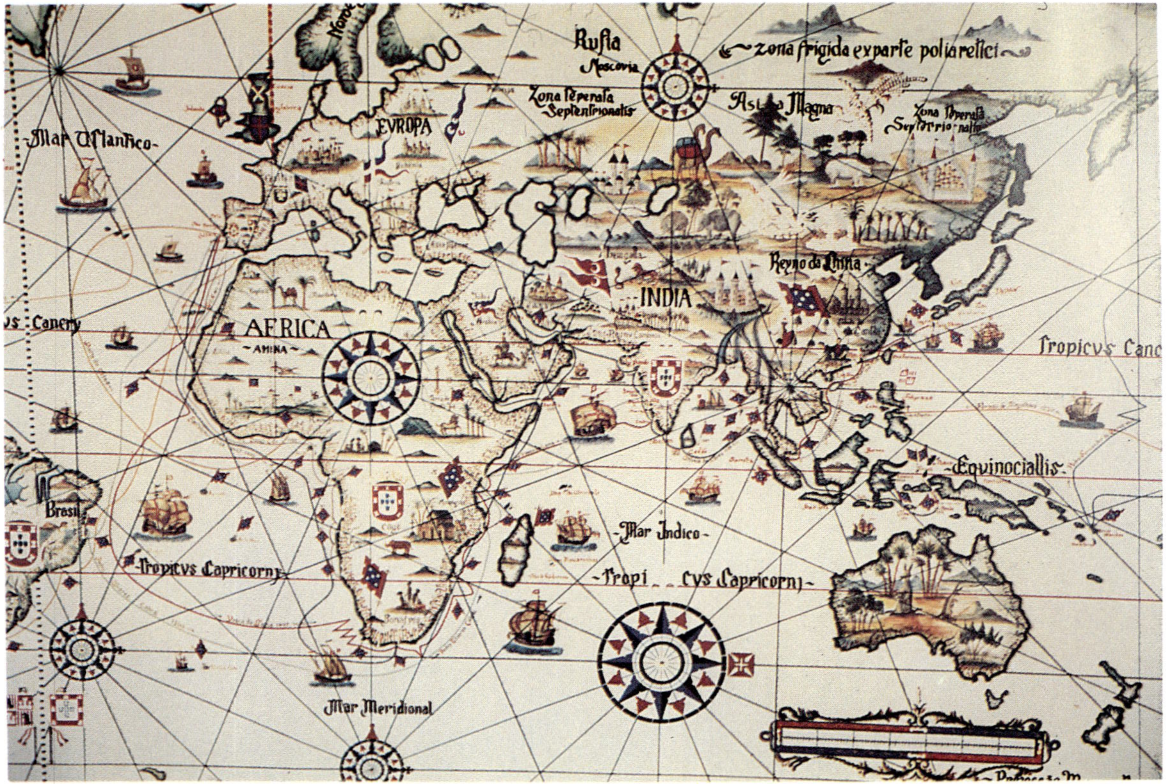

Plate 1 A world map showing Geographical Discoveries and overseas Trade Routes to the East. Collection, *Museu da Marinha*, Lisbon.

Chapter - 1

Indo-Portuguese Trade at the Dawn of the Seventeenth Century

In this introductory chapter an attempt will be made to highlight the organisation of the Portuguese trade and its various offices, in Portugal, the *Carreira da India*, (the sea-link between Lisbon and Goa), Portuguese organisation and diplomacy of trade in India, direction of trade, commodity composition of the trade, the various branches of Portuguese trade, its financiers and finances and finally, the monopoly of the trade at the end of the sixteenth century. All of this, I propose with the aim of placing the study of Portuguese trade in the seventeenth century in its proper perspective.

To govern their far-flung empire, the Portuguese set up a comparatively elaborate administrative hierarchy. At the top was the king of Portugal, in Lisbon, (and between 1580 and 1640, in Madrid and Valladolid). The trade with the East, including the supply of the ships, crews and provision was organised by the *Casa da India* (henceforth it will be referred as India House).(1) In the beginning of the sixteenth century, there was a *Feitor* (Factor), a treasurer, three scribes and many other workers who operated this organisation. But later, as trade flourished, the number of the employees was increased substantially. During the last decades of the century, there was a factor, three treasurer one to deal with money, one for spices and for the House of Guiné and Mina.(2) This number was again increased in the early decades of the seventeenth century to meet the increased work load. The number of the employees was as follows: one *Provedor* (purveyor) or *Feitor*, in charge of the India House itself, six clerks, one *Juiz do peso* (Judge of weight), two guards for the House itself, one porter, seven messengers, thirty workers to carry loads, one chaplain, four evaluators of goods and their prices, two goldsmiths for the evaluation of precious stones and metals, two pharmacists for the evaluation of drugs, one sailor with scribe for the excursion from the House at the time of the arrival of ships from India to fetch their *Caderno da Carga* (cargo diary). All the employees were subject to the authority of the *Feitor*, or the Factor.(3)

The subjugation of Portugal in 1580 by Philip II of Spain gave a new turn to the history of Portuguese trade and commerce. At the beginning, according to the terms of the agreement of the Union made at Tomar in 1581, the Spanish and the Portuguese colonial empires were to be kept separate and each administered by its own officials.(4) The affairs of the *Estado da India* (A general term used for all the commercial set-up in the East especially for India) was left untouched to function under the administration of India House at Lisbon. But, by a decree of November 20, 1591, the king, finally abolished the old financial offices functioning under the authority of the India House and created a new *Conselho da Fazenda* (council of finance) consisting men of his own choice. The India House and spice trade were placed under its jurisdiction and it soon became the centre around which all the agencies of Portugal's metropolitan and overseas government had to revolve.(5) The *India* House, which was long the suprem e house to decide the Asian affairs throughout the sixteenth century, now became subordinate one, at the dawn of the seventeenth century.(6) Before this change, the factor of the India House was responsible only to the king of Portugal. But, due to this new arrangement, he was to give all the reports of the India House to the Minister of the Council of Finance. It was the duty of the factor to sign all the papers and registers regarding every matter of the India House.(7) He was responsible for sending all the accounts of the India House to the Finance minister by the end of every month containing all the information about the loading and unloading of goods, its selling, income and expenditure on trade.(8) After processing the reports the Minister was responsible to send them to the king. Minister was the only competent authority, after the king, to oversee the affairs of both the crown and that of the colonial dominions both the East and the West. This minister, who had the general power to look after the revenue and customs of the crown, also tallied the income and expenditure of the India House. The sale of pepper, spices and various other products of the East was also the concern of the Council. As the India House was subordinate to this Council, other matters like the construction of the ships, it's provisioning and various similar activities became the responsibility of the Council of Finance. Its jurisdiction was very vast in practice. In brief, this council was responsible for all the affairs of the crown as well as the Portuguese settlements in Asia and Africa.(9)

In 1600, the old Castilian *Consejo De las Indias* (Council of the Indies) was changed into the Council of Chamber of India and was given additional powers from the Council of Finance. In fact this was done to lighten the senior council's burden. The main work of this office was for consultation regarding the provisions and goods to be sent for the overseas territories, to select and appoint the trust worthy officials for the colonial domains.(10) Apart from the power of the India House and its factor, the functions remained the same in the seventeenth century as they were in the sixteenth century.(11) Here, it is desirable to throw some light in brief on the function of the India House in connection with the Indo-Portuguese Trade.

Yet in practice the India house had played a very important role in conduction of the trade with India. All the outgoing ships were furnished by it with the commodities, needed for the consumption of the crew and officials sailing for India in the annual fleets.(12) The India house served as a housing of foreign affair and overseas administration. It was the duty of its Factor to keep records and the list of those persons leaving for India along with the merchandises and the cash for the purchase of oriental goods sent on the annual ships.(13) As soon as the Factor was informed about the arrival of the ships from India, he appointed the necessary guards for their unloading and to prevent any smuggling or black-marketing.(14) Nobody, even the officials, were allowed to take anything either from the ships or from the India House at the time of their unloading.(15) The captains of the ships and scribes were required to entrust the *Caderno da Carga* to the Factor of the India house and then goods were unloaded according to what was written in those books and stored in the warehouse. After this, commodities were weighed in the presence of the *Juíz do peso* and registered by the scribes and then kept in the warehouse.(16) The merchandise belonging to the private merchants and the *Quintaladas* and *Liberdades* of the officials taking part in this maritime enterprise was also kept in the storeroom of the India House in the same manner. On all the private goods, a fixed amount of custom duty was levied.(17) The percentage of custom duty charged in the seventeenth century varied as per the commodities.(18) Till the third decade of the sixteenth century the goods were sold wholesale as well as at retail at the India House. But after 1530, only wholesale was permitted. Since then India House continued to be only a wholesale market place. Later, at the end of the century, merchants were required to make contract in advance and obtain permits from the *Conselho da Fazenda*.(19) Some times this could be done at the time of the arrival of the ship's. The prices for the sale of goods were fixed by the India House. But, during the early decades of the sixteenth century, some private merchants sold their goods on different prices than they were fixed by the India House.(20) The Factor of the India House was to submit accounts of the sale and stocks of the goods at the end of every month to the Minister of the Council of Finance, as it has already been mentioned earlier.(21)

So far as the officials of the *Carreira da India* were concerned, there was a *Capitão Mor* (captain-in-chief) to look after the activities of other captains. Apart from the captains, their were soldiers, porters, sailors, clergymen, doctors, overseers, merchants, and passengers going for the purpose of staying in India to work in the Portuguese settlements and the factories.(22)

The ships were fitted out not only by the king but also by the Portuguese officials.(23) Nobility and the merchant community consisted of both, Portuguese and foreign nationals. The owner of the ships were expected to equip them, but the officers and crew of the ships were only appointed subject to the approval of the crown.(24) The officers of the ships also took part in this overseas trade as per their status.(25) The captains and other employees of *Carreira da India* were paid a salary in cash by the India House, but, still, they were entitled to carry certain quantity of Indian goods by way of *Liberdades* (26) and *Quintaladas* (27) as was the case from the early sixteenth century.(28)

Normally, ships destined for India left Lisbon every year by the end of March or the beginning of April and arrived at the Indian coast by the end of September.(29) The ships were loaded with the commodities at the Indian ports during the months of October and November. The return voyage to Portugal was either in the second half of the month of December or at latest by the beginning of January.(30)

Diplomacy of the Portuguese Trade

At the time of the union of the crowns- Spain and Portugal, after the death of Cardinal King Henry in 1580, the king of Spain had gained title to at least fifteen fortresses and factories of considerable importance on the western coast of India.(31) Diu,

Daman, Bassein, Surat, Chaul, and Dabhol, to the north of Goa, and to the south, Onor, Bhatkal, Barcelor, Cannanore, Calicut, Cranganore, Cochin, Kayamkulam and Quilon were most important of all the ports the Portuguese possessed in the East. There were various fortress and factories on the eastern coast of India too.(32) Among these, there was a trading factory in the port of Massulipattam to control the textile trade from Golconda. In Bengal, Hugli, Chinsura and Chittagong were very important ports where they possessed factories and had acquired the textiles and silk trade supplying various commodities. In the eastern archipelago, Malacca and the Molucca islands were governed from its base in Macao from where they controlled the trade of that region and acquired hot spices. Ceylon had been another important island where Portuguese had at least three fortresses and factories and a very lucrative trade in cinnamon. They possessed two trading posts in the Persian Gulf: Muscat at the mouth and Hormuz a little inside. Both were so strategically situated that it was difficult for any non-authorised vessels to escape the sight of the Portuguese patrol ships in the Gulf. In Africa: Mozambique, Mombassa, Angola and various other trading post were under Portuguese control could be named as important.(33)

The area that has been chosen for this study is the Western Coast of India: from Quilon, in the south to Diu, in the north, with Goa as its capital. The greater part of this area falls into four main divisions: The region of Malabar in the extreme south which was divided among many small kingdoms; next to it lies the territory of Kanara also fragmented into different petty kingdoms but at the beginning of the seventeenth century they were subjugated and ruled mainly by the Nayakas of Ikkeri; further north was Konkan, partially under the Ahmadnagar and partially under Bijapur kingdoms; finally, to the extreme north in the Gulf of Cambay was the regions of Gujarat ruled by the Mughals.

Vasco da Gama, soon after arriving at the port of Calicut, had antagonised this kingdom, but established political and commercial relations with the neighbouring kingdoms. His policies were followed by his predecessors, who widened their relations with the states on the Malabar coasts.(34) Portuguese diplomatic relations with all the above mentioned states, have been discussed under the following rubric.

Portuguese-Malabar Relations

The first ruler with whom the Portuguese came into contact

on the southwestern coast of India was Zamorin, the king of Calicut. Vasco da Gama who reached Calicut on May 20, 1498,(35) had to face, in the beginning, a very different reaction from the one he had expected.(36) Somehow, it was not until 1513 that the Portuguese Governor, Affonso de Albuquerque, was allowed to establish a fort and a factory in Calicut (37) one which was abandoned in 1525.(38) A further diplomatic rapprochement, however, took place only in 1531 during the time of Nuno da Cunha, the Portuguese Viceroy.(39) The Portuguese-Zamorin relations, thus remained inconsistent between friendship and hostility throughout the sixteenth century. The Zamorin, under his renowned admiral, the Kunjali Marakkars(40), had long been harassing the Portuguese shipping and trade as their arrival was a severe blow to his own trade and commerce as well as his economy.(41) It was only in 1599, that the Zamorin and the Portuguese combined against the Kunjalis, whose repeated successes towards the end of the century had made them arrogant and disloyal.(42) Both the said powers were successful in taming the Kunjali menace in 1600, forcing the Kunjali himself to surrender to his erstwhile master, the Zamorin.(43) Contrary to the treaty between the Zamorin and the Portuguese admirals, André Furtado, the Kunjali was handed over as a prisoner to the Portuguese who brought him to Goa where he was hanged.(44) The Portuguese-Zamorin treaty was not destined to last. Unlike in Calicut, the Portuguese were welcomed in the states of Cochin, Cannanore, and Quilon. These were the states where the Portuguese power and influence was greatest, and their commerce flourished throughout the sixteenth century. There was hardly any time when these territories could afford to become hostile to their ally. The rulers of Cannanore and Cochin, long hostile to Calicut in fact felt themselves menaced by the suddenly relations between the Zamorin and the Portuguese in 1513 (45) and 1599 (46), and complained to the King of Portugal against the promises made to them in the earlier years of the century.(47) However, they continued to be a faithful allies of the Portuguese till they fell into the hands of the Dutch.

Portuguese-Kanara Relations

The next region in the north of Malabar was Kanara, which played an important role in the Portuguese activities on the western coast of India. More than half a century after the arrival of Vasco da Gama at Calicut, the ruler of Vijay Nagar, Rama Raya, was crushingly defeated at Talikota in 1565 by an alliance of

Muslim Sultanates- Bijapur, Golconda, Bidar and Ahmadnagar-(48) and his empire broke into number of autonomous Hindu principalities, of which Tanjore, Madura and Ikkeri were the most important. "Kanara, too, was cast adrift, but it remained politically fragmented until during the first quarter of the seventeenth century, when it fell under the control of the Nayakas of Ikkeri".(49) During the sixteenth century no major incident took place, which could become a cause of much concern of the Portuguese in that region. However, about the time of the Talikota war, the Portuguese had begun, as a matter of policy, to purchase some of their Indian pepper in Kanara instead of depending exclusively on the Malabar region.(50) Kanara, therefore, took on a new importance to them in the second half of the sixteenth century, and to consolidate their interests in the region, they seized control during 1568-69 of the three coastal towns of Onor (Honawar), Barcelore and Mangalore, and established fortresses and factories at each.(51) Even before this, the Portuguese had concluded a treaty with the ruler of Gersoppa for the supply of pepper in 1540.(52)

Konkan-Portuguese Relations

When the power of Bider declined, the ports of the Konkan- Chaul, Danda Rajapur or Rajpur, Dabhol, Goa and Bhatkal- were divided between the Sultans of Ahmadnagar and Bijapur. The first port to fall into the Portuguese hands was Goa. This port, formerly ruled by the Sultans of Bijapur, was conquered by Afonso de Albuquerque in 1510 and the foundation was laid for a Portuguese colony there.(53) Later, in 1530 Goa was made the Portuguese Asian capital and commercial centre. Peace between the Portuguese and the Bijapuri Sultan was later restored by treaty.(54) During the course of time, Martim de Souse, the Portuguese governor, also captured the surrounding territories of Goa Bardez and Salsete also belonging to the said Sultan.(55) This act of the Portuguese of course offended the Sultan anew. In the meantime the Portuguese had already occupied other ports on the Konkan coast belonging to the Sultans of Bijapur and Ahmadnagar.(56) The increasing power of the Portuguese forced the two Sultans Ali Adil Khan of Bijapur and the Sultan of Ahmadnagar to unite to drive the Portuguese out of their territories. Thus in 1570, they unsuccessfully attacked Goa, Chaul, the Portuguese strongholds.(57) Peace was restored by a treaty in 1575.(58) Henceforth, both these powers enjoyed peace until Bijapur negotiated with the Dutch in the seventeenth century.(59) During the ensuing years of peace, especially in the early decades of the seventeenth century, Bijapur and Ahmadnagar were of much importance for the textiles of Balaghat, which were traded to the Portuguese in exchange for the other commodities.(60)

Portuguese-Gujarati Relations

The Gujaratis were quick to realise the consequence of the Portuguese trade on their economy as early 1507. In that year, the Sultan of Gujarat, along with his allies the Egyptians, the Zamorin of Calicut, the Sultans of Ahmadnagar and Bijapur, delivered a setback to the Portuguese off Chaul.(61) However, the Portuguese trapped their fleet in 1509 inside the port of Diu and decisively defeated them.(62) By treaty, Malik Ayaz, the Governor of Diu and the Sultan of Ahmadnagar thereupon agreed to pay tribute to the king of Portugal.(63) Later, the relation between the Gujarati Sultan and the Portuguese authorities was stabilised by exchange of embassies.(64) The Portuguese, from their side then attempted to gain control the territory of Diu and construct a fort there.(65) They tried, through diplomacy and sporadic coastal raids, to change Sultan's mind, but he refused to budge. During the reign of Bahadur Shah (1526-37), eventually the port city of Bassein was ceded to the Portuguese and a site was granted for the building of a fort on the island of Diu during 1534-35.(66) But only after the death of Sultan Bahadur Shah, the dream of the Portuguese could become true. Finally, in 1546, after various raids, they were successful in occupying the whole island. (67) Besides Diu and Bassein, the Portuguese seized control of Daman in 1559.(68) After the death of Bahadur Shah, his successors allowed the state to slip in to anarchy and their power disappeared completely.(69) At last it fell into the hands of the Mughals in 1572-73.(70) Surat and Cambay were the two main Gujarati ports which came into the hands of the Mughals at the time of their occupation.(71) At first, it appeared as though the Portuguese and the Mughals would clash, but after some preliminary hostilities, Akbar, the Mughal Emperor, and the Portuguese Viceroy realised that the peace would be a better choice.(72) Later, their relations became more amicable and embassies were exchanged. Akbar tacitly acknowledged the Portuguese supremacy on the sea by accepting a free *Cartaz* (a license or passport issued for the ships to ply in the Indian Ocean) for his ship to go to Mecca annually.(73) The subsequent Jesuit missionaries to the Mughal court during 1582, 1590 and 1596 respectively, made the relations between the two even more friendly.(74) The Portuguese-Mughal relations cooled only during the early decades of the seventeenth century when the Dutch and the English East India Companies representatives appeared and the Mughals extended support to them.(75)

To control and exploit brisk trade in the Indian Ocean and the Arabian Sea, the Portuguese extended the scope of outposts and settlements. Ceylon was made tributary to the king of Portugal in 1507, (76) but not actually occupied until around 1519. The ruler of Hormuz in the Persian gulf had submitted himself to the Portuguese suzerainty in 1508 paying 15,000 Ashrafis annually as tribute and a fortress was established there (77) which remained in Portuguese possession until it fell into the hands of the English in 1622.(78) The foothold in Hormuz helped them to stop the flow of spices from the Malabar coast through the Persian Gulf. Another port of importance in this Gulf was Muscat , which the Portuguese occupied during this time.(79) After their occupancy of these ports they were in full control of the Persian Gulf.(80) Malacca was another port in South East Asia that the Portuguese brought under their control in 1511 and drove out its ruler. A Portuguese fortress along with a factory was quickly constructed there.(81)

Thus in a short span of time the Portuguese were in a position to occupy in all the key points in the Indian Ocean save Aden, which they twice failed to captured, and controlled the trade in the East by 'force'. Their power was most seriously challenged until by the other European nations at the dawn of the seventeenth century. This will be discussed in the next chapter.

Oganisation of the Portuguese Trade in India

The head of the Portuguese *Estado da India* was the viceroy or governor the title depending upon the nominee's degree of nobility. He was resident until 1530 in Cochin and later in Goa. A viceroy enjoyed slightly higher social status than did a governor, but their function and powers were identical. They were the undisputed heads of the civil and military government of the whole state, responsible only to the king and God.(82) To assist him in Goa, the governor had at first a loosely organised council. These were not institutionalised, they were called into existence more or less at the whim of the governor or viceroy, to give him advice only on specific, usually, military matters. The Members were always *Fidalgos* but there was no fixed member ship or procedure.(83)

During the second half of the sixteenth century, this council evolved and became more institutionalised as the *Conselho do Estado* (Council of State). Its members were governor or viceroy as president, the archbishop of Goa, two or three older *Fidalgos* resident in Goa, the head of the High Court, the captain of the city of Goa, and the *Vedor da Fazenda* (Inspector of the Finance), which was dominated by officials and met regularly in the seventeenth century to decide the economic matters, specially, related to trade. The governor was also entitled to attend sittings of *Mesa da Relação*, or the High Court.(84) The cash and commodities brought from Portugal for the purchase of Indian commodities, along with a list of the items required to be bought, were handed over to the viceroy and then it was to be given to the *Vedor da Fazenda* at Goa for necessary action. The *Vedor da Fazenda* with the consent his own officials, then transmitted orders to the factors or governor of respective factories from where goods were to be brought. If the amount brought from Portugal was insufficient to meet the requirements of the crown, a meeting of ministers of the *Conselho da Fazenda* was to be called and there, it was to be decided how to arrange things. However, *Vedor da Fazenda* had advance knowledge of the crown's needs. He usually sent orders to the factories to have merchandises purchased and ready before the arrival of the ships from Portugal, making down payment from the treasury.

There was also the municipal council, selected by the Portuguese and Eurasian population, and at time an influential force on the Government.(85) As professor M.N. Pearson has observed, four areas of authority can be distinguished: in the financial matters the Vedor and later the *Conselho da Fazenda*; in religious affairs, the clerics; in legal, the High Court; and in local government the municipal council. Only over the first did the government exercise appreciable control. However, the Governor with the *Conselho do Estado* did control military matters and external relations, in a manner befitting the head.(86)

Each fortress had a factory with a Factor, two scribes, a *Juíz do peso*, two treasurers, one for spices and other for money matters, one *Língua* or interpreter, and various guards and porters. At the time of loading and unloading of the ships, the factory employed more personnel for this work. All the officials of a factory were under the authority of factor.(87) The factor was responsible to the Captain or the Governor of the fort or directly to the Viceroy and provided to him reports of the factory's purchase and sale.(88)

Before the loading of ships, he was to prepare a log of the commodities to be sent to the capital and obtain a receipt of the same from the captain or the factor of the ships.(89) All the captains of the forts were subject to the authority of viceroy or governor of the state responsible for the entire area under his jurisdiction.(90) Thus all the fortresses and the factories were enchained to each other from top to bottom. In addition to being the office of the factor, the factory, especially at Goa, served as store house for the merchandise brought from Portugal as well as spices and other commodities collected from various parts of India, Ceylon, and south-east Asia and awaiting transhipment to Portugal. Similarly, as the ships depended on the monsoon, they had to depart before the harvest seasons of the pepper and other spices. Therefore, these goods had to be purchase for in advance and as indicated were stored in the factories so that there would be enough cargo at the time of the arrival of the ships in September or October every year.(91)

The intermediaries, particularly the local merchants and the Portuguese settlers, played an important role in the Portuguese trade on the western coast of India. They contacted the cultivators directly by going from one place to the other, giving rice, cloths and cash in exchange for pepper, cinnamon and various other items destined for Lisbon. The Muslim and Jewish merchants also collected cloths from Cambay and the Coromandel Coast and brought them to the Spice Islands in the eastern archipelago to exchange for pepper and spices and a handsome profit. In certain cases, they themselves stored the commodities thus purchased from the cultivators and entrusted to the Portuguese at the time of the arrival of the ships on the Indian coast. The factors of the respective factories visited the store of these intermediaries and paid cash in advance to get merchandises at the time of loading of the homeward bound ships of the *Carreira da India*.(92)

Due attention was paid by both, factor and viceroy to the loading of ships bound for Portugal. After the ships were loaded, the factor of Goa handed over the *Caderno da Carga* to the captain of the vessels and took receipt, as has been discussed earlier, before they left the Mandovi bound for Europe. In due course, they were to be handed over to the factor of the India House.

Indian merchants and ruler interested in sending their ships loaded with Indian commodities from one port to the other in India or other countries were forced to take *Cartazes* from the Portuguese maritime authorities in India. Similarly, those ships wishing to sail to India also needed the same sort of permit, failing which, the ships were subject to capture by the Portuguese.(93) Hence, the *Cartaz* can be defined as safe conduct issued for the Indian Ocean and the Arabian sea to the merchants ships so that they could navigate and enter the ports for loading and unloading without any trouble. The fee charged for issuing the *Cartaz* was negligible, a few Rupees (94) only, (95) but it did oblige the ships concern to call at a Portuguese port, both coming and going to pay duties.(96) There were free *Cartazes* also. These were given to the local rulers for political reasons. Mughal emperors were given one *Cartaz* a year for their ship to go to the Read Sea.(97)

The Portuguese maintained several fleets of warships to check on *Cartazes* and to impress local rulers of the coastal areas of India as well as to combat pirates.(98) The duties of these armadas were also to guard the ships trading under Portuguese auspices. Later, these merchants' ships sailed in convoys, accompanied by a small fleet of warships to deal with the pirates. At the end of the sixteenth century, the Portuguese were obliged to institute a new form of trade control, the *Cafila* or the Caravan, (99) of a small merchant ships guarded by a Portuguese fleet. In 1596 it was made compulsory. The viceroy, Matias de Albuquerque, decreed that all the ships trading on the coast of India must travel in *Cafilas*, The basis of this rule was the threat of the Kunjali Marakkars of Malabar, and later, the presence of the Protestant Europeans.(100) But, occasionally, merchant ships came to Goa unguarded. This practice was in evidence throughout the seventeenth century. At any rate, the escort fleet had two functions: to protect the merchant ships from the pirates and to make sure none of these ships slipped away to trade outside the Portuguese system.(101)

The most important customhouse on the western coast of India was of course Goa. The Portuguese attempted, with some success, to make it the focus for trade from all over Asia and Europe. In the north, Diu, Daman, and Chaul were other customhouses of considerable importance.(102) The duties levied on all these ports and customhouses will be discussed in detail in the forthcoming chapters.

Direction of Trade

Normally, pepper, ginger, and other spices were grown in the regions of Malabar, and Kanara, cinnamon in Ceylon, mace, nutmegs and cloves came from Moluccas and Banda Islands via Malacca. Gujarat, Bijapur, Golconda, and Bengal were famous for their textiles, both silk and cotton. From Persia came horses and better quality carpets, both prime items of Portuguese trade. Ivory, slaves, precious metals and stones, coral, and various other goods were brought from Mozambique, Mombassa, Angola and other places in Africa.

During the first half of the sixteenth century, the Portuguese collected their supply of spices specially pepper, ginger and inferior quality cinnamon from the coastal regions of Malabar and considerable quantity from Malacca.(103) The Portuguese, as has been seen, maintained a fortress and a factory on each of their settlements. In Malabar, for example, they had factories at Cannanore, Calicut (intermittently), Cranganore, Cochin, and Quilon. In these places they maintained a weighing house along with all the necessary officials. Quilon's weighing house was located in the vicinity of Kayamkulam. Pepper and other spices were brought from places throughout these regions to the weighing houses and after completing the formalities, they were carefully packed in sacks and kept in the factory warehouse. After the arrival of ships to carry them they were loaded in the presence of the factor. So far as Malabar was concerned, the Portuguese were successful in handling the spice trade for the whole of the sixteenth century with an exception of Calicut, with which the Portuguese could never maintain peace for any length of time. Even after their capture of Malacca, they were unable to enjoy full control of its trade owing to the competition of the Chinese and Achinese merchants who operated from their bases in its straits, as well as the general problems of transport.

Kanara was known to the Portuguese even before the war of Talikota, after their establishment in Onor, Barcelore and Mangalore, they insisted upon obtaining some of their supplies from this area instead of relying entirely on the Malabar coast as was the case in the first half of the sixteenth century.(104)

Some thirty-five miles upstream from Onor, near the town of Gersoppa, the Portuguese maintained a weighing house where pepper was weighed and bought. From here pepper was brought by river to the fortress at Onor for transhipment aboard coastal vessels to Goa.

About fifty mile south of Onor and a few miles up the Kidnaper estuary, lay the city of Barcelore (presently known as Basrur). Here also the Portuguese maintained a fortress and a factory so as to command the river approaches. Portuguese Barcelore was a thriving trading centre exporting rice, textiles, saltpetre and iron, importing corals, exotic piece goods, horses and elephants. (105)

The most southerly of the Portuguese strongholds on the Kanara coast was the fortress of Mangalore, a town situated near the mouth of the Netravali River, and between the territories of Banguel or Bangher to the north, and Olala to the south, independent petty principalities until the rise of Ikkeri. The principal export from both Barcelore and Mangalore was rice, for provisioning the vice regal capital, its outpost, and its fleets. According to Bocarro, Barcelore and Mangalore together comprised "the sole granary by which Goa, Malacca, Muscat, Mozambique and Mombassa were supplied".(106)

The Portuguese settlements in Kanara regions held important implications for the purchase of pepper in their official trade. It widened the area for their acquisition of this particular commodity. Kanara pepper, certainly, reduced the dependence of the Portuguese merchants on Cochin and other Malabar outlets. Until the rise of Ikkeri, the Portuguese purchased Kanara pepper either directly from private dealers or from petty rulers on contracts.(107) But in the seventeenth century, as it will be seen later, this situation changed considerably at the time of the rise of Venkatappa Naka, who came to dominate this region.

Apart from spices, Gujarati, and Bengali textiles were of considerable importance during the sixteenth century.(108) This commodity was especially bought from the port towns of Cambay, Daman and Surat where it was brought from the various cities and villages of Gujarat, for exchange with spices and many other items in local demand. A substantial quantity of cloth was exported to Portugal during this century.(109) In Bengal, Chittagong was the major entrepot of textiles from the various regions of India.(110) In general, the Portuguese export of textiles from India to Portugal, somehow, was inconsequential in comparison with the other goods, but it swiftly rose to importance in the first half of the seventeenth century.(111)

Commodity Composition and the Volume of Trade

During the sixteenth century, pepper, ginger, clove, cinnamon, Mace, nutmeg and various types of textiles were the major items of the Portuguese trade.(112) Among these, pepper and other spices had quickly acquired the prime importance. But apart from the spices, textiles were of considerable importance in the Portuguese trade, though primarily of utility within Asia as an item of exchange for other commodities.

It is determined by historians that during the first decade of the sixteenth century, the Portuguese exported from Malabar about 25,000 to 30,000 quintals of spices of all sorts annually to Lisbon. (113) Towards the end of the same decade, about 40,000 quintals of pepper were collected and exported to Portugal in one year from Cochin.(114)

The production of spices in Asia and demand for them in Europe roughly doubled during the second half of the sixteenth century, and European prices Likewise increased two to three fold. The cargoes carried by the Portuguese around the Cape of Good Hope have been estimated at an annual total of between 40,000 and 50,000 quintals.(115) In the first three decades, around 60,000, and later under the 'New Era of the contract trade', (1570-1598), 70,000 quintal.(116) The proportion of pepper in these cargoes oscillated between 10,000 and 45,000 quintals, but for long it fluctuated around 16,000 to 26,000 quintals as can be seen in the Table1.1 provided below for the last few decades of the century:

Table 1.1

EXPORT OF PEPPER FROM INDIA TO PORTUGAL IN QUINTALS 1586-1601

Year	Volume Exported	Sources (For all the years)
1587	10, 378.5	BSGL, (Mss) India House, Res. *Maço* 4, Nº 88.
1588	22, 963.5	Docs. 6/6, 6/8, 7/1, 12/a,
1589-26	840.0	16/13; Luíz de F. Falcão, *op. cit.*, pp. 57; AGS,
1590-23	682.0	*Secretarias provinciales*, cod., 1571.pp. 1445;
1592	9, 940.0	*APO-CR*, Fasciculo 3, pp. 52-54; Azevedo, *op. cit.*,
1593	4, 994.0	pp. 107-15; Lach, *Asia in the Making of... op. cit.*
1594	6, 516.0	pp. 131-41; Boxer, *op. cit.* pp. 59-60.
1595	17, 611.0	
1596	2, 714.0	
1597	16, 927.0	
1598	7, 895.5	
1597-1601	30, 390.5	
Total	180, 582.0	Average, 12, 056 quintals per year.

The other spices i.e. cinnamon, clove, mace, nutmegs, ginger, etc., accounted for between, 5,000 and 10,000 quintals in these yearly shipments.(117) Apart from pepper, the Portuguese export from south-east Asian regions of mace, nutmeg, cinnamon, and ginger increased somewhat in the second half of the sixteenth century, since their value roughly trebled during that period. The crown did not ultimately derived much profit from the cloves and nutmegs, owing to the great cost of fitting out the annual carracks or galleon sent to fetch out spices from the Moluccas and from Banda, respectively, and owing to the cost of maintaining the precariously held forts at Amboina, Ternate and Tidore.(118)

As regard to cinnamon, the Portuguese were able to exercise a more effective monopoly in this commodity than in any other spices since the best variety grew only in the lowland districts of Ceylon, which were under the Portuguese control. Moreover, the Sinhalese had no merchant ship of their own. Inferior varieties were grown in Malabar and in Mindanao, but, as Linschoten observed in 1592, "the cinnamon of the island of Ceylon as the best and finest in the world, and is at least three times dearer in price".(119) The crown should, therefore, have profited greatly from the royal monopoly in this spice. But in actual practice the chief profits were reaped by the governors and officials who embezzled or traded in cinnamon, despite all legislation enacted at Goa and Lisbon to prevent such mall-practices.(120)

Textiles were purchase from Gujarat and Bengal mostly for the trans-coastal trade, as well as to carry them to Portugal.(121) A very meagre quantity of Indian cloths was exported in the early sixteenth century. (122) The volume of its export increased considerably in the second half of the century, (123) though lack of documentation enables me to go into details.

Various Branches of the Portuguese Trade

The Portuguese developed a very thriving trade with countries other than Portugal. They, in order to get their supplies ready for the annual cargo ships, maintained a very brisk trade with all Indian ports on both the western and eastern coasts. Every year their ships sailed to Gujarat with spices and various necessary goods for bringing back divers types of cloths and drugs to Goa.(124) Ships carrying cloths and food grains sailed towards Kanara and Malabar for the purchase of different kinds of spices and pepper to be sent to Portugal. (125) From the Coromandel and Bengali ports the Portuguese and the local merchants brought numerous varieties of textiles, silk, both in crude and woven, by supplying mostly, pepper and spices brought from Malacca and other South-East Asian countries.(126) Though Indian merchants and ruler who used to send their ships loaded with goods from their respective ports to regions in Africa, Arabia, Persia, and South-East Asia now had to pay considerable amount of customs duties to the Portuguese under the *Cartaz* system. The Portuguese also sent their ships loaded with Indian goods to all these places to maintain their monopoly as well as to acquire goods and profits for crown and state.(127) The following were inter-national trade routes over which Portuguese ships plied every year, carrying combinations of merchandises.

Goa-Hormuz-Muscat

Pepper, ginger, nutmeg, rice, and copper, collected from the different regions of India and brought to Goa, were in great demand in Arabia and Persia. Portuguese vessels took these items every year to these ports in the month of October or November and returned with Persian horses, Larins, and silver in the months between December and March.(128) Normally, ships touched both these ports in one trip.

Goa-African Coasts

In Africa, Portuguese possessed various centres and colonies that derived much revenue and wealth by its trade. Mozambique, Mombassa, Sofala and Angola were the most important among their settlements there.(129) However, various commodities like ivory, gold and some precious metals were brought from there to Goa in Portuguese ships in exchange for Indian spices, cloths and food grains.(130)

Goa-Ceylon

As has been remarked earlier, the cinnamon was very much in demand, not only for export to Portugal and other European countries but also in Asia as well it was needed for daily consumption and use. Cinnamon, in the end of the sixteenth century, like pepper in the early century had been declared as the commodity of royal monopoly as the significant profits were increased in its trade. Therefore, ships loaded with cinnamon were brought to Goa for the distribution in India as well as to take it to Portugal. In Ceylon, Portuguese ports like Jaffna, Kandy, and Colombo were provided with the Indian commodities like textiles, rice and copper every year.(131) There was also an important trade between Ceylon and Goa in elephants, though in fact these were immediately redistributed to the princely courts.

Goa-Malacca

In South-East Asia, Malacca served as capital for the collection of spices from the surrounding regions. All sorts of spices like pepper, cinnamon, brew, clove, nutmegs and so on were collected from various islands in this area and brought to Malacca, one of the major strongholds of the Portuguese during the end of the sixteenth century. Gujarati textiles and copper from Cochin and Portugal had been in demand of these regions for centuries. The convenient times of departure for Malacca were between August and May and the return trips were made during the months of September and January.(132)

Finance and Financiers

Within a couple of years, after the return of Vasco da Gama, the king Dom Manuel I, had realised that the monopoly of trade he dreamt of would hardly be possible without sufficient cash in gold or silver that was needed for the purchase of eastern goods, and that bringing up the huge amounts of these precious metals required for the eastern enterprise was beyond the crowns capabilities. Therefore, after consultation with his ministers, he was bound to pursue other means of obtaining the cash. He invited the Portuguese as well as the foreign merchant bankers to invest money or outfit their own ships under the Portuguese flags. His offer was welcomed by the Portuguese and the foreign bankers and merchants because Portugal was already threatening to under mine the old trading system, of which Venice was the Western terminus. Moreover, the king offered important privileges. Among the foreign merchant bankers, the Germans and the Italians came forth with investments and settled their business headquarters in Lisbon.(133) Among the Germans were the Welsers, the Fugers, the Herwarts, the Hochstetters, the Imhofs, the Hisrschovogel and so on, to name only the most prominent financiers of the Portuguese trade during the sixteenth century.(134) The Italian financiers, especially the Florentines, also occupied an important place among the financiers connected with the Portuguese trade during the sixteenth century.(135) Bartolomeu Marchioni, Gualterotti, Frescobaldi, Girolamo Sernigi, Giovanni Francisco de Affaitati, Lucas Geraldi were among the greatest business magnates and financiers of this period.(136) Many of these merchants had their factories and agents throughout Europe. The majority of those bankers, had their own establishments in Lisbon too.(137) These contractors used to advance money on loan under contract or at simple interest. Sometimes they sent their own ships under the Portuguese maritime regulations. They not only took part in financing the trade and commerce but also, from time to time, gave money on credit for other state affairs. Until 1570, this trade arrangement continued. But somewhere around 1550 or shortly thereafter, Venetian efforts to stimulate the revival of their trade began succeeding,(138) and at the same time the kings unsuccessful efforts to prevent the illegal trade through his own system thwarted the Portuguese monopoly and forced the king to change course and initiate a new system of contract trade giving all facilities to the contractors. The difference between this contract trade and the previous sort was that now the trading powers were given completely over to the contractors, whereas earlier, it was functioned through the government officials without their direct involvement. The main intention behind this was to monopolise the trade using the contractors' men and equipment because the government was unable to bear the whole cost of the import. However, under this condition, the king and his advisors expected that at least 50,000 to 60,000 quintals of pepper and spices should be imported, while half of it was to be given to the India House without charging any expenditure against it.(139) The other half was to be sold to the contractors at the rate of 32 *Cruzados* (about 45 Ashrafis) which they bought in India at the rate of 6 o 10 Ashrafis. Thus, it was thought to be a more profitable business. It was a great shock in the world market when, in the last month of 1575, the pepper contract was handed over to Konrad Rott, an Augsburg merchant who had long been doing business in the Iberian peninsula though he was not a leading merchant.(140) Rott committed himself to buy at least 12,000 quintals of pepper in first year and 20,000 thereafter, at 47-48 Ashrafis per quintal.(141) As part of his contract, he had to provide an immediate loan of several hundred thousand ducats at a moderate rate of interest to the king of Portugal.(142) This was to be repaid in pepper deliveries during the last years of the contract. Rott soon realised that this enterprise was beyond his capacity to carry out successfully alone. Therefore, he sought a partner. He sold three-eighths of his contract to Giacomo dei Bardi & Company of Florence. As if his obligations were not already overwhelming, he took over an India contract in 1578 with the Cardinal King Henry that looked towards the establishment of a world monopoly. In other words, Rott anticipated operating a monopoly, which the king of Portugal had found difficult to maintain.(143) Rott divided his contract into thirty shares, keeping twelve and a half for himself. Of the remainder, he sold ten to the Portuguese firms and seven and a half to Italians. Soon after his enterprise was organised in southern Europe, Roh entered into negotiations with the Elector of Augustus of Saxony in 1579 to establish a centre in Leipzig from where pepper would be sold to Germany, the Netherlands, the Baltic States, and Poland. But soon all Rott's expectations and plans to control the spice trade of northern Europe through Leipzig collapsed. By 1580, he became bankrupt and his India contract was taken over by Giovanni Rovelasca, an Italian merchant from Milan.(144)

The bankruptcy of Rott coincided with the Union of the two crowns Spain and Portugal under Philip II (and Philip I in Portugal) after the death of Cardinal Henry. In terms of empire and commerce, Philip now saw the possibility of controlling within his realm the riches of Asia, Africa, and America along with some of finest ports in Europe. His Dutch subjects, however, continued their successful resistance and were supported, after 1580, by England and France.(145)

The part of the Indian contract originally concluded by Konrad Rott had been taken over, as has been mentioned earlier, by Rovelasca after 1580. Rovelasca, supported by the Italians and perhaps by a Spanish branch of the Fugers, managed the Indian contract until 1585.(146)

With the expiration of the Rott-Rovellasca contract in 1586, Philip II now apparently hope to conclude a new arrangements for the distribution of spices in Europe. But the continuous war with Netherlands and the outbreak of war with England paralysed his plans. Forced by the circumstances, he already began as early as 1581 to negotiate with Venice to take Portuguese pepper.(147) In 1585, he offered to the Venetians 30,000 quintals of pepper per year at a decreased rate of 30 Ducats (about 40 Ashrafis) per quintal at Lisbon. But his offer was refused, probably because the Venetians feared objections from the Turks. Similar offers were subsequently refused by the Milanese, Genoan and Florence.

While seeking to find a buyer for the European contract, Philip II concluded a new India trading contract in 1586. Giovanni Rovelasca, with his Italian associates, continued to be the contractor, though the negotiations in Spain were now conducted by one Giraldo Paris, a noble of Liburg and a copper trader. In the agreement signed at Valencia on February 15, 1586, the new contractors stipulated that for a period of six years they would equip five vessels each year to sail to India and Malacca carrying 170,000 ducats for the purchase of pepper. They agreed to deliver 30,000 quintals of pepper to Lisbon each year.(148) Finally the Weslers took five-twelfth's share in the enterprise. In the following year, Octavian and Philip Edward originally the Fugers' secretaries, bought a one-quarter interest in the Indian contract.(149)

In an effort to regularise the distribution of pepper in Europe and in the hope of collecting the debts owed to them, a group of the king's creditors agreed in March, 1591, under pressure from the crown, to form a syndicate for the purposes of signing a European contract with Philip. This was divided into thirty-two shares twelve belonging to André Ximenés, a Portuguese merchant of Italian origin and a banker doing business at Lisbon and Antwerp. The remainder were divided as follows: Fugers seven, Welsers five, Rovelasca four, and the Spanish merchants Francisco and Pedro Malvenda of Bouggos four.(150) These merchants sold their shares after 1591 to Lubeck, Middleburg, Amsterdam, and Danzig, for northern cities, Hamburg in the last decade of the sixteenth century became the most important point of distribution for the pepper trade. (151) Evidently, it proved to be one of the safest places for the merchants to operate during the disruption attending the Anglo-Dutch-Spanish war. But the lower price and the big stock of pepper in Venice after 1592 kept the Portuguese pepper out of the Italian markets. The situation in Asian and African continents was taking a new turn favourable to the revival of Venice-Arabian trade and to the decline of commercial relations between Italy and the Iberian states.(152)

The great contractors of *Carreira da India* trade, having suffered losses on their pepper contract of 1592-1598 and 1599, in Antwerp and Florence, were retiring from the trade with India in the face of Dutch competition in Asia, sinking their fortunes.(153) But still there were daring merchant contractors such as Afonso Vaaz de Souza, António Rodrigues da Veiga, Duarte Ximenẹs and Gaspar Ximenés (cousins of Ximenés d'Aragão), all continued to participate in the Asian trade till the third decade of the seventeenth century.(154) But, by then, the principal family fortunes in Lisbon, Antwerp, and Florence had retired from the trade with India.(155) It will be too early to conclude that Goa-Lisbon trade was already declined as it has been believed by many historians. On the contrary, in Lisbon and elsewhere, a new generation of more aggressive merchants carried on the Asiatic trade, and from these successful Lisbon merchants of the private trade with India the crown later recruited its leading bankers. For the while, Ximenés d'Aragão and their associates in the contracts were concentrating on the monopoly of spices, a host of merchants was plying the private free trade in other Asian commodities that lay outside the crowns monopoly.(156)

However, towards the end of the sixteenth century, the international turbulence made the task of the old contractors even more hazardous for their supply of pepper to *Casa da India*. Contrary to the contract they were never in a position to deliver in the 30,000 quintals of pepper.(157)

Financing of Trade in India

In India, when the Portuguese first arrived, they faced the immediate problem of ready cash to pay for the commodities. After their settlements in Cochin and Cannanore, they were in a position to solve this problem to a considerable extent with the help of the rulers of these areas. The king of Cochin stood as a guarantee and obtained the spices on credit for the fleet of João de Nova during 1501-1502.(158) The Portuguese owed a sum of 10,000 Cruzados to the monarch in 1513 and therefore, Afonso de Albuquerque had to pay it by selling 1,000 quintals of copper at Gujarat.(159) The practice of taking loan or getting commodities on credit with the help of the kings of Cochin continued even in the second half of the sixteenth century. (160) The king of Cannanore also procured commodities on credit. In 1513 he delivered 4,000 quintals of ginger to the Portuguese factor at Cannanore on credit. (161) Later, the Portuguese settlers on the Malabar coast, especially those in Cochin and Cannanore, too advanced money to the nominees of the king of Portugal for the purchase of commodities on the Malabar coast.(162) It was reported that the Portuguese settlers in Cochin were more prompt in giving loans to the Portuguese government than those settled in Goa.(163) Very few local merchants were found having direct contacts with the Portuguese merchants in the sixteenth century.(164) Thus, it can be assumed that during most of the sixteenth century the Portuguese official had to depend on the local kings to obtain the supplies on credit or getting the cash on interest by the local creditors.(165)

Trade and it's Profit

As the Portuguese were the monopoly holders throughout the sixteenth century, both in India and in Europe they purchased the Indian commodities at a lesser price but disposed them off at the highest possible one in Europe but certainly lower than it was available in Italy before the discovery of the Cape route to India. During the early sixteenth century, one quintals of pepper of Malabar cost at the most 2.5 Cruzados (about five Ashrafis) and after reaching at Lisbon, including all such expenditure as freight and other charges, it was valued at about six Cruzados. At this time, the sale price per quintal of pepper was twenty-two Cruzados. Thus the profit earned was 16.41 Cruzados or almost 300 %(166). A little later, the margin went up to between 300 and 500 percent as has been suggested by one historian.(167) Between 1580 and 1585, pepper prices rose sharply in Europe and thus increased the profits, but thereafter they trailed off until about 1592.(168) At about this time the international trade rivalry had already started, chiefly the revival of the Venetian trade through the old trade routes via Alexandria as well as Aleppo and Beirut. This competition not only drove up the prices of spices in India, but also led to a considerable decline in their sale price in Europe, thus decreasing the profits. For instance, in the last decade of the sixteenth century, the pepper cost sixteen Cruzados a quintal after reaching Lisbon, and was sold to the contractors with the rate of 36 Cruzados, which meant a mere profit of 125 percent.(169) Thus the profit and loss could be judged through this brief discussion.

Monopoly of the Trade in India and Europe

The right of the Portuguese issuance of *Cartazes* was granted by the several Papal Bulls in the early sixteenth century.(170) Though the high seas were common to all (since there was no public route), this law was not acceptable to the Indians. It was valid only in Europe, and to the Christians who by faith and baptism became member of the Roman Church. According to the Portuguese, though the Hindus and the Muslims, being outside the law of Jesus Christ and being condemned to eternal damnation, had no right to the high seas. Or at least, the chronicler, João de Barros argued that there was no *Mare Libervm* in India. In other words, the Indian Ocean became *Mare Clausvm* by the arrival of the Portuguese, a "Christian" power.(171) It was in the light of these consideration that he explained the necessity of *Cartazes* for the ships in Indian Ocean or more specifically for non Christian travellers in the Ocean.(172) But this theory was refuted by the Dutch and the English in the end of the sixteenth century.

Conclusion

A brief survey such as this one of the sixteenth century environment of Asia in general and India in particular, together with the Portuguese trade to the dawn of the seventeenth century, leads one to conclude that the bureaucratic structure of the Portuguese trade which started at the dawn of the sixteenth century passed through many vicissitudes. In the beginning, the Portuguese trade was open for all, but later when it flourished, it became monopolistic. Meanwhile, the officials of the India House increased in number according to the requirement. Later, when the Spanish ruler took over the sovereignty as the king of Portugal, he implemented new rules regarding overseas trade of India. He replaced the old financial houses by a new council of Finance probably because he wanted to secure his own royalty by appointing his own men. The India House, once a supreme house was made subordinate to the *Conselho da Fazenda*. The *Conselho da India* was changed into the *Conselho da Câmara da India*. However, these changes had certain deep-rooted effects on the Portuguese trade in India during the seventeenth century, which will be discussed in the following chapters.

The Portuguese relation with the Indian states in regard to the supply of their goods also had important implications for the Portuguese trade. In fact, in the beginning, Portuguese captains and officials tried to establish their trade monopoly by force of arms, but later they realised that this would be next to impossible while at the same time maintaining a peaceful trade and flow of commodities in such sharp competition from the local merchants and rulers. Therefore, to some extent, especially with Cochin, Cannanore and Quilon in the beginning and later, after gaining their footholds there, they brought other states under their control. Since their relations with most Indian states were based mostly on gunpoint, it was very difficult for them to maintain a stable atmosphere for any length of time. This was probably the main reason that the Indian as well as Arabian states, except for Cochin, Cannanore and Quilon, could never have any friendly relations with the Iberians. The Portuguese control of the seas through various fortresses and factories, plus the imposition of *Cartazes*, always kept the Indian states in unrest and seeking to find some way to break through the restraints. And when the other European reached, they welcomed them. Obviously, they thought the European rivals might be able to help them against the Portuguese monopolists. Various regions like Malabar, Kanara and Gujarat on the west coast, and Coromandel and Bengal on the eastern, were the main producing centres of the spices, pepper, cloths and other sorts of merchandise mentioned above. Portuguese merchants collected all the goods required by them from all these above mentioned regions and brought to Goa for reshipment to Portugal.

Various commodities, pepper, cinnamon, ginger, clove, mace, nutmegs and many sorts of spices and drugs were exported in the beginning of the sixteenth century by the Portuguese. Later, textiles were also included in their exports, though in very limited quantity until the last decades of the century. Till the end of the century, the trade flourished and volume of the trading commodities increased year by year. But in the last decade, when European competitors, like the Dutch and the English, started taking more interest, their volume of trade started dwindling. This rivalry decreased the demand for the Indian goods provided by the Portuguese in the northern Europe, which had been the major centres for supply by the Portuguese. Now these two nations began providing the same commodities in which the Portuguese earned more than 300 to 500 percent of profit while carrying them only to their country and before reshipment. In India itself they maintained several routes as their monopoly, and thus profited considerably. Their negotiation with curious countries of south-east Asia, Ceylon, Persia and, finally, with the coastal cities and regions of Africa made their condition financially sound, but even out of these profits they were not able to run such a huge maritime enterprise as that of India. To maintain this Indian commerce, the Portuguese king had to seek various means and sources of financing. The king even welcomed Catholic foreigners to part in his overseas business. Many nationals, mainly Germans and Italians, took a very active part in this trade by advancing their money on loan or sending their ships to carry goods in the name of the king of Portugal. Only with the help of these foreigners simultaneously with the new Christians could the king enjoy the monopoly he dreamt of. But toward the end of the century they feared having more transactions with the Portuguese because of the growing European political turmoil and the Inquisition. This forced the Portuguese authorities to search for new sources and means of financing their enterprise at the dawn of the seventeenth century.

Notes

Indo-Portuguese Trade at the Dawn of the Seventeeth Century

1. F. P. Mendes da Luz, *Regimentos da* India House, p. 32
2. *Ibid.*, p. 27
3. Damião Peres, *Regimentos das Cazas da India e Minas*, p. 3
4. F. Mendes da Luz, *O Conselho da India*, pp. 6979; F.D. Lach, *Asia in the Making of Europe*, Vol. I, Book I, p. 135; C.R. Boxer, *The Portu guese Sea-borne Empire*, pp. 10-78.
5. Da Luz, *O Conselho...*, pp. 81-82.
6. *Ibid.*, pp. 2728.
7. Damião Peres, *Regimentos...*, p. 40
8. *Ibid.*, p. 47
9. Da Luz, *O Conselho...*, pp. 81-82
10. *Ibid.*, pp. 27-28
11. For the functions of the India House see M.N. Pearson, *Merchants and Rulers in Gujarat*, pp. 33-56; K.S. Mathew, *The Portuguese Trade with India in the Sixteenth Century*, pp. 29-77
12. Da Luz, *Regimentos...*, pp. 55-58
13. *Ibid*, p. 27
14. *Ibid*, p. 44
15. *Ibid*, pp. 30, 45
16. *Ibid*, pp. 46-67
17. *Ibid*, p. 27
18. In the early sixteenth century it was 1/20 1/4 percent. Mathew, *Portu guese Trade...*, pp. 123-140
19. Damião Peres, *Regimentos ...*, pp. 63-66
20. Mathew, *Portuguese Trade...*, p. 123
21. Da Luz, *Regimentos...*, p. 47
22. *Ibid*, pp. 49-50
23. *Ibid*, p. 34
24. Diogo de Couto, *Década da Asia*, X.I. p 19
25. Mathew, *Portuguese Trade...*, pp. 29-77
26. *Liberdade*, literally means 'Liberty'. It was a kind of entitlement given to the officials on board which allowed them to carry a certain quan tity of spices without paying any duty.
27. It was also an entitlement probably given to lower category offi cials.
28. Da Luz, *Regimentos..*, p. 55

29. Luís de Figueredo Falcão, (Secretary of the King Philip II), *Livro em que se contém toda a fazenda e real património dos reinos de Portugal, India e ilhas adjacente e outras particularidades*, pp. 183-90; Pearson, *Merchants and Rulers..*, p. 7
30. V.M. Godinho, *Os descobrimentos e a economia mundial*, vol. I, pp.
28- 30; Pearson, *Merchants and Rulers..*, p. 7
31. *APO-BP*, tomo IV, Vol. II, parte I, Goa, 1937, pp. 103-360; *BSGL*, Res. maço nº3,4, (Passim); A.B. de Sousa, *SPHMMI*, vol. I, (passim); Figueredo Falcão, *Livro em que* ... (passim)
32. George D. Winius, "The Shadow Empire of Goa in the Bay of Ben gal" in *Itinerario*, 1983-2, pp. 83-101
33. *APO-BP*, Tomo IV, Vol. II, parte I, Goa, 1937, pp. 103-360; BSGL, *Res.* Maço nº3,4, (Passim); A.B. de Sousa, *SPHMMI*, vol. I, (passim); Figueredo Falcão, *Livro em que* ... (passim)
34. Mathew, *Portuguese Trade*, pp. 27-77; Pearson, *Merchants and Rul ers...*, pp. 57-112; Lach, *Asia in the*, vol. I, Part I, pp. 338-437: and refer to F. Note. Number - 31
35. Barros, *Década*, I, part, p. 438; Mathew, *Portuguese Trade...*, pp. 42-43
36. Alexander and Costa Paiva, *Roteiro da viagem de Vasco da Gama em MCCCXCVII*, pp. 42-51, 63-65; Mathew, *Portuguese Trade*, pp. 43-45; Panikkar, A History of Kerala, 1498-1801, pp. 38-40; R.S. Whiteway, *The Rise of Portuguese Power in India*, pp. 90-103; F.C. Danvers, *The Portuguese in India*, vol. I, pp. 100-105
37. Afonso de Albuquerque, *Cartas de Afonso de Albuquerque*, tomo III, pp. 73-84; Judice Biker, (ed.) *Collecção de tratados e concertos de pazes que o estado da India Portuguesa fez com os reis e senhores em que teve nas partes da Asia e Africa oriental desde o princípio da conquista até ao fim do século XVIII*, tomo I, pp. 10-24
38. Barros, *Décadas*... III, part II, pp. 451-52
39. *Ibid*, tomo IV, part I, pp. 470-75
40. In the Portuguese documents they have been mentioned as '*Piratas*' (pirates). In fact they were the traditional captains and admirals of the Zamorin of Calicut. See O.K. Nambiar, *The Kunjali Admirals of Calicut*, (passim)
41. Nambiar, *The Kunjali..* (passim); Panikkar, *A History of.* pp. 95-128, see also his *Asia and the Western Dominance*, 1498-1945, (Passim)
42. Biker, *Collecção de tratados..* tomo I, pp. 186-189; Nambiar, *The Kunjali*...pp. 116-119; Manuel de Faria e Sousa, *Asia Portuguesa*, vol. V, pp. 193-197
43. Faria e Sousa, *Asia...*, vol. V, pp. 206-213; Nambiar, *The Kunjali...*, pp. 132-34
44. Faria e Sousa, *Asia...*, vol. V, pp. 214-225; Biker, *Collecção...*, tomo I, pp. 186-89

45. Biker, *Collecção...*, tomo I, pp. 10-14
46. Faria e Sousa, *Asia...* vol. V, pp. 193-200; Biker, *Collecção..*, tomo I, pp. 186-89
47. Faria e Sousa, *Asia..* vol. I, pp. 142-50; Mathew, *Portuguese Trade...*, pp. 48-50
48. Nilakanta Sastri, *A History of South India*, pp. 291-97; R. Sewel, *A Forgotten Empire*, pp. 10-78; A.R. Disney, *Twilight of the Pepper Em pire*, p. 23
49. Disney, *Twilight of the Pepper..*, p. 2
50. Disney, *Twilight of the Pepper..*, pp. 35; Simão Botelho, "Tombo do estado da India", in *SPHIP*, (ed.) A.J. Lima Felner, pp. 258-59
51. *HAG*, cod., 4460, pp. 20-60; *BSGL*, Res. Maço nº 3, 4
52. Biker, *Collecção...*, tomo I, pp. 96-97.
53. Cartas, *op.cit.*, tomo I, p. 21; Faria e Sousa, *op.cit.*, vol. I pp. 293-300; P.S.S. Pissurlenkar, *Tentativos dos portugueses para a ocupação do Concão*, separata dos *Anais* II série, vol. 6, Lisboa, 1955, pp. 425-426; Whiteway, *op.cit.*, pp. 130-35; Pearson, *op.cit.*, pp. 30-33; Boxer, *Por tuguese Seaborne...*, pp. 46-47; Mathew, *Portuguese Trade...* p. 59;
54. Faria e Sousa, *op.cit.*, vol. I, pp. 300-310; *Cartas*, tomo I, pp. 21ff.
55. *Ibid*, pp. 117-125; Whiteway, *op.cit.*, pp. 285-86; Biker, *Collecção...*,tomo I, pp. 116-118, 122-27.
56. N. Alexander Kyd, *History of Konkan*, London, 1899, p. 38.
57. Couto, *Década*, no. IX, p. 290
58. Biker, *Collecção...*, tomo I, pp. 160-80
59. See Chapter 2, part I
60. See Chapter 4
61. Faria e Sousa, *op.cit.*, vol. I, pp. 232-40; Mathew, *Portuguese Trade...* pp. 39-40; Lach, *op.cit.*, pp. 392-93; Whiteway, *op.cit.*, pp. 110-127; Boxer, *The Portuguese Seaborne...* pp. 46-47.
62. Faria e Sousa, *op.cit.*, vol. I, pp. 257-79; R. B. Serjeant, *The Portuguese Off the South Arabian Coast*, Oxford, 1963, pp. 44-45; Whiteway, *op.cit.*, pp. 124-26.
63. *Ibid.*
64. M. S. Commissariat, *A History of Gujarat*, London 1938, vol. I, pp. 293.
65. Whiteway, *op.cit.*, pp. 128-78; Lach, *op.cit.*, pp. 394.
66. Biker, *Collecção...*, tomo I, pp. 63-83, 103-108.
67. *Ibid.*, pp. 127-30
68. Faria Sousa, *op.cit.*, vol. III, pp. 284-90
69. Commissariat, *op.cit.*, vol. I, pp. 290-350.
70. Couto, *Década*, IX, cap. XIII, p. 69.

71. Couto, *Década*, IX, cap. XIII, p. 70-78; Danvers, *Portuguese in India*, vol. II, p. 4; Commissariat, *A History of Gujarat*, vol. I, pp. 290-350
72. *Ibid*
73. Couto, *Década*, IX, cap. XIII, p. 76-80; HAG, *Consultas do serviços de partes*, códice 1043, fls. 47-49.
74. Sir Edward Maclagan, *Os Jesuitas e o grão Mogol*, Porto 1946, pp. 29-79.
75. *Ibid*; And also See Chapter 2, part I.
76. Faria e Sousa, *op.cit.*, vol. I, pp. 220-230; Mathew, *op.cit.*, p. 59.
77. Faria e Sousa, *op.cit.*, vol. I, pp. 233-50; Barros, *Da Asia de...*, Década II[a], parte I[a], pp. 109-120; Whiteway, *The Rise of...*, p. 119
78. See Chapter 2, part III.
79. Barros, *Década* II, pp. 20-57, 119-20; Whiteway, *The Rise of...*, p. 119
80. Barros, *Década* II, pp. 20-57, 119-20
81. *Ibid*, p. 40
82. Pearson, *Merchants and Rulers..*, pp. 33-35
83. *Ibid.*
84. Mendes da Luz, *O conselho...*, (passim); Boxer, *The Portuguese Sea borne...*, p. 42-44; Whiteway, *op.cit.*, pp. 58-75; J.B. Harrison, *New Cambridge Modern History*, vol. III, pp. 532-34.
85. Pearson, *Merchants and Rulers..*, pp. 34-35.
86. *Ibid*; Also see for details Mendes da Luz, *O conselho...*, (passim)
87. Damião Peres, *Regimentos...*, pp. 29-30.
88. *Ibid.*; Mathew, *Portuguese Trade...*, p. 90.
89. *Ibid.*
90. *Cartas*, tomo II, p. 271; Barros, *Década*, part I, p. 254.
91. Mathew, *Portuguese Trade...*, p. 91
92. *Ibid.*, pp. 29-77; Pearson, *Merchants and Rulers..*, pp. 33-36.
93. Mathew, *Portuguese Trade...*, p. 29-77; Pearson, *Merchants and Rul ers..*, pp. 33-56; W.H. Moreland, *From Akbar to Aurangzeb*, N. Delhi, 1972, p. 7; *Cartaz* can be defined as a kind of safe-conduct issued for the Indian and the Arabian seas to the private merchant's ships so that they could navigate and enter into the Portuguese ports for loading and unloading without trouble.
94. *Rupees*, that was current at the Mughal Period.
95. HAG, *Regimentos e Instruções*, cod. 1420, fl. 122v-124
96. Pearson, *Merchants and Rulers..*, p. 43.
97. Pearson, *Merchants and Rulers..*, p. 43; Moreland, *From Akbar to Aurangzeb*, p. 9.
98. Pearson, *Merchants and Rulers..*, p. 41; Faria e Sousa, vol. IV, pp. 27-28.

99. A group of people, merchants or ships travelling together from one port to the other.
100. Couto, *Década*, vol. VIII, cap. 30.
101. Pietro Della Valle, *The Travel of Pietro Della Valle in* India, London, 1892, vol. I, pp. 385-86, 393-94.
102. HAG, *Fortalezas*, cod. 4460, fls. 412; *APO-BP*., tomo IV, vol. II, part I, pp. 279-80; Pearson, *Merchants and Rulers*.., pp. 43-44.
103. J. L Azevedo, *Épocas de Portugal Económico*, Lisboa, (Passim) Mathew, *Portuguese Trade*..., (passim); Pearson, *Merchants and Rulers*.., (pas sim); V.M. Godinho, *Os Descobrimentos*..., (passim).
104. Disney, *Twilight of the Pepper*..., pp. 25
105. HAG, cod. 4460, fls. 20-60; BSGL, *Res*. Maço nº. 3 & 4 (passim) *APO-BP*, *op.cit*., pp. 307-320; Da Luz, in *Stvdia 6, Das cidades*..., pp. 40-42; Disney, *Twilight of the Pepper*..., p. 5.
106. HAG, cod. 7786, fls. 288-89; *APO-BP*, *op.cit*., pp. 316; Disney, *Twi light of the Pepper*..., p. 5
107. *SPHI*, pp. 257-58.
108. Duarte Barbosa, *The Book of Duarte Barbosa*, vol. II, pp. 182-84; Tomé Pires, *The Suma Oriental of Tomé Pires*, vol. I, pp. 43-44.
109. Mathew, *Portuguese Trade*..., (passim); Pearson, *Merchants and Rul ers*.., (passim)
110. Duarte Barbosa, *The Book of*..., vol. II, pp. 182-84; Tomé Pires, *The Suma Oriental*..., vol. I, pp. 43-44.
111. See Chapter IV.
112. Azevedo, *Épocas de Portugal*..., pp. 89-173; Mathew, *Portuguese Trade*..., Chapt. IV; Pearson, *Merchants and Rulers*.., Chapt. II; Godinho, *Os Descobrimentos* vols. II, III; Disney, *Twilight of the Pep per*..., pp. 16-49; Boxer, *The Portuguese Seaborne*..., pp. 39-64.
113. Mathew, *Portuguese Trade*..., pp. 113-14.
114. AGS, cod. 1571, *op.cit*., p. 14.
115. Azevedo, *Épocas de Portugal*..., pp. 107-115.
116. Lach, *Asia in the Making of*..., pp. 131-41.
117. BSGL, *Res*. Maço No. 4 No, 88 (passim); Falcão, *op.cit*., (passim); Boxer, *The Portuguese Seaborne*..., pp. 62-63; Mathew, *Portuguese Trade*..., pp. 13-120
118. Boxer, *The Portuguese Seaborne*..., pp. 61-63
119. Boxer, *The Portuguese Seaborne*..., pp. 61-63; J. H. Van Linschoten, *The Voyages of John Huyghen Van Linschoten to the East Indies*, vol. II, pp. 77-78.
120. Boxer, *The Portuguese Seaborne*..., pp. 61-63.
121. ANTT, *Chancelaria de D. Manuel*, cod. 38, fls. 125-126v.

122. Mathew, *Portuguese Trade...*, pp. 133-34.
123. Boxer, *The Portuguese Seaborne...*, pp. 61-65; Pearson, *Merchants and Rulers..*, Chapt. II.
124. *Cartas, op.cit.*, tomo I, pp. 265, 272-73, 424; Mathew, *Portuguese Trade...*, pp.146-47; Boxer, *The Portuguese Seaborne...*, pp. 44-48.
125. Boxer, *The Portuguese Seaborne...*, pp. 41-60.
126. *Cartas*, tomo I, pp. 52, 425; Boxer, *The Portuguese Seaborne...* pp. 41-50.
127. Mathew, *Portuguese Trade...*, pp. 146-48.
128. *Cartas*, tomo I, pp. 272, 425; Boxer, *The Portuguese Seaborne*...pp. 40-41, 44, 57, 59; Mathew, *Portuguese Trade...*, pp. 146; Whiteway, *The Rise of Portuguese...*, pp. 43-44, 49-50.
129. Barbosa, *op.cit.*, vol. I, (passim)
130. *Cartas*, tomo I, pp. 266-69, 283; *APO-BP*, tomo IV, vol. II, part I, pp. 20-21, 51, 58-59; Boxer, *The Portuguese Seaborne...* pp. 55-57.
131. *Cartas*, tomo I, pp. 266-269, 28, 256; Boxer, *The Portuguese Seaborne*...pp.62-63; Mathew, *Portuguese Trade...*, pp. 148.
132. *Cartas*, tomo I, pp. 425; Pearson, *Merchants and Rulers...* pp. 18; Mathew, *Portuguese Trade...*, pp. 147.
133. Mathew, *Portuguese Trade..*, pp. 61-63, see for details of their share of money in the contract.
134. *Ibid.*
135. Mathew, *Portuguese Trade..*, pp. 61-63; Virginia Rau,*Um Grande mercador banquario Italiano em Portugal*, Separata de Estudos Italianos em Portugal, No. 24, 1965 (passim)
136. *Ibid.*
137. *Ibid.*
138. F.C. Lane, *Venice and History*, pp. 25-34; Lach, *Asia in the Making of Europe...*, Vol. I, Book I, p. 132-34.
139. Azevedo, *Épocas de...*, pp. 10-78.
140. BSGL, India House, Res. Maço 4, N. 88, docs. 6/6, 6/8, 7/1, 12/ 16/ 13; AGS, *Secretarias provinicales*, cod. 1571, pp. 14-45; *APO-CR*, fasc. 3, pp. 52-54; Azevedo, *Épocas de*...(Passim) ; Lach, *Asia in the Making of Europe...*, vol. I, Book I, p. 134-38; James C. Boyajian, *Portuguese Bankers at the Court of Spain* 1626-1650, See preface and first two chapters.
141. *Ibid.*
142. *Ibid.*
143. *Ibid.*
144. *Ibid.*
145. *Ibid.*

146. *Ibid.*
147. *Ibid.*
148. AGS, *op. cit*, cod. 1571, pp. 14-30.
149. *Ibid.*
150. Lach, *Asia in the Making of...*, Vol. I, Book I, p. 138-39; Also see the documents used in Table 1.1.
151. Lach, *Asia in the Making of ...*, Vol. I, Book I, p. 138-42.
152. *Ibid.*
153. AGS, *op.cit.*, cod. 1571, pp. 14-30; Lach, *Asia in the Making of...*, vol. I, Book I, p. 135-38.
154. Boyajian, *Portuguese Bankers...*, pp. 27; Lach, *Asia in the Making of...*, vol. I, Book I, pp. 134-38.
155. *Ibid.*
156. See Table 1.1
157. Disney, *Twilight of the Pepper...*, (Passim); Boxer, *The Great Ship...*, pp. 211-71.
158. Mathew, *Portuguese Trade..*, pp. 18182.
159. *Cartas*, tomo III, pp. 39697.
160. AGS, *op.cit.*, cod. 1571, pp. 2021.
161. *Cartas...*, tomo III, pp. 49.
162. *Ibid.* p. 397.
163. Mathew, *Portuguese Trade..*, pp. 181.
164. *Ibid.*
165. Mathew, *Portuguese Trade...*, pp. 42-59, 181-92.
166. *Ibid.* 197-98.
167. Azevedo, *Épocas de...*, pp. 10-78; *SPHI*, *op.cit.*, pp. 34-35
168. BSGL, *Res.* Maço No. 4, No, 88, doc. 6/6; Falcão, *op.cit.*, pp. 75-80.
169. See documents used in table 1.1.
170. Barros, *Década*, I, part II, pp. 1417.
171. *Ibid.*
172. *Ibid.* p. 15.

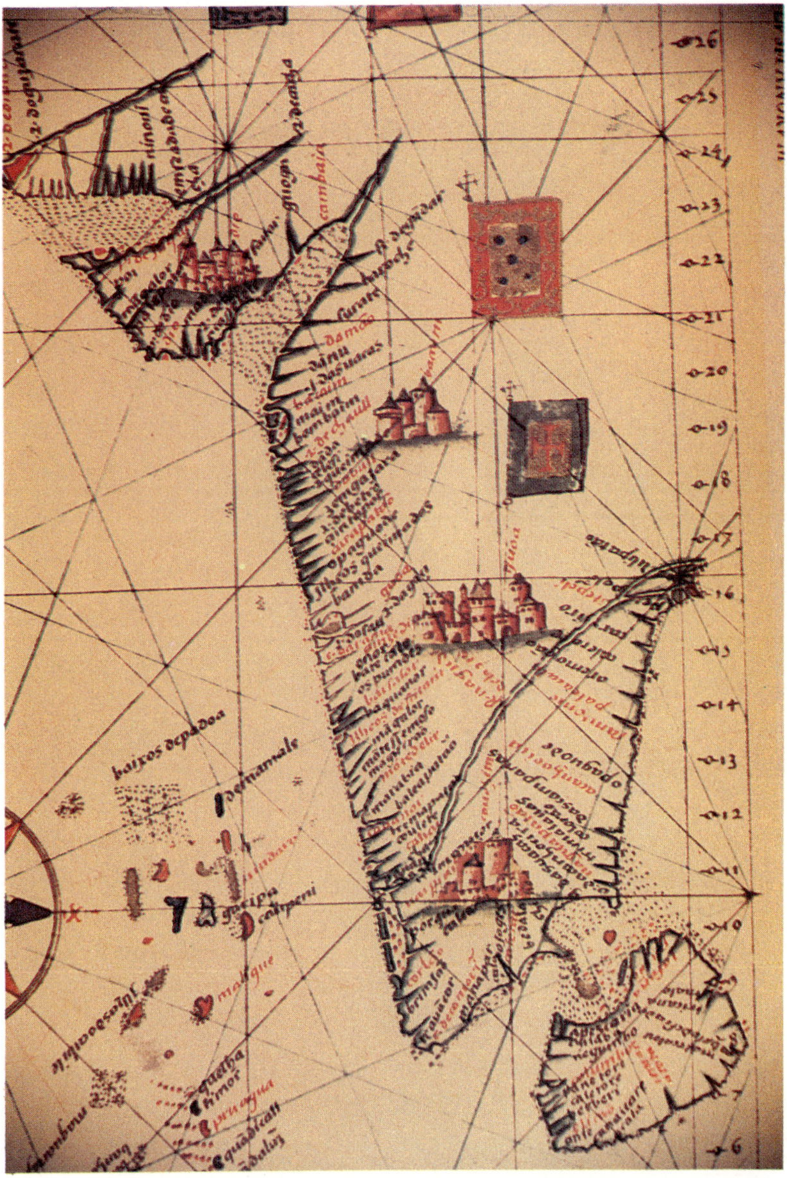

Plate 2 A Sixteenth Century Map of Western Coast of India. *F. Vaz Dourado*

CHAPTER- 2

Commercial Contacts and International Rivalries During the Seventeenth Century on the Indian Coast

In the sixteenth century, the Portuguese were powerful enough to overawe the native powers with their maritime might. Indian rulers were generally unhappy with the Portuguese highhandedness and their monopolistic tendencies. During the first seventy years or so, both singly and in combination, they made several unsuccessful attempts to drive away their intruders. But during the seventeenth century, a notable change can be found in their relation with the Portuguese due to the arrival of other European powers. From the beginning of the seventeenth century, the Zamorin of Calicut joined hands with the Dutch against the Portuguese and provided pepper and other spices from his territories. During this time only, as has been seen earlier, Venkatappa Nayak was expanding his power and became a threat to their existence. The Portuguese, in order to maintain their supply of pepper, accepted some of his overbearing demands. Bijapuri and Ahmadnagar Sultans who had already tried to expel the Portuguese from their lands of Goa and Chaul, also invited the Dutch and offered various rights and privileges of trade in their kingdoms in hopes of overthrowing the Portuguese. The emergence of the Marathas about the middle of the seventeenth century as a paramount power likewise disturbed the existing balance of the Portuguese. Mughal-Portuguese relations also became estranged due to the Mughal patronage to the English and later the Dutch in their empire during the second decade of the century. In the beginning, the Dutch and the English, in their efforts to ruin the Portuguese, remained united till 1635. But after 1635, the situation changed entirely. The English, fearing the increasing successes of the Dutch, joined hands with the Portuguese against the later. The Dutch, on the other hand, remained aggressive until they ousted the Portuguese from the Malabar spice producing areas and became master. Keeping these broad outlooks in mind, this chapter has been divided into three main subchapters:

i) Portuguese relations with the Indian states,

ii) Portuguese relations with the Dutch and finally,

iii) Portuguese relations with the English.

Part I: Potuguese Relations with the Indian States

For the convenience of study, this subchapter has also been divided into the following sections:

(a) Portuguese Relations with the Malabar States

Malabar was the first region on the Indian soil where the Portuguese established their footholds. It was also the first place in which its power began to fail. The so called 'pirate king', the Kunjali Marakkar, was yet to be hanged at Goa when the Zamorin-Portuguese confederacy broke in 1604, upon the Zamorin's entering into negotiations with the Dutch Admiral Van der Hagen to overthrow their settlements and factories not only from the Calicut but from the whole Indian subcontinent.(1) Although the Portuguese formal diplomatic relations and their factory at Calicut remained in existence for some time, neither side could continue their friendly relations for long time out of mutual suspicion.(2) In 1614, troubles arose between the Portuguese and the Calicut ruler when the Zamorin attacked and captured the town of Cranganore.(3) In this war the Zamorin was helped by the ruler of Parur who was also indisposed towards the Portuguese.(4) This ally commenced a series of attacks on the Portuguese shipping between Cochin and Paliporto. Even the king of Cochin was not on goods terms with the Portuguese at this time. Because of these strained relations, probably, it was believed in Goa that all was done at the instigation of the ruler of Cochin.(5) After a considerable loss on both sides, peace was restored through embassies between the two.(6) Thereafter, it seems. that no untoward incident took place from that sector to disturb the peace of the Portuguese.

In the mean time, the Portuguese were challenged on the seas, both by the Dutch and the English. Their appearance changed the whole situation. The Portuguese fought a losing battle and in spite of heavy odds, maintained their position for some time as defenders. However, it was quite obvious that the Portuguese were weakening their power gradually. Their naval insufficiency in the Arabian Sea was exposed to every local ruler of Malabar. As might be expected, the opposition, even from the minor principalities on the Malabar Coast, increased.(7)

The nominal authority of the Portuguese in Malabar and their control of trade, through Cochin, Quilon and Cannanore, continued for the first half of the seventeenth century before it fell in the hands of the Dutch.(8)

(b) Portuguese-Kanara Relations

Portuguese settlements at Onor, Barcelore, and Mangalore proved to be a major stumbling block to the initial stages of the expansion of Venkatappa Nayak in the early seventeenth century. At this time, the Portuguese authorities were very cautious in their response. They were aware of the danger for their commercial and trading settlements, but were reluctant to enter into open war. That is why they tried to check the increasing power of Venkatappa Nayak by encouraging threatened princes of Onor and Mangalore to enter into a defensive alliance.(9) However, these measures proved to be unsuccessful. Therefore, by early 1618, they had to involve themselves directly through the provision of troops, artillery and ammunitions to their ally and close neighbour at Mangalore, the king of Banguel.(10) Though in the beginning they were successful, in late 1618 they suffered a serious defeat near Mangalore, losing their commanders, Francisco de Miranda Henrique and Luis de Brito de Melo. It is because of the heavy pressure from the Dutch at Surat on the western coast of India and Jakarta, that they were obliged to seek peace.(11) They forced the king of Banguel to accept even the unfavourable terms from Venkatappa Nayak and his ally, the Queen of Olala. In 1623, the Portuguese sent a peace embassy to the court of Venkatappa.(12) Pietro Della Valle, the Italian traveller, who also accompanied the embassy, was very critical of it and remarked in the weakening position of the Portuguese in India during this period. He had roundly criticised the Rani of Olala, when he met her while on the road, and described her as "rather a dirty kitchen wench, or laundress, than a delicate and noble queen".(13) His comments certainly reveal the poor naval and military power of the Portuguese and their inability to deal with the problems in Kanara in the early decades of the seventeenth century.

The Nayak, realising the weakness of the Portuguese on the seas and seeing his own power increase day by day over the neighbouring territories, proceeded to insist that the Portuguese buy most of their pepper from him on his terms and conditions, and at a very high price.(14) This policy was later continued by Virabhadra Nayak, when the Portuguese political and economic condition had deteriorated even further because of the Dutch and the English encroachment on their settlements and shipping. The Portuguese authorities, keeping in view their position and the growing power of the Nayakas of Ikkeri, arranged the contracts as advantageously as possible to get their terms fulfilled and their consignment ready for the annual fleet thus avoided the enmity from the Nayak.(15) The ruler of Ikkeri became the major concern of the Portuguese to keep peace with, especially when the threat from the Dutch and the English were increasing. In 1629, the Portuguese viceroy, the Count of Linhares, in order to strengthen his position at Barcelore, established a new fortress at Cambolim. Virabhadra Nayak considered this fortress a barrier to the harmonious relations between him and the Portuguese. It was indeed one of the most strategically located forts in the region and had many advantages over Barcelore and possessed a better water supply. It was favourably situated for controlling both, the adjacent paddy lands and the sea.(16) The Count of Linhares, in fact, intended to transfer the factory of Barcelore to the new site, but in reality, both the places continued to be occupied until 1653-54, when Barcelore was ceded to the Nayak of Ikkeri.(17) After this, there was hardly any occasion for the Portuguese to reoccupy it because of the increasing menace of the Dutch and their attacks on Ceylon, the territories of Malabar and weaknesses of their own maritime power.

(c) Portuguese-Bijapuri Relations

The dawn of the seventeenth century saw the commencement of peaceful relations between the Portuguese and the Sultan of Bijapur. It was only through his mediation that the treaty between the Portuguese and the Sultan of Ahmadnagar could be negotiated. But soon good relations between the two ended when the Sultan of Bijapur approached the British for a pact to drive out the Portuguese and extended his facilities to them. But he did not succeed in his attempt because of the "Go slow" policy of the English".(18) The hostility took a new turn when the Portuguese captured two vessels belonging to Bijapur in the Persian Gulf and killed all crew members.(19) Adil Shah responded by detaining the Portuguese revenue comptroller of Muscat.(20) Portuguese became more aggressive and seized another vessel.(21) The situation grew more serious when the Sultan withdrew his ambassador from Goa, closed all the ports for the Portuguese and threatened to attack the provinces of Bardes and Salssete.(22) The Portuguese quickly realised the consequence of this hostile atmosphere when the Bijapuri Sultan extended his support to the Dutch and hampered their textile trade from the territory of Balaghat. This soon led to negotiation with him.(23) Portuguese and the Sultan came still closer in 1632 when Bijapur was invaded by the Mughals.(24) In such circumstances, Bijapuri Sultan asked Goa for help, to which the Portuguese viceroy Linhares agreed immediately, being aware of the consequences of the defeat of Bijapur on his own territories. But according to a letter Linhares wrote on November 29, 1634, to the King of Portugal, it is indicated that he was quite hesitant to take any real steps against the Mughals on account of the latter's power and wrath.(25)

In 1635, Luso-Bijapuri relation again became estranged as the Sultan negotiated with the Dutch to overthrow the Portuguese and provided them facilities at the ports of Dabhol, Karwar, Rajapur and Vengurla. Moreover, the facilities for the construction of a fortress and a factory at nearby Vengurla brought the clouds of disaster for the Portuguese strongholds.(26) After the Dutch obtained their base at Vengurla, their blockade of Goa during 1637-41 became intractable and this particularly aggravated the situation of the Portuguese. The Dutch and the Bijapuri Sultan, both decided to invade Goa by land and the sea. But the Adil Shah's engagements in Kanara saved the Portuguese at Goa.(27) Soon after this, the Portuguese had to face continuous harassment from the Dutch through their blockading the ports of Goa and colony. (28)

(d) Portuguese-Ahmadnagar Relations

Portuguese Ahmadnagar relations took a new turn in the first half of the seventeenth century. After the rise of Malik Amber, the Abyssinian minister, the situation changed considerably. Malik Amber joined hands with the Portuguese to face the new threat of the Mughals on one frontier and to save the northern ports of the Portuguese on the other.(29)

In 1604, Malik Amber granted the right to the Portuguese to collect half of the land revenue in Chaul in response to their help against the Mughals.(30) This new arrangement did not continue for long time as the Portuguese relations with the peasants were not cordial. Malik Amber tried to put an end to these problems by himself but the Portuguese did not agree. This resulted in hostility between the two, which lasted for several years.(31) Yet in 1609, the governor of Chaul sent a fleet to cruise the sea against the ships belonging to Malik Amber, and prevented his obtaining relief from Ahmadnagar. Soon after this, they united through the mediation of Ibrahim Adil Shah due to the Mughal attack in 1615.(32) Misfortune, however, stalked the Ahmadnagar kingdom. Malik Amber died in 1627 and was succeeded by his son, Fateh Muhammad Khan. In the north, the Mughal emperor, Shah Jahan, ascended the throne. Ahmadnagar and Bijapur were more divided than before. This enabled Shah Jahan to subdue Ahmadnagar once and for all in 1637.(33) Thus, Ahmadnagar's problems became the problems of the Mughals.

(e) Portuguese-Maratha Relations

The emergence of the Martha as a threat to Portuguese by the end of the first half of the seventeenth century was less an effect of their activities than those of the other rivals. The rise of Martha as a power occurred soon after 1624 under the leadership of Shahji, father of Shivaji. Shivaji's first thirty years passed through many adventures and troubles but his firm and determined character stood him well. For a man of Shivaji's mettle, his problems were not insurmountable.

All the early successes of Shivaji were not of great importance to the Portuguese. But once his ambitions turned towards the Portuguese territories, Bassein and Chaul, they became alert. Meanwhile, Shivaji had already prepared his navy to face any challenge from the sea. His navy was built up under renegade Portuguese nationals, fugitives escaped from the prison and fortune seekers. This was in 1658 when Shivaji was in the vicinity of Chaul. By this time some of his acts irritated the Portuguese.(34) In 1659, a fleet of twenty war ships of Shivaji were ready for sail in three different ports; Bhivandi, Kalyan and Panvel. Luís Leitão Viegas, a Portuguese national, was commander of the fleet. Shivaji asked him to seek permission from the Portuguese authorities for their departure. But the Portuguese had already made up their minds regarding Shivaji. They not only prohibited the fleet from sailing but also tried to scuttle Shivaji's effort to build a navy.(35) The reason behind this was that the Portuguese wanted to help their friend Siddi Rajapuri, with whom Shivaji was at war and was ready to send his fleet against Siddi. Secondly, Portuguese officers feared a threat to their own sea power. Therefore, no permission was granted for sailing, even out of the ports. In fact, they even succeeded in persuading Viegas and three hundred other fellow compatriot, who were assisting Shivaji in his navy, to desert him at once.(36) This was a severe blow to Shivaji's ambitions but he was not a man to be prevented from reaching his goal. Till the end of his life he remained a threat to the Portuguese sea power.

For the convenience of study of the Portuguese-Maratha relations, the period has been divided into two parts: from 1657-1667, when the Marathas and the Portuguese maintained on the whole cordial relations, despite some misunderstanding and conflict, and 1668-1680, when Shivaji became more fearless and his attacks on the Portuguese vicinities became more intensive and serious. Since the second phase lies beyond the period of the present study, the discussion here is confined to the first only.

In the first phase, the Portuguese followed a varying policy of friendship, hostility, or neutrality towards the Marathas, depending upon the circumstances and in accordance with who their enemies were.

In the context of Shivaji-Bijapuri-Portuguese relations there was hardly any time when Shivaji got Portuguese support against Adil Shah of Bijapur. They were always cautious about the balance of power in Deccan. This was during the time when the Dutch were also very active on the western coast. Their navy was a permanent threat for the Portuguese colonies and trade; therefore, Portuguese chose to behave very diplomatically towards the Marathas, while at others they remained inactive.(37) By the end of 1664, Shivaji had occupied Kudal, Perne and Bicholim of the Adil Shah's territories. The holders of these areas, mostly Desais, were given shelter in Goa, from where they made inroads into the Maratha territory. The basis for the Portuguese policy was that the Dessais' were vassals of Bijapuri Shah and, as pér the agreement, ought to be supported by the Portuguese.(38)

In 1665, after the treaty with the Mughal General, Raja Jai Singh, Shivaji directed his attention towards Khwas Khan, Adil Shah's general, and defeated him on the Konkan coast. At this time the Portuguese officers kept themselves at a distance. Again in 1666, when Shivaji attacked Ponda, which was then under the Adil Shah, the Portuguese secretly aided the Adil Shah with ammunition and provision for his garrison and thus they contributed to the successful resistance to Shivaji.(39)

Maratha-Mughal-Portuguese relation were governed by a different set of factors and as such varied from those discussions above. Here the Portuguese were sympathetic and helpful to Shivaji. The Portuguese were then at war with the Dutch in the southern ports of Malabar and Kanara. In other word Portuguese needed help rather than an enemy, on both land and sea. Another consideration was to keep the Mughal power out of reach, for if the Mughals were successful against Adil Shah and Shivaji, they would next be knocking at Goa's door. Thus in 1663, Shivaji sought and found shelter with the Portuguese authorities in Bassein and Chaul. Besides these two places, shelter was provided to his forces in Goa, while arms and ammunition were also delivered to them. On the other hand, the Portuguese instructed their officers in Bassein and Chaul not to supply any provision to the Mughals and thereby obliged them to retreat.(40)

In January 1664, when Shivaji attacked and looted the city of Surat, the Portuguese authorities not only expressed their happiness but also are said to have actually helped his forces. In fact Portuguese soldiers were observed plundering Surat with the Marathas, and when the Mughals, complained to the Viceroy at Goa, the later blandly replied that they were not his men, but deserters.(41) In 1665, Jai Singh, the Mughal general, sought Portuguese aid against Shivaji, and in particular he asked for some artillery. Further more, he requested them not only not to extend help to Shivaji, but also not to return his ships they had captured. None of these demands were accepted. Although they promised not to give any assistance to Shivaji, the Portuguese accepted Shivaji's request for shelter. The Portuguese also provided him ammunitions and food grains.(42)

A nominal change is noticeable in the policy of the Portuguese after 1665. Shivaji's surrender to the Mughals created suspicion and uneasiness in their mind. From then on, they hesitated to give him outright help. After his escape from Agra in 1666, Shivaji again inquired of them whether he could find refuge in Portuguese territory along with his treasure. The reply was dubious, expressing, powerless-ness to face such a mighty ruler as Aurangzeb.(43)

In fact, it is evident from a letter of the Viceroy to Jai Singh, dated 29th April, 1667, that the Portuguese were willing to give up the cause of Shivaji in return for the ports that might be captured from him.(44) However, these eventualities came to nothing, and the Portuguese once again reconciled with Shivaji and wrote to him that they preferred his friendship than the Mughals.(45) Such were the ups and downs in the Portuguese policies towards Shivaji vis-à-vis the Mughals. The conflicting forces against which they were called to hold their own position, created considerable problems to the maintenance of the Portuguese colonies and ports in India.

(f) Portuguese-Mughal Relations

Portuguese-Mughal relation became estranged after the death of Akbar due to various causes, namely Mughal attacks on the Deccan states as well as the arrival of the English ambassador, Captain Hawkins, in 1608 on a diplomatic mission.(46) His main aim was to get trading facilities in the Mughal lands including their ports. There was no attempt from the Portuguese side to stop the development of ties between the English and the Mughals. The English succeeded in their endeavours and got some concession for their trade in Surat. They were received with great honour and respect.(47)

In 1609, the new Viceroy of the Portuguese at Goa, André Furtado Mendonça, called upon the Mughal embassy at Goa for renewal of cordial relations. However, the attempt for friendly ties did not last long because of the Portuguese attack on the English ships in 1612.(48) The Mughal Governor was furious at this act. Further deterioration set in when the Portuguese ships looted one of the Mughal ships off Surat and burnt it. This operation was carried out under the command of Luís de Brito de Mello from the fortress of Diu.(49) All the booty and prisoners were brought to Goa after the burning of the ship.(50) In response, Mughals confiscated Portuguese lands within their territories and burnt a large many villages in Daman and its any adjacent areas where Portuguese were to be found.(51)

Peace was restored in June 1615 between the two powers through Embassies and negotiation, and shipping regularised from Surat to Mecca through the *Cartaz* system. The following were the terms and conditions of the treaty.(52)

1. That, the Mughal emperor should not extend any facility to the Dutch and the English, who came in the guise of merchants to capture the Indian land.

2. That the Mughal emperor and his men shall not have any commercial or other type of relations, like giving provisions, within their territories.

3. That, they should be asked to leave the port and the Indian Ocean within the period of three months.

4. That, the emperor should give all permission to the Portuguese, for the disembarkations of the artillery and necessary ammunitions, and take them back whenever it would be required.

5. And that, the English, who are at present in the city should go out with their merchandises and belongings. This treaty, to some extent, made the Portuguese position stabilised for some time and reveals the fact that till this time the Portuguese had their maritime power secured and maintained.

Portuguese-Mughal relation remained quite till 1632 when Shah Jahan, the Mughal emperor, ordered an attack on the Portuguese settlements at Hoogly in Bengal where they had been settled since 1579 on the strength of a *Farman* from Akbar.(53) Shah Jahan's dislike for the Portuguese goes back to 1622 when he was a rebel and was not taken seriously by the Portuguese.(54) His opportunity came in 1632 when Portuguese settlers in Bengal were accused by the governor of Hoogly, Qasim Khan, of gross interference in the local matters. The Mughal governor thereupon attacked Hoogly with great force. Portuguese settlements were destroyed and were made prisoners. Out of some 300 Portuguese and 600 local Christians, it is difficult to estimate how many survived.(55) Nevertheless, through the effort of Father João de Cruz, one of the prisoners of war, peace was restored at Hoogly. Shah Jahan issued a *Farman* releasing all prisoners and returning all booty captured during the war.(56)

In 1635, Shah Jahan launched another expedition to the south, resulting in permanent subjugation of Ahmadnagar in 1637.(57) Bijapur also obliged to pay tribute every year to render help against the rising power of Marathas under the leadership of Shahji, father of Shivaji. However, war against Bijapur had to be renewed in 1657 because of the negligence on the part of its ruler in the payment of tribute for so many years. The expedition against Bijapur was disrupted by the war of succession to the throne of Mughals in 1658. (58) It was not until 1686 that the Bijapur dynasty finally fell into the hands of Mughals.

Thus the political turmoils involved a lot of money and forces contributing greatly to the weakening of the Portuguese power and their trade. Their expenditures for defence doubtlessly affected their financial position and shaped their investments in commercial activities.

Notes

Part-I

Commercial Ccontacts and International Rivalries During the Seventeeth Century on the Indian Coast

1. P.S.S. Pissurlenkar, 'Fragmentos Históricos' in *BIVG*, Nº 47, p. 61; Kail, *The Dutch in India*...pp. 30-31;*The Dutch in Malabar-Selection From the Records of the Madras Government*, No. 13, pp. 68. (Hence forth cited as *The Dutch in Malabar Records*...)
2. Portuguese Factory at Calicut continued till 1614 for the purpose of issuing *Cartazes*, F.P. de Laval, *Viagem de Francisco Pyrard de Laval*, vol. I, pp. 405-406.
3. Danvers, *Portuguese in...*, vol. II, p. 168; Panikkar, *Asia and the Western...*, pp. 149-151.
4. Panikkar, *Asia and the Western...*, pp. 150.
5. Danvers, *Portuguese in...*, vol. II, p. 168; Panikkar, *Asia and the Western...*, pp. 149-151.
6. Danvers, *Portuguese in...*, vol. II, p. 183-84.
7. Panikkar, *A History of Kerala...*, pp. 132-35.
8. *Ibid.*
9. Disney, *Twilight of the Pepper...*, p. 6; Della Valle, *The Travel of Pietro della Valle...*, vol. II, pp. 212-19.
10. *ACE*, vol. I, docs. 11-18.
11. Disney, *Twilight of the Pepper...*, p. 6
12. *ACE*, vol. I, docs. 13; Della Valle, *The Travel of Pietro della Valle...*, vol. II, pp. 314-15.
13. Della Valle, *The Travel of Pietro della Valle...*, vol. II, pp. 253-54, 307
14. *Ibid.*, pp. 250-315.
15. *ACE*, vol. I, docs. 38.
16. Disney, *Twilight of the Pepper...*, p. 78.
17. *APO-BP*, Tomo IV, Vol. II, parte I, pp. 311-313; *ACE*, vol. II, pp. 79-83.
18. Bocarro, *Década* 13 da *História da Índia...*, part I, p. 202.
19. *ACE*, vol. I, docs. 76.
20. *Ibid.*
21. *Ibid.*
22. *Ibid.*
23. *India*, cx. 3, doc. 64; *LML*, cod. I, pp. 23/75, 183-185v; cod. 4, p. 66/157; cod. 9, p. 43/102.
24. *ACE*, vol. I, pp. 414, 416, 556-57.
25. *Ibid.*; *LMG*, cod. 19a, fl. 55

26. *ACE*, vol. II, pp. 312-315, 318.
27. *Ibid.*
28. See Chapter II, part II.
29. Boxer, *Portuguese Seaborne...*, p. 136.
30. *APO-BP*, Tomo IV, Vol. II, parte III, pp. 17-24, 48-77, 85-92, 106-12; 218-22, 250-59, 303-8; P. M. Joshi, *History of Mediaeval Deccan*, Vol. I, pp. 265-66.
31. *Ibid.*
32. *Ibid.*
33. Nayeem, *External Relations...*, pp. 95-96.
34. Lobato, *Relações Luso-Marata...*, p. 19; Shastry, *A Note on Portuguese...*, pp.110-112
35. Delduque da Costa, *Os Portugueses e os...*, in *BIVG*, No. 20, p. 4; Shastry, '*A Note on Portuguese...*, pp. 110-112.
36. Shastry, '*A Note on Portuguese*'..., pp. 111.
37. Shastry, '*A Note on Portuguese*'..., pp. 112.
38. Pissurlenkar, 'Português e Marata', *BIVG*, N°. I, pp. 4898; No. 2, pp. 6692; No. 3, pp. 66-92; No. 6, pp. 80-89.
39. *ACE*, vol. IV, pp. 151-53.
40. Delduque da Costa, *Os Portugueses e os...*, in *BIVG*, No. 20, p. 48.
41. Pissurlenkar, 'Português e Marata', *BIVG* No. I, pp. 48-98;No. 2, pp. 66-92; No. 3, pp. 66-92; No. 6, pp. 80-89.
42. Shastry, 'A Note on Portuguese'..., pp. 113
43. Biker, *Tratados e concertos de pazes...* Vol. IV, pp. 131-132.
44. *Ibid.*
45. Shastry, '*A Note on Portuguese*'..., pp. 10-15.
46. S. Purchas, *His Pilgrims...*, Vol. I, p. 206; W. Foster, *The Embassy of Sir Thomas Roe...*, (passim).
47. S. Purchas, *His Pilgrims...* , Vol. I, p. 206
48. Boca, *Década* 13..., part I, pp. 200-204. 49. *Ibid.* pp. 189-192.
50. *Ibid.*
51. *Ibid.*, pp. 200-201.
52. Biker, Vol. I, pp. 189.
53. Campos, *History of the Portuguese...*, pp. 4546.
54. *Ibid.*. p. 129.
55. *Ibid.*. p. 14346.
56. *Ibid.*. p. 142-44.
57. Tripathi, *The Rise and Fall...*, pp. 447-453.
58. *Ibid.*. p. 470-76.

Part II: Portuguese-Dutch Relations

The union of Portugal with the castilian patrimony in 1580, yielded Philip II important colonial possessions in Asia and Africa.(1) Consequently, his enemies also became the enemies of the Portuguese colonial empire.(2) It was the Dutch who through their V.O.C., or the United East India Company, made the life unpleasant for the Portuguese in the Indian Ocean where once they used to breath freely. The entire sea and its coastal areas became a scene of bloodshed through almost continent warfare. It is usually assumed that what set the whole process off was the confiscation in Lisbon of the Dutch cargoes and ships by Philip II and the closure of the Iberian ports in 1585, 1595 and 1597. This seems to have prompted the Dutch to search for the sources from which these goods came.(3) In order to make themselves masters of the lucrative trade of Asia, the Dutch ruined the whole set-up of the Portuguese there.(4)

The Luso-Dutch struggle, which began with raids of the Dutch on the Principe and São Tomé in 1598-99, ended with the capture of Cochin and other settlements on the Malabar coast in 1663.(5) The V.O.C., which had been founded in 1602, successfully gained control of the trade of cloves, mace, nutmegs of Moluccas and Malacca around 1641,(6) of the cinnamon of coastal Ceylon between 1655-58(7) and of pepper of Malabar during 1659-63.(8) In the meantime, they had secured the textiles and indigo trade of the eastern and western coast of India, especially Surat and Massulipattam.(9) The Dutch, by 1663 had also displaced the Portuguese in securing the lion's share of the trade in Asian waters between Japan and Arabia.(10) The Dutch, before starting their expedition to the Indian territories, attempted to gain clear picture of economic and political condition of the Portuguese state of India. The Itinerário of Jan Huygan Van Linschoten, an Amsterdammer, proved to be very useful for the above purpose. It afforded not only a fair idea of the commercial situation, but indicated that the Portuguese claims to be the 'Lord of the Conquest Navigation and Commerce of Ethiopia, Persia and India' was not so effective as the title was when assumed by the King Dom Manuel I in 1501.(11) It also showed the location of the Portuguese settlements where the Dutch had the best chances of achieving success, like those of the Indonesian Archipelago, which also coincided with the production area of the spices, and commodities most in demand (12) Linschoten, during his thirteen years of service to the

Archbishop of Goa, Dom Vicente da Fonseca, collected much information about the traffic of the Portuguese trade and political condition.(13) Apart from that some of the Dutch merchants of Amsterdam, sent one Cornelis de Houtman, to India and to the Moluccas to collect details about the trade. Houtman return to Holland in 1597 with only a modest cargo of spices, but with the signal that the coast was clear.(14)

Being equipped with all the primary information about the trading companies of such a far off land, the Dutch merchants succeeded in obtaining permission of the States General for the organisation of a trading company in Amsterdam in 1602, named as *Vereenigde OestIndische Compagnie*, already mentioned as the V.O.C.(15), with a capital of 6,590,000 florins.(16) The Company through its 17 directors, variously referred to as *Heeren XVII* or the 'Seventeen Lords' was empowered to conclude treaties with foreign powers, build fortresses, factories and strongholds, and wage war against the Portuguese in the Indies, who under papal authority had claimed the sovereignty of the Eastern Seas.(17) Presumably, the wave of Protestant revolt that was gaining ground in the low countries and the inveterate enmity towards the Spanish throne prompted the Dutch to call relevance of the Papal Bulls in question and flout the Portuguese supremacy by capturing the Portuguese galleon, Santa Catarina, in the Straits of Malacca in 1603, which was loaded with valuable cargo. The step taken by the Dutch commander, Heemskerk, in capturing the ship was justified by the theorist Hugo Grotius through his work *De Jure Predae* written during 1604-5 and the famous chapter XII of the same published separately in 1608 under the title *Mare Libervm*, attacking the monopolistic attitude of the Portuguese.(18) As mentioned above, Pope Alexander VI had issued a number of bulls in 1493 granting the Portuguese the right to the territories already discovered or to be discovered. But Grotius very clearly denied the right of the Portuguese eastern lands and seas based on the papal grants. Since, the Pope could not have any temporal authority and even granted that he could have, it was entirely irrelevant in case of Asiatic powers as they did not belong to the Church.(19) He even disagreed with the argument that the Portuguese, on the basis of war and conquest had right to India except in case of Goa.(20)

However, once the work of Grotius was published and began to be discussed, the Portuguese took up the challenge and Frei Serafim de Freitas came up with *De Justo Império Lusitanorvm*

Asiatico, published in 1625 from Valladolid. Freitas justified the right of the Portuguese to the East especially India on the basis of the propagation of the Christianity in the non-Christian areas and thus disallowed the objections proposed by Gortius.(21) Naturally, however, whatever justification proposed by the Freitas fell on the deaf ears of the Dutch. Thus begun the war for the monopoly of the eastern commerce and continued nearly for a century to overthrow the Portuguese possessions and trade.

Although the forerunners of the United Company had made several previous voyages, the first venture of the Dutch VOC was under Steven Van der Hagen who left Holland in the 18th of December, 1603, with a fleet of thirteen ships besides one which had started in the early part of the year. Van der Hagen had instructions for initiating friendly relationships with the Indian states like, Cambay, Dabul, Calicut and Ceylon. Van der Hagen was to make sure that he got all sorts of facilities against the Spanish, Portuguese and their allies in the Indian Ocean.(22) He brought two letters for the Mughal emperor, in the Portuguese language.(23) After nine month, the Dutch fleet anchored of the port of Goa and tried unsuccessfully to capture four Portuguese galleons in the Mandovi River. They remained there for 23 days without any further luck. Later, Van der Hagen sailed towards Cannanore and tried to open negotiation but in vain. The King of this port, being one of the oldest friends of the Portuguese, did not pay any heed to the Dutch commander. The King Philip III (II of Portugal), incidentally, was much pleased with the behaviour meted out to the Dutch by the ruler of Cannanore, and wrote a very pleased letter to him.(24) On the contrary, the Dutch general was received very cordially by the ruler of Calicut, the Zamorin. Van der Hagen reached the Calicut roads on 29 October, 1604, where on 11th November, they concluded a treaty of loyalty and friendship towards each other against the Portuguese. The main aim of this treaty was the expulsion of the Portuguese not only from the roads of Calicut, but also from the whole Indian coast. Moreover, the Dutch were allowed to construct a fortress in his land.(25)

Only now did the Portuguese realise the consequence of the appearance of the Dutch in the East. From this date onwards any formal relations between the Dutch and the Portuguese came to an end and changed into hostility. It was a treaty, which indicated the commencement of war in support of the Indian Princes of Malabar coast against the Portuguese. It (adherents) patently became a barrier to the collection of pepper for the Portuguese from the territory of Calicut as well as from its adherents, the whole coast of Malabar. For from this date onwards, at least from these regions, no pepper was forthcoming throughout the period under review.(26) Moreover, Van der Hagen promised to the Zamorin to give active support as soon as the new fleet from Holland arrived.(27)

Here it should perhaps be mentioned that prior to the landing of Van der Hagen on the Calicut coast, two Dutch merchants, a Hans Wolf and a certain Lafer, were sent to Surat to explore the commercial potential of Northwest India.(28) They landed and settled at the port of Surat in Gujarat. Later, in route towards the south, they were made prisoners and brought to Goa, where they were executed.(29) The very incident gave birth to a serious conflict. The Dutch replied to it by burning a Portuguese ship off Chaul which only dramatised the state of Portuguese-Dutch relations.(30) Soon after this incident, the Dutch proceeded towards the port town of Surat and attempted to send an ambassador to the court of the Mughal Governor, seeking *Farman* for the trading facilities at this port. But their mission did not succeed because of the arrival of the Portuguese ships under the command of Dom Pedro de Mascarenhas, who had been sent out in search of the Dutch ships to gain revenge. One Dutch ship somehow managed to escape the Portuguese net.

Other Dutch ships, returning from the north, sailed to Cochin and burnt two Portuguese ships on their way. Later, they proceeded towards the Coromandel Coast and reached Massulipattam, known for textiles, early in 1605.This port belonged to the Sultan of Golconda where they already had a factor named Issac Eyloff Pieter, to deal in the affairs of textiles trade. Here, Van der Hagen was assisted by a Jew, named, Azelan in their dealings with the Sultan. The Dutch were, finally, successful in getting permission for the establishment of a trading factory and ousting the Portuguese who were residing in this region for the purpose of trade. The permission was sought in August, 1606.(31) While this development was taking place in the eastern coast, on the west, the Dutch Admiral was active in blockading Goa and setting up a factory once again in the territory of Surat. David Van Deynsen and Pieter Van Dam, were sent there to handle the business. Deynsen was sent to Surat in May, 1606. But he was so frustrated there by the harassments created by the Portuguese with the help of the local authorities that he committed suicide in December, 1607.(32) What Pieter Van Dam achieved is not Known. It is reported that after the death of Deynsen, the Dutch factory disappeared from Surat till 1616, when it was re-established by Pieter Van der Broeck with the help of local authorities.(33)

In 1607, two fleets, one under Caerden and another under Verhoff, left the port of Amsterdam on different dates and reached Goa on 19th of September and blockaded till the end of October, 1608. Verhoff, however, did not succeed in capturing any vessels and sailed off towards Calicut, where he renewed the treaty with the Zamorin made by Van der Hagen in 1604.(34) The Dutch thus doggedly attacked the Portuguese shipping and their settlements on the Western coast. Being rich and organised, they managed to sent a fleet of twelve ships every year from Amsterdam, where as the Portuguese government was hardly in a position of sending more than four or five ships. The Dutch Company had such quantities of vessels, even from the beginning of the century that before one could reach India another started from the port of Amsterdam.

This superiority certainly helped them later during the time of siege of Goa, Malacca or Ceylon. While they blockaded one port, another fleet was available to attack a different part of the Portuguese settlements which shall be seen later. Moreover, during their siege they attempted to get hold of the Portuguese trade and its commodities, their ships moving without fear of Portuguese reprisal.(35)

In the early seventeenth century, the Dutch were successful in establishing a factory on the port of Negapattam. The Nayak of Jinji, under whose jurisdiction Negapattam or Devanampattam was, received the Dutch with much care and respects and permitted them to build a town on the same place where they landed.(36) This factory was later transferred to the fort of Tirupapuliyr, near the city of Cuddalore.(37) During this period some other important events took place. The English were quite active at the Mughal court and port on one hand, while on the other the Mughal attacked the territories of Diu, Daman, Bassein and Chaul, (38) while they requested the Dutch at Massulipattam for help against the Portuguese. In return, the Mughals promised to give the port city of Daman to them.(39) The whole situation forced the Portuguese viceroy to conclude a peace treaty with the Mughals in June, 1615 as already has been mentioned in the previous part.(40)

But this treaty did not last long. As soon as the new Mughal

Governor took charge of the port city of Surat, the whole situation changed. He was a great admirer of the English and the Dutch and had confidence in their naval power which was more visible in the Indian Ocean by this time. Therefore, he did not bother to observe the treaty just concluded with the Portuguese.(41)

After this threatening development, a coalescence of interests between the Dutch, the English and Mughals, the Portuguese tightened their security around the entrance to Surat. They blockaded the port in order to hinder the departure of the Dutch and the English ships loaded with commodities bound for their home lands.(42) In 1622, the king of Portugal wrote a letter to the Dutch and the English commanders in-chief to stop their activities in the Indian waters and warned them about their further steps.(43) In the same year, Dutch ships blockaded the port of Goa and tried to contact the local merchants for which the Portuguese viceroy issued preventive orders.(44) Furthermore, the Dutch tried to enter into negotiations with the Sultan of Bijapur against the Portuguese.(45) The Portuguese, nevertheless, soon realised the significance of this relationships, and they tried to check on this development also. Because the Bijapuri Sultan himself was interested in this truce, it became difficult for the Portuguese to prevent its progress. In fact the combined forces of the Dutch and the English not only attended to ruin their maritime trade and commerce by attacking and blockading their ports but also spoiled their relations with the neighbouring states.

In 1623, with the threats of the Dutch navy still mounting, the Portuguese equipped the forts of Goa with all the necessary provisions.(46) At the same time, another Dutch armada appeared off Quilon and checked the movements of the Portuguese ships which the captain of the Portuguese fort there duly reported to the viceroy.(47) All these troubles prevented the Portuguese fleet from sailing for Lisbon.(48) Besides this, the Portuguese viceroy was unable to provision to other ports such as Surat, and Dabhol where the joint armadas of the Dutch and the English consisting twenty big ships had laid their siege to prevent the egress and ingresses of the Portuguese shipping to Goa from any part of their colonies.(49) Similarly, the fort of Quilon was also in danger, as just recounted. Moreover, during 1622 in the Far East, Macao was also attacked though unsuccessfully, by the united forces of the Dutch and the English.(50) The Dutch and the English were well prepared and aggressive, while Portuguese resources were meagre. However, when the Portuguese state sources of income failed to provide the increasing demands to meet the coast of defence, the Portuguese authorities sought help from the *Fidalgos* of Goa, to provide the cost of expenditure occurred due to the Dutch wars.(51) The only action left for the Portuguese was to create some trouble among the European allies, while trying to hinder their relations with the neighbouring states.(52)

In October, 1626, a joint attacked by the Dutch and the English was launched on the island of Bombay and caused heavy damage to property and life. Then the allied armada sailed away.(53) In other encounter, one Simão de Oliveira captured three Dutch Galleons near Goa in 1626.(54) The same year a Dutch captain concluded a peace treaty with the King of Achin, promised all sorts of help against the Portuguese.(55)

In 1627, one big Portuguese ship was built with local resources and furnished with arms and ammunitions.(56) Further, Bombay was fortified and instructions were given to hinder the English and the Dutch trade from Surat.(57) It was reported that the Dutch again tried to enter and occupy the port of Paliaporto, fifty leagues from Cochin.(58) It was felt that if the Dutch were successful there, the next attack would certainly be on Cochin, somehow, though, Portuguese were successful in repelling them. In 1631, that the Portuguese crown sent 50,000 Cruzados (or 100,000 Ashrafis) for the building of Armadas to face the challenge of the Dutch.(59) The worsening situation in Portuguese India has been properly mentioned in one of the letters by the Portuguese viceroy to the King of Portugal.(60)

By 1633, the Dutch were discovered to have trade relations with the Bijapuri states. In reality, there had been one dissatisfied Portuguese merchant, Tomé da Costa, who had started trading with the Dutch in the territory of the Adil Shah.(61) The rapid progress made by the Dutch had made the English jealous and suspicious towards their friendship. In 1635, the political situation in the Indian maritime states took a new turn. The English and Portuguese conflict ended by a truce concluded between these two nations.(62) While the Portuguese were busy in negotiations, the Dutch were preparing for a powerful attack on Goa from both the sides, land and sea, with the help of the Sultan of Bijapur. (63) For this reason, in 1636, the Dutch commander, Jacob Cooper, sent an ambassador, Jan Van Twist, to the court of Mohammed Adil Shah, Sultan of Bijapur, to conclude a political and commercial treaty against the

Portuguese.(64) In this treaty it was decided that the Dutch ships would blockade from the sea side while the Adil Shah's forces would march from land to press the attack.(65) It was decided in the treaty that the territory of Goa and its adjacent lands shall be handed over to the Sultan. In return, the Dutch were to be given a site for construction of a fort at Vengurla, plus privileges of trade in the Bijapur territories and half of the revenue of the Mandovi and adjacent areas of Goa.(66) In this instance, all the efforts of the Portuguese to hinder the friendly relations between the two failed because of their recent hostile behaviour in capturing one of the Bijapuri ships off the port of Dabhol which was about to sail towards Mocha and Persia. Thus, as soon as the Portuguese viceroy, Pedro da Silva, received this news of the Dutch progress in the neighbouring states, he became impatient and sent António Monis Barreto, as an ambassador to the court of the Adil Shah, on a mission of friendship with a request for the expulsion of the Dutch from Vengurla as well as from other regions of his territories. But this mission proved to be unsuccessful because of the intervention of one Mustafa Khan took revenge by attacking one of the richly laden ships of the Portuguese returning from Muscat.(67)

The Dutch settlement at Vengurla was highly dangerous for the Portuguese and helpful to the Dutch. This was the reason that as soon as they settled themselves there, they plotted a co-ordinated attack on Goa. The Dutch blockaded Goa twice between 1637 and 1638. Meanwhile, in 1638, the Dutch signed a treaty with the King of Kandy and, at his invitation moved into Ceylon. António Telles de Menezes, the Portuguese commander, was given orders to face the Dutch. He had to fight several battles between February, 1637 and January, 1638.(68) The first two were not decisive but affected the Portuguese commercial shipping. No ship could sail during this period to Portugal nor could arrive in this port. In appearance the fight may have been stand-offs, but they did expose the maritime weakness of the Portuguese to the Dutch. The Dutch ships remained before Goa till the 3rd of May, when they gave up hope of the arrival of any ship from any part of the empire, they sailed towards Batavia before the Monsoon. They returned in October when Portuguese were expecting ships from Portugal as well as from coastal regions of India, laden with Indian commodities.(69) This time, the Dutch naval forces were led by Adam Westerwolt. He had sixteenth men of war in the mouth of the Mandovi to blockade them. They were again successful in their mission. In order to clear the way, the Portuguese galleons and other vessels went to meet the Dutch ships and provisions, under the commander ships of Anthonie Caen, remaining in the Mandovi roads till February, 1639. This time no unpleasant event took place except the annual fleet could not sail again for Portugal.(70) On 30 September, 1639, they again blockaded the port of Mormugoa and burnt three Galleons, *Bom Jesus, São Sebastião* and *São Boa Ventura,* some of the best naval ships the Portuguese had. Their blockade of Goa port, however, continued intermittently, but successfully, till 1641.(71) The last siege of Goa took place in 1644, and thereafter the Dutch change their direction of attack towards different Portuguese settlements.(72)

The Dutch appearance to blockade this Portuguese capital was so frequent and decisive that it deserted the whole city for about four years with its trade throttled and ingress of the cargo ships at a standstill.(73) This was the picture of the Portuguese capital during (1637-41). On the other hand in Malacca, the Dutch had intensified their blockade for about six to seven years during 1634-41, (74) and fighting was escalating in Ceylon, where the Portuguese needed many arms and provisions to face the Dutch challenge. But it was difficult for the capital to send any help as this, too, was badly besieged by them as has already been pointed out. The co-ordinated fighting on the three fronts gave the Dutch two results, their victory over the Islands of Malacca, their gain in Ceylon and financial ruin of the Goan capital. It is curious that while the Portuguese bled in India and South-East Asia, at the same time in Portugal, they proclaimed independence under the banner of Dom João IV, against the Spanish rule of almost sixty years.(75) Not long after Portugal had proclaimed her independence, ten year truce was signed between Dom João IV and the United Provinces, (The Dutch Netherlands) on 12th June, 1641, in which following terms and conditions were stipulated: (76)

- In the East, and in all the Islands and seas under the jurisdiction granted by the States General to the East India Company,

- The aforesaid treaty was to come into force one year after the date of its signature. Should, however, the proclamation of peace reach any of these lands after the year had expired,

- All acts of hostility were to be cease at once: all the kings, sovereigns, and nations in the East Indies who might be friends of, or in confederation with the States General, or the East India Company of the United provinces were to be included in this treaty,

- All the Portuguese ships from Portugal to those parts, and vice-versa, were not to be molested by the Dutch fleets, but to have perfect freedom on seas for the space of ten years; and,

- At the same time the ships of the United Provinces were also to be similarly free from molestation on the part of the Portuguese,

- The Dutch and the Portuguese were to aid each other, should occasion arise, while this treaty lasted.(76)

It was not before 2nd of March 1643, that the Dutch commissioner, Pieter Boreel, arrived in India with the news and a copy of truce, and, proceeded first to Galle in Ceylon where, however, he declined to publish it on the ground that the Dutch were entirely hemmed in these at that time. He thought it best that fight should continue. He then proceeded to Goa, where he arrived on the Ist. of April, and, here also, he refused to publish the armistice unless the Portuguese would give up the spice lands around Galle, giving various reasons including one that the Galle was not included in the treaty. He, however, left Goa without proclaiming the truce and proceeded to Galle, where he reached on 8th May, 1643.(77) The armistice was published on 10 November, 1644, in Goa, but only after the home government in The Hague, had exerted pressure on the V.O.C. to do so. A provincial treaty was shortly afterwards concluded between the King of Portugal and the States General, respecting certain doubts as to the jurisdiction of the territories and fortress of Galle, which was signed at Hague, on 27th March, 1645. Under this agreement, the possessors of the fort were to have the use of the lands in the same way as they had at the time the treaty of 1641 was signed, but they were not to grow Cinnamon while the dispute lasted, during which time, however, the King of Portugal agreed to deliver annually to the Dutch, at the said port, 600 quintals of that spice.(78) Under this treaty all vessels and goods seized, as well as places and forts taken by either party, since the treaty of 1641 was proclaimed, were to be immediately restored.(79)

It seems that none of the parties were interested in following the terms of the treaty. And thus the fights for the share of lands and merchandise continued even after the truce was published. The V.O.C. saw no reason to stop the war in the Island of Ceylon for the occupancy of the land and the monopoly of the cinnamon trade. From the Portuguese side, a sizeable amount, (about 20-30% of the total cost of the Portuguese defence expenditure) was spent every year to save the Island, but the Portuguese could only resist and fall back until 1656, when they handed over the keys of Colombo to the Dutch and finally in 1658 were expelled from the Island of Ceylon.(80)

Soon after their establishment in Ceylon, the Dutch turned their attentions towards the Malabar Coast, the spice land.(81) In December, 1658, the Dutch Admiral, Ryklof Van Goens, attacked the fort of Quilon and captured it. After establishing strong garrisons there he returned Colombo. But his victory did not last long, and the Portuguese forces again occupied that land on 14th of April, 1659, with the help of the Queen of Quilon. The very next year, the Dutch forces again tried to sieze this territory, but failed. Once again, with a large force they attacked this city with the help of Zamorin. The Dutch reached Azhikode, near Cranganore, on February 10, 1661.(82) This first joint attack of Zamorin and the Dutch was launched on Paliaporto or Pallipuram, a very important location for serving as a forward base against Cochin. After a heavy fight, this port fell into their hands, after which the Dutch, according to their treaty, handed it over to Zamorin.(83)

Immediately after the capture of Quilon, the Dutch troops proceeded to Cranganore, where they landed under the command of Rijklof Van Goens, at the end of December. On the morning of 15th January, 1662, after fifteen days heavy fighting the fortress of Cranganore was surrendered to the Dutch.(84)

They did not plan immediately to attack the kingdom of Cochin. In the mean time the Portuguese fortified and equipped the fort with necessary provisions. The Dutch, realising the weakness of their army for the capture of this fort, entered into negotiations with the leading chiefs on the coastal regions of Malabar.(85)

At this time, kingdom of Cochin was passing through a state of civil war. This situation leaded the Dutch for the intervention into the local politics and took the causes of the dispossessed princess. In 1661, after the capture of the fort of Cranganore, when the Dutch Admiral Van Goen was in Pallipuram, a rebel chief who supported the exile prince, approached him and entered into secret negotiation.(86) Thus the Dutch got the right opportunity to interfere in the Cochin's local politics. This chief and the claimant of the Cochin state, Vira Kerala Varma reproached the Dutch governor for the expulsion of the Portuguese from Cochin and requested their restoration. The Dutch governor also agreed this.(87) In this negotiation, the Zamorin of Calicut was also assisting the cause of the exile prince. After this agreement both parties planned to attack Cochin. The Zamorin was to attack Cochin from the north, and other supporters of the exiled Princess from the south.The Dutch Admiral was to attack from the sea.

Cochin was immediately attacked after the arrival of the Dutch Admiral, Van Goen, from Quilon, after its recapture in 1661, on Ist. of January, 1662, along with thirty ships. First an attack was made on the Cochin palace, which was completely successful. Adriaan Van Rhede entered the palace and captured the Rani, Gangadhara Lakshmi, the puppet set up by the Portuguese on the Cochin throne; she was later handed over to the Zamorin as prisoner. Three, out of the five, incumbent Tanur princes died in the fight. The next attempt was to cross the backwaters and establish the newly returned Rajahs on the aimed land. Somehow, the Dutch, along with their allies could not succeed in their attempt and withdrew temporarily. (88) The Dutch returned as soon as the monsoon was over.(89) They established a blockade with the help of the Palliyam chief and the prince of the dissatisfied branch. The Rajah of Proccad helped Portuguese. Desertion weakened the ranks of the Portuguese and close blockade was maintained from the seaside. In this hour of peril, the Portuguese inside the fort showed great heroism. Though reduced to extremity, and with no hopes of relief from Goa, they held on to the very last. Thus, at the last moment, the Portuguese commander, Inácio Sermento, handed over the keys of the town to the Dutch Admiral.(90) After this the Portuguese flags ceased to fly over the Malabar coast.(91) Thus, as one historian has mentioned, "vanished the glory of Vasco da Gama and Albuquerque"(92).

After the capture of Cochin, the Dutch proceeded towards Cannanore. They carried on the siege for several days over there. In the mean time the Portuguese commander heard the news of the surrender of Cochin and entertaining no reasonable hope of relief, capitulated to the enemy on the 13th of February, 1663.(93)

Soon after the terrible lost of the Portuguese possessions on the Malabar Coast, the news arrived that the peace had been concluded between the States General and the King of Portugal. The treaty was signed on the Ist. of August, 1661 and was ratified by the King of Portugal and the States General on 24th May and 4th December, 1662, respectively.(94) On the ground that the towns and fortresses of Cochin and Cannanore had been captured subsequent to the signing of the treaty, the surrender of those places was claimed by the Portuguese from the Dutch, to which, however, they replied that hostilities would only cease when both parties had assented to and ratified the treaty, its publication of which did not take place until the 14th of March, 1663. (95) This question was again raised in 1666 by the Portuguese ambassador to Holland, but he was unable to obtain any satisfactory reply.(96) The main idea behind all the political details is that I wanted to stress on the fact that how all this political upheavals affected the Portuguese commercial activities in the Indian Ocean.

Notes

Part-II

Portuguese-Dutch Relations

1. B. W. Diffe and Winius, *Foundation of the Portuguese Empire*, 1415-1580, Oxford, 1977, vol. I, pp. 427-29
2. *The Dutch in Malabar...*, doc...N°13, p. 67
3. Kail, *The Dutch in.*, p. 11
4. *The Dutch in Malabar...*, N°13, pp. 57
5. Boxer, *Portuguese..*, pp. 110-12
6. *LML*, 47, pp. 7474v, 129-129v; *LML*, 48, pp. 70-71; cod. 49, pp.136-39
7. *India*, cx. 19, doc. 23; cx.22, docs. 60, 129; cx. 23, docs. 16, 112, 119; cx. 24, doc. 34; *Cambridge History of India*, vol. V, Cambridge, 1929, pp. 47-49
8. *India*, cx. 25, docs. 147, 148, 183; cx. 26, docs. 13, 17, 41, 126, 151, 217; Danvers, *op.cit.*, vol. II. pp. 327-29; *The Dutch in Malabar...*, doc.., p.103
9. Pissurlenkar, in *BIVG*, n°47, 194⁰0 p. 63; A.B. Radwan, *The Dutch in Western India, 1601-1632*, Calcutta, 1978, pp. 21-22
10. See foot note N°8
11. Barros, *Década*, I, Part II, pp. 11-19; ANTT, Maço 7 de Bulas N° 29; Gavetas, 17, Maço, 6; Kail, *The Dutch in*, p. 12; Mathew, *Portuguese Trade...* , pp.62-63.
12. M.A.P. Melink Roelfez, *Asian Trade and European Influence Between 1500 and about 1630*, The Hague, 1962, p.173; Kail, *The Dutch in..* pp.105-106
13. Linschoten, *Itinerario..*,vol. I, and II (passim); *The Dutch in Malabar* doc. N° 13, pp.56; *Cambridge History*, vol. V, pp. 282-9; Kail, *op.cit.* p.11
14. *APO-BP*. tomo, IV, Vol.II, part II, pp. 231-32; *The Dutch in Malabar...*, doc.., p. 6; *Cambridge History*, vol.V, p. 28; Kail, *The Dutch in...*, p. 12
15. A Company for trading in the west Indies was formed in 1621, Kail, *The Dutch in...*, p. 13

16. *The Dutch in Malabar...*, doc.. p. 68; *Cambridge History*, pp. 30-31; Kail, *The Dutch in ...*, p.13
17. Refer foot N° 11
18. Hugo Grotius, *The Freedom of the Sea (Mare Librum)* or the Right which belongs to the Dutch to take part in the East Indian trade, Oxford, 1916, (passim)
19. *Ibid.*,p. 16
20. *Ibid.*, p. 20
21. Frei Serafim de Freitas. *Do Justo Império Asiático dos Portugueses*, Lis bon, 1961, vol. II, pp. 90-91
22. Pissurlenkar, *Loc.cit.* p. 59; *The Dutch in Malabar...*, doc., p.6; Kail, *The Dutch in ..*,p. 30; Radwan, pp. 22-23.
23. During this period Portuguese Language was the medium of com munication of Europeans on the ports of India. David Lopes, *A Expansão da Lingua Portuguesa no Oriente nos séculos XVI, XVII e, XVIII*, p. 28; p.32
24. *LMG*, cod. 6, p. 116; *The Cambridge History*, Vol. V, p. 31
25. Pissurlenkar, *Fragmentos...*, p. 61; *The Dutch in Malabar*, doc., p. 68; Kail, *The Dutch in...* p. 30-31.
26. See Chapter 3.
27. *The Dutch in Malabar...*, doc., p. 67.
28. Kail, *The Dutch in...*p. 30; Radwan, *The Dutch in Western India*, pp. 21-22.
29. *Ibid.*
30. *The Dutch in Malabar...*, doc., p. 12-15.
31. *The Dutch in Malabar...*, doc., p. 67; Kail, *The Dutch...* pp. 3132; Danvers, *The Portuguese*, vol. II. pp. 137-38; Winius, *The Fatal His tory of Ceylon..* p. VIII.
32. Radwan, *The Dutch in Western India*, pp. 21-22; Kail, *The Dutch in...* p. 37-38; Kail gives the date of his death some times in the summer of 1608, Radwan reports his death took place at Burhanpur where he went on a business trip in 1607.
33. Radwan, *The Dutch in Western India*, pp. 25; Kail, *The Dutch in...* p. 40-45.
34. Pissurlenkar, *Fragmentos...*, p. 62-63.
35. V. Ribeiro, *Fatalidade Histórica...*, p. 259.
36. Kail, *The Dutch in...* p. 37-39.
37. *Ibid.*
38. Bocarro, *Década* 13, vol. I, pp. 200, 301.
39. Moreland, *From Akbar to ...*, p. 37.
40. Biker, *Tratado...*, tomo I, pp. 189-90.
41. HAG, cod. 779, fl. 55v; *Monumenta Historiae...*, *JBHS*, vol. II, Nos. 1 & 2, pp. 151-52, 154.

42. *LML*, cod. 13, fl. 446/91.
43. *LML*, cod. 16, fls. 23/5354v.
44. *LML*, cod. 17, fls. 174/44.
45. *LML*, cod. 17, fls. 13/34v.
46. *LML*, cod.17. fls. 14/45.
47. *LML*, cod. 17, fls. 53/12v14.
48. *LML*, cod. 17, fls. 186/50v.
49. *LML*, cod. 17. fls. 173/43.
50. *LML*, cod. 20. fls. 7/13, 38/75.
51. *APO-BP*. tomo, IV, Vol.II, part I, pp. 188-89. 52. *LML*, cod. 23. fls. 9/17.
53. *LML*, cod. 23. fls. 10/19.
54. *LML*, cod. 24. fls. 204/69-69v.
55. *LML*, cod. 24. fls. 399/185.
56. *LML*, cod. 26. fl. 16/34.
57. *LML*, cod. 28. fl. 7/12.
58. *LML*, cod. 29. fls. 124/24547.
59. *LML*, cod. 30. fls. 246/248, 314/263-64; cod. 32, fl. 16/31.
60. *LML*, cod. 32. fls. 36/1112; Boxer, *The Portuguese Seaborne...*, p. 111.
61. Danvers, *The Portuguese*, vol. II. pp. 257.
62. *LML*, cod. 40. fls. 62/13435; Danvers, *The Portuguese*, vol. II. pp. 258-59, 26163.
63. *LML*, cod. 38. fls. 46/100-101; Danvers, *The Portuguese*, vol. II. pp. 258-59, 261-63.
64. Pissurlenkar, *Fragmentos...*, p. 67.
65. Pissurlenkar, *Fragmentos...*, p. 70; *LML*, cod. 48. fls. 245/199-199v.
66. *LML*, cod. 40, fls. 100/209-210v, 110/229; cod. 42, fls. 26/2426v, 48/3637v; Boxer, O Geral do Mar...in *BIVG*, No. 37,
67. *LML*, cod. 42, fl. 76/52v; Danvers, *The Portuguese*, vol. II. pp. 258-59, 261-63.
68. *LML*, cod. 41, fls. 1/12; cod. 42, fls. 56-60; cod. 43, fls. 1/12v; cod. 44, fls. 94/194-194v, 245, 105/25052v; cod. 45, fls. 25/2525v, 181/185-86, 182/187-88v, 221/269-76.
69. *LML*, cod. 46, fl. 142/151-152, 197; Danvers, *The Portuguese*, vol. II. pp. 267-268.
70. *LML*, cod. 50, fl. 89/132.
71. *LML*, cod. 47, fls. 22-22v, 48/89-89v, 41/7474v; cod. 48, fls. 88/70-72v; cod. 49, fls. 47/62-64, 82/136-39.
72. *LML*, cod. 47, 41/74-74v, 68/129-129v; cod. 48, fls. 88/70-72v; cod. 49, fls. 82/136-39.

73. *LML*, cod. 49, fls. 82/136-39, 105/248-250; Pissurlenkar, *Fragmentos...*, p. 73.
74. *LML*, cod. 49, fls. 58/87; cod. 48, fls. 208/156-56v; Danvers, *The Por tuguese*, vol. II. pp. 275-76.
75. *Ibid.*
76. *LML*, cod. 48, fls. 253/205; cod. 50, fls. 67/100v, 117v; cod. 51, fl. 49/107, 140/354, 141/356-57, 142/358-359; Danvers, *The Portuguese*, vol. II. pp. 281-85.
77. *LML*, cod. 50, fls. 24/73-74, 25/84v, 104-140, 151-274v; cod. 51, fl. 1/117/35; *India*, cx. 15, docs. 8, 32, 115, 125.
78. *LML*, cod. 50, fls. 24/73-74, 25/84v, 104-140, 151-274v; cod. 51, fl. 1/117/35; *India*, cx. 15, docs. 8, 32, 115, 125: cod. 54, fl. 83/171; Danvers, *The Portuguese*, vol. II. pp. 289.
79. *India*, cx. 19, docs. 23; cx. 22, docs. 60, 129; cx. 23, docs. 16, 112, 119; cx. 24, doc. 34; *The Cambridge History*, Vol. V, p. 47-49.
80. *India*, cx. 24, docs. 68, 138; *The Dutch in Malabar...*, No 13, pp. 89; Danvers, *The Portuguese...*, vol. II. pp. 323-325.
82. *India*, cx. 25, doc. 45; Danvers, *The Portuguese...*, vol. II. pp. 325-26.
83. *India*, cx. 25, docs. 24, 27, 40, 78, 132, 134.
84. *India*, cx. 25, doc. 148; Danvers, *The Portuguese...*, vol. II. pp. 15859; Panikkar, *Malabar and the Portuguese...*, pp. 150-70
85. *India*, cx. 25, docs. 45, 78; Panikkar, *Malabar and the Portuguese...*,, pp. 115, 657.
86. *India*, cx. 25, docs. 45, 78; Panikkar, *Malabar and the Portuguese...*,, pp. 156-57.
87. *The Dutch in Malabar...*, No 13, pp. 11-12; Danvers, *The Portuguese...*, vol. II. pp. 325-26.
88. *The Dutch in Malabar...*, No 13, pp. 11-12.
89. *India*, cx. 25, docs. 147, 148, 183; cx. 26, docs. 13, 17, 41, 126, 151, 217; *The Dutch in Malabar...*, No 13, pp. 103; Danvers, *The Portuguese...*, vol. II. pp. 327-29.
90. *India*, cx. 27, doc. 41; *The Dutch in Malabar...*, No 13, pp. 103; Danvers, *The Portuguese...*, vol. II. pp. 329.
91. *India*, cx. 25, docs. 147, 148, 183; cx. 26, docs. 13, 17, 41, 126, 151, 217; *The Dutch in Malabar...*, No 13, pp. 103; Danvers, *The Portuguese...*, vol. II. pp. 327-29.
92. Panikkar, *Malabar and the Portuguese...*, pp. 161.
93. *India*, cx. 26, doc. 224; cx. 27, doc. 96; *The Dutch in Malabar...*, No 13, pp. 103
94. *Ibid.*
95. *Ibid.*

Part III: Portuguese-English Relations

There is a significant difference in the manner in which the English and the Dutch proceeded, respectively, to undermine Portuguese colonial settlements. The Dutch in their efforts to establish and expand their trade, proceeded to overthrow Portuguese settlements and trade before involving themselves exclusively in commerce. The English on the contrary, first laid the network of trade and then occupied territorial bases for consolidation and expansion. The aim of both these powers, however, was the same, that is, to oust the Portuguese from the field of international trade.

The English-Portuguese relation can be examined in two phases: 1600-1635, and 1636-1665. The first phase is one of instability since relations between them fluctuated from outright belligerence to cordiality. This seems to be explained by the fact that the first phase was a period when the English were trying to secure a commercial footing in the Indian subcontinent but had to reckon with the presence of Portuguese naval power. Hence, in the nature of things, adjustments between them involved both, hostilities and compromises. However, from 1636 onwards these take a different turn, mostly because of the increasing Dutch menace in the Indian Ocean,(1) towards cooperation and friendship.

Like the Dutch, the English, were able to secure the lucrative trade of India, but without much loss to life and money. They peacefully acquired textiles and Indigo from Surat, Cambay, and Sindh on the coastal areas; Ahmadabad, Agra and Lahore in the hinterland, partially by *Farmans* which they occasionally received from the Mughal Emperors and partially by fighting the Portuguese off the mouth of Tapti river.(2) After 1635, they also got a share in the pepper, spices and copper trade of Malabar, Kanara and of South-East Asian spice Islands, and cinnamon of Ceylon.(3)

The acquisition of Bombay by the English in the second half of the seventeenth century contributed greatly to these commercial successes. Bombay, received as a dowry by Charles II of England in his marriage to Infant Catarina of Portugal, was supposed to be a symbol of union and friendship between the two crowns. In effect it proved to be a commercial and territorial loss to the Portuguese. The post 1663 period saw the tragic end of Portuguese maritime power.

Keeping in view this broad outline, an attempt has been made to throw some light on the events of this period; the English appearance and its effect on the Portuguese trade and commerce;

the way in which the English secured control of the Indian spices and textile trade and elimination of Portuguese domination over Indian waters. The wealth brought by the Portuguese in the sixteenth century from the Eastern trade raised an earnest desire in England to obtain a share in it. But before setting forth to the unknown Indian subcontinent, the English, like the Dutch, needed some basic knowledge about the political and commercial position of the East. Towards this end, in 1583 Ralph Fitch, and three other adventurers, were sent to the East Indies. The account they brought back home of the extensive Indian Kingdoms and the grandeur of its cities, gave visions of a rich source of commerce to the English merchants.(4)

In 1586, Cavendish, another English traveller to India, further broadened the picture in his accounts. In 1591, a fleet of three ships under captain Raymond was sent from London. The expedition met with disaster and the only ship managed to reach India, sank on the homeward journey. Its commander Captain James Lancaster, however, survived to take back the experience that proved vital in the establishment of a permanent intercourse with the East. Another fleet, sponsored by private merchants in 1596, was equally unsuccessful. It may be recalled that it was about this time that the *Itinerário* of Huygen Van Linschoten was published, and Houtman, the Dutch merchant, returned with sufficient information and cargoes from India. All these news gave encouragement to the English to persist in their efforts even after four unsuccessful ventures.(5)

In the few remaining years of the sixteenth century, the English employed as many as forty ships to explore the Indian Ocean. It was the success of the early voyages of Houtman, the Dutch merchant that aroused the desires of the English, and in 1599, a number of principal merchants of London formed an association for trading with India, subscribing 30,000 Libras. Finally they sought a charter from the Queen to undertake the venture to the Eastern seas, along with certain privileges and exemptions. Initially the Queen was reluctant to grant these on the grounds that they might arouse rivalry and misunderstanding between England and Spain.(6) However, the merchants made her believe that the ports and territories they had planned to trade with, were different from the Spanish or the Portuguese. Convinced by these arguments, the Queen granted a Charter for a period of fifteen years to the Company to trade with all the places in India not claimed by the European nations, and to punish by fine and forfeiture such of Her Majesty's subject who should engage in the Indian trade without a licence.(7) The Charter conceded to the merchants the right to purchase land from the natives for factories. The land was, thenceforward, to be treated as private property; also to make bylaws for themselves and their servants, not different from the laws of England. Further it exempted the merchants from payment of customs duties either on export or import for a period of four years.(8) Thus, the English entered into the eastern trade. Irrespective of the fact whether they intruded into Portuguese territories or not, their presence was sufficient to obstruct the Portuguese monopoly.

The Company began by appointing a Governor and twenty-four directors. They purchased five ships, large and small and manned them with 440 mariners. Thirty-six factors in different capacities accompanied the fleet, which was commanded by Sir James Lancaster, a commander of an earlier abortive expedition.(9)

Though the objectives of the English Company supposedly were commercial, they were quick to participate in local politics and internal affairs. On the very first voyage, during the year 1601, the commander of the fleet, Lancaster, concluded treaties with the Kings of Achin and Bantam and controlled large supply of pepper on the west coast, whereby the English secured exemption from customs duties and permission to build a factory and to be ruled by their own laws.(10) On the same voyage, Lancaster, together with a Dutch officer, launched an attack on the Portuguese and captured a richly laden vessel.(11) After this other three subsequent voyages were also made to the Eastern Islands. But for a long time they directly made their visits to India, being chiefly undertaken as the means of exchanging their European commodities. But subordinate traffic soon became important enough to attract notice on its own account.

The English like the Dutch, to justify their presence and right of trade with the Asian countries, brought different views and refuted both the theories of the Portuguese and the Dutch simultaneously. According to the English theorist, William Welwood, who published the booklet *An Abridgement of All the Sea-Laws* in 1613,(12) the Indian Ocean was neither *Mare Clausvm*, as the Portuguese had claimed in the light of the papal bulls, nor was it *Mare Libervm* as Hugo Grotius proclaimed.(13) According to him, it was open to the English trade and expansion of territories. John Selden, another theorist, had defended the right of the English Crown to appropriate the sea as well as land, and also denied the idea of *Mare Liberum*. Thus, both, the Portuguese and the Dutch claims for the dominion of the Indian Ocean and the adjacent areas, were challenged by the English and, they went on trading with the Indian port-towns. The first attempt of the English to establish themselves on the western coast of India did not come before 20th August, 1609 when Captain Hawkins landed at Surat on a political mission to the court of Jehangir, the Mughal Emperor. His main aim was to obtain permission for establishing a trading factory at Surat and commercial privileges in that area.(14) But his efforts were thwarted by the intervention of the Portuguese Jesuits at the Mughal court and the hostility of Mukarrab Khan, the Governor of Surat.(15) By 1610, the Company had gained an upper hand in the seas and hence, despite their failure at Agra they persisted in their effort. On 16 September, 1611, Sir Henry Middleton, commander of the fleet approached Surat from the mouth of the Tapti river. The Admiral of the Portuguese fleet protested against this intrusion into an area over which they had exclusive rights. Sir Henry tried to work out a peaceful compromise, two months passed in negotiations, at the end of which the Portuguese moved down the river to attack the English. The Portuguese fleet was repelled and the English gained entry into the port of Surat.(16) Nevertheless, the overbearing temper of Middleton, invited the wrath of the Mughal Governor himself, who ordered him to quit the port without allowing him to complete his transaction or even to collect his debts. Though Middleton left the port, he replied to the insult by harassing all Indian shipping in the region of the Red sea. A large number of Indian vessels were detained and compelled to part with their merchandise in exchange for English goods for which they had little use.(17)

The next expedition, in 1612, under Captain Thomas Best was more successful. He not only gained the goodwill of the Mughals but also managed to get all sorts of facilities for the security of the English and in their trade.(18)

While Captain Best was concluding the treaty with the Mughals, his fleet was attacked by a very large Portuguese force and obliged to engage in battle, fought partly on the Tapti and partly on the open sea for several days. In the end, the Portuguese returned to Goa, while the English consolidated their position at Surat.(19)

The peace proved short-lived and in 1615 the Portuguese attacked the English ships under the command of Captain Downton, at the mouth of tapti. It was a desperate bid to revive their power and dwindling trade. Moreover, royal orders regarding the expulsion of the English were followed.(20) The battle lasted for a number of days and the Portuguese were once again beaten with considerable loss to both, life and prestige.(21)

The repeated success of the English made them masters of the sea. Besides, it also convinced the Mughal authorities that they were people to be reckoned with in the Indian waters. Consequently, the English were extended all trade facilities as well as protection to life and property at Surat.(22)

Evidence of the increased importance of the Company was offered by the acceptance of Sir Thomas Roe as the English ambassador to the court of the Great Mughal, Jehangir. In 1615, Roe sailed from England with the sole purpose of promoting English commercial interest. He spent two years trying to get a *Farman* that would strengthen the English position in India.(23) Unfortunately, due to the opposition of Mukarrab Khan, the inimical reports of the Portuguese, as well as the internal bickering of the Company's factors, the concessions he received were not in proportion to the high rank of his mission.(24) Even then it had to its credit the major achievements of securing a general permission for establishing factories throughout the Empire, especially in Bengal, Sindh, and Surat. They were also provided with legal immunity from certain exaction, and facilities in the transport of goods through all the ports of India.(25) This directly led to a considerable increase in the English commercial authority and their influence in India.

In 1618, Luso-English relations again became hostile because of the seizure of three ships and two flyboats of the Portuguese by the English off the St. Helena, on their way to Goa from Lisbon. They seized all the goods and the money valued at 90,000 ducats as compensation for the damage inflicted by the Portuguese viceroy, Dom Jerónimo de Azevedo on the four English ships off the Surat port during the 1612-13 fight.

By this time the Dutch and the English had already joined hands against the Portuguese. Though several attempts were made by the Portuguese viceroy, on the instructions received from the King of Portugal, to hinder this friend ship and their progress in the Indian trade, all those efforts ended in a fiasco.(26) By 1622, the English had entered into an agreement with Shah Abbas and established commercial ties with Persia. Not surprisingly, the Portuguese oppose the agreement and the English faced them in more than one naval engagement. In alliance with Shah Abbas, the English led an attack on Hormuz then in the possession of the Portuguese. The capture of the Island was due to the exertions of the English fleet, and they were paid with a share in the booty and permission to establish a factory at Gombroom. Various other concessions were conceded to the Company.(27)

Misfortunes now began to fall heavily upon the Portuguese and 'the stars in their course fought against them'. Not only they beset by enemies in distant possessions, but also the elements appeared to have turned against them in preventing the arrival of reinforcements.

In January, 1623, three English and four Dutch vessels comprising the defence fleet, blockaded Goa ports with the aim of obstructing the Portuguese from sending any ship to Portugal. After achieving their objectives, the blockade was lifted and fleet retired from the port on 19th March, 1623.(28) In the same year several attempts were made by the allied forces to hinder the Portuguese commerce. There were almost twenty enemy ships in the vicinity of Dabhol till Surat to obstruct the Portuguese ships coming from Mozambique as well as those coming from Portugal.(29) During the same period Macao was raided by both these forces and caused heavy damages before any help could reach.(30) In the month of January 1625, they again blockaded Surat with twelve ships that made it impossible for the Portuguese to get out any ship from this area. Therefore, they had to send words to Cochin to get few ships for their annual trip to Portugal.(31) Still the worst condition arose when the allied forces launched a furious attack on the Island of Bombay and caused heavy damage to property and life over there. Somehow, the arrival of the Portuguese ships from Surat saved the city from falling into their hands.(32)

Though naval engagements between the Portuguese and the allied forces especially on the part of the English continued till 1635, they were less frequent compared with the preceding ten years.(33) It seems that the English became very dissatisfied with the increasing power and success of the Dutch during this period which resulted in a peace treaty between these two nations. The English President William Methwold travelled to Goa from Surat for signing this truce with the viceroy extended them commercial facilities even in their ports.(34)

Eventually the two companies agreed to be merged for five years. An act of parliament was passed to form a new company, with powers to enforce obedience from the English subjects under strict sanctions.(35)

The opening of the Portuguese ports to English commercial interests clearly signified the dwindling strength of the Portuguese sea power. Equally significant is the fact that the English now acquired a place in the commercial traffic of the Portuguese, carrying away considerable quantities of pepper, cinnamon and other commodities of interest to them. Some times the Portuguese used English ships to carry their own goods.

After this period the Luso-English relation took a friendly turn and they promised to help each other against the increasing menace of the Dutch. But it is very hard to find any occasion when the English helped Portuguese. They did utilise the opportunity for increasing their commerce.

The Portuguese out of necessities did employ English ships bottom for their own goods. For instance, by the end of 1635, the English merchants brought a huge quantity of iron, muskets, cannon balls, anchors and various other things for the foundation of artillery to used against the Dutch.(37) All these goods were brought from China under the treaty concluded between them. Taking advantage of the opportunity, the English president did not hesitate to send an ambassador to the court of Virabhadra Nayak for the negotiation and purchase of pepper in 1637.(38) This was the time when the Dutch ships were in the vicinity of Goa waiting to attack the Portuguese ships. Therefore no sooner did the Portuguese get the news of the progress of English in Kanara state, the Portuguese Viceroy issued order to prevent their activities. Another reason also involved in this is that the English merchants had robbed a Portuguese ship near Diu.(39) The Portuguese Viceroy sent an ambassador, Martim Teixeira de Azevedo to the court of Virabhadra Nayak for the purpose of fixing the price of pepper and to request the expulsion of the English ambassador from their.(40) Another important event of this period is this that the English and the Dutch started collecting taxes on the movements of the local Indian merchant's ships. In other words they began issuing passes for the ships plying in the surroundings of Surat.(41) Since the taxes were collected by the Dutch and the English at the gun points, the income of the Portuguese *Estado da India* decreased substantially.(42) The Portuguese Viceroy orders in respect of the

Kanara merchants dealing in pepper to not exchange copper with pepper as the quality of their copper was very poor.(43) On one hand the Portuguese officers were carrying prohibitary orders against the English, on the other hand the English President was requested to carry almost 1,000 Khandi of rice in their ships to Malacca where the Dutch soldiers had laid siege since 1634.(44) It seems that the Portuguese were passing through a very confusing state of affairs. Nevertheless, they were bound to get the support of the English ships for their own goods especially items of defence viz. arms and ammunitions, but they were hesitant also to allow them to carry free trade which normally they did using the good opportunity of war between the Dutch and the English. Contrary to it the Portuguęse official were found negotiating with the English merchants for 1,000 quintals of cinnamon from Ceylon, of course at a higher rate then normally paid by the marine officials for their *Quintaladas* or *Liberdades*, that is 45-50 Ashrafis per quintal.(45) Thus, English merchants got share in the cinnamon trade in 1641 making use of the weak conditions of the Portuguese caused by the Dutch. But, again in 1643 orders were issued to stop trade in cinnamon with foreigners, keeping in view the monopoly of the said commodity.(46) On the contrary the English went on expanding their business in all the commodities one by one but rather peacefully.(47) They continued strengthening their commercial ties with neighbouring states particularly with those having strained relations with the Portuguese government.

With the passage of time Luso-English relations became increasingly cordial. Soon after Portugal's declaration of Independence from Spain in 1640-41, the English Company president sent a good will mission to Goa, forging closer ties. As a result, English trade in Portuguese territories was regularised further and they made new contract for larger quantities of goods.(48) A source of added strength was the grant of a fresh Charter confirming their possession, including Saint Helena. The latter had been occupied by the English after it was abandoned by the Dutch. The Charter envisaged the right to make war and peace with all people except Christians, to raise troops in England for their service, although they were used against the Portuguese only in the name of friendship. England's position improved further in 1662. The territory of Bombay was transferred to them as dowry to the princess Infanta Catarina in her marriage with Charles II.(49) The Earl of Marlborough was sent out with five ships to take possession of it, and Sir A. Shipmand to act as Governor on the King's port. But

Bombay was not acquired until 1665-67.(50) The delay occurred on the Portuguese side, first on account of a dispute regarding the extent of the cession and, afterwards, due to objection to the validity of the new Governor's commission. There was also disagreement between the King's Governor of Bombay and the President of Surat. In 1668, the king decided to put an end to the dispute by granting Bombay to the Company. Except for a token sum of ten Libra for quitrent, the transfer was full and complete.

Thus, the English became controller of trade in the Indian commodities very tactfully though not as much as the Dutch mastering over the same. A glance at the volume of English trade will reveal the exact position occupied by the English East India Company and how it helped in the decay of the Portuguese Eastern commerce and settlements.

Thus, this chapter reveals the facts about the political situation of the Indian subcontinent, which certainly affected the Portuguese position in the Indian Ocean. The threat posed by the Dutch and the English in the early decades of the century added to the anarchy of the Portuguese commerce and territorial bases that apparently ruined the Portuguese maritime trade.

The Dawn of the seventeenth century itself witnessed the disturbed relations of the Portuguese with the various neighbouring states. Zamorin, the century old enemy, did not loose the opportunity to join hands with the Dutch against the Portuguese. The Sultan of Bijapur was the next to welcome the Dutch during the second decade of the century. The Mughals came along giving more concessions and support to the new traders in comparison with the Portuguese. The relation with the Nayakas of Ikkeri, always fluctuated between friendship and hostility. The rise of Marathas added fuels to the fire. It seems, none of the Indian rulers or states were interested in supporting the Portuguese. In other words, those who had been friends, were waiting for an opportunity to take revenge on the Portuguese for their atrocities, now had two powerful maritime nation for their supports. Except Cochin, Cannanore and Quilon, joined hands with the other European powers against the Portuguese. In the end, after the fall of these territories into the hands of the Dutch, the Portuguese claims of the 'Lords of Navigation, Conquest and trade with Ethiopia, Arabia, Persia and India', came to an end.

Notes
Part III
Portuguese-English Relations

1. Refer to Chapter 2, part II.
2. *LML*, cod. 7, fls. 37-45; cod. 11, fls. 83-84, 135-136; cod. 12, fls. 78; *India*, cx. 4, doc. 192.
3. *LML*, cod. 34, fls. 34; cod. 35, fls. 25-25v; cod. 35, fls. 102-103v, 385-91; cod. 40, fls. 116-117v, 138-139, 189, 365, 373; cod. 41, fls. 22-23v; cod. 42, fls. 41; cod. 44, fls. 426-427v; *ACF*, cod. 1162, fls. 147-147v.
4. J. H. Talboys Wheeler, *Early Travels in India*, pp. VII-XVIII; M. Elphinistone, *The Rise of the British Power in the East*, pp. 289; Danvers, *The Portuguese...*,vol. II, pp. 109-110.
5. Elphinistone, *The Rise of..*, p. 29; Danvers, *The Portuguese..*,pp. 10-59; Talboys, *Travels..*, pp. VIIXVIII.
6. Danvers, *The Portuguese..*, vol. II, pp. 109-110.
7. *Ibid.*
8. *Ibid.*
9. *Ibid.*
10. Danvers, *Letters Received by East India Company from its Servants in the East*, Vol. I, pp. 14; Danvers, *The Portuguese..*, Vol. II, pp. 110; Moreland, *From Akbar to Aurangzeb*, pp. 15, 18.
11. Elphinistone, *The Rise of...*, p. 31.
12. Mathew, *Maritime Trade of Maharashtra..*, P. 5.
13. Grotius took up the challenge and wrote the reply to Welwood's attack though it was to published then and was under the title, *Defensio Capitis Quinti Maris Liberi oppugnanti a Gulielmo Welwood Juris Civilis Professore capitis XXVIIe jus Libri scripti Anglica sermone cui Titulum fecit Compendium Legum Maritimarum*. Ref. James Brown Scott ed. *The Freedom of the Seas*, Nova York, 1916, pp. viiiix; Serafim de Freitas, defended the right of the Portuguese seas by writing *De Justo império Lusitanorum Asiatico*, translated from Latin to Portu guese by Miguel Pinto de Meneses, entitled *De Justo Império Asiatico dos Portugueses*, Lisboa, 1960.
14. Talboys, *Travels*, pp. 34; Purchas, *His Pilgrimage...*, vol. I 206.
15. Talboys, *Travels*, pp. 34-35.
16. *LML* , cod. 7, fls. 19/37, 20/39-42, 21/43$_v$-44, 22/45-45$_v$; Danvers, *Letters Received...* vol. I, pp. 138-141, 144-46, 155-58; Danvers, *Portu guese..*, Vol. II, pp. 152-54.
17. *India*, cx. 2, doc. 87; Talboys, *Travels*, pp. 46-47.

18. *LML*, cod. 7, fls. 22/45-45$_v$; Talboys, *Travels*, pp. 49-50.
19. Hamilton, *The Trade Relations...*, p. 17.
20. *Ibid.*
21. Danvers, *Letters Received...* vol.II,p. 107 ; Danvers, *Portuguese..*, Vol.II, pp.170-174.
22. HAG, *Livro das Pazes* nº 1, fl. 1; *Livro das cartas*, cod. 779, fls. 55-55$_v$; Hamilton, *The Trade Relations...*, p. 16-17.
23. Delduque da Costa, 'Os Portugueses e os reis da India', *BIVG*, No. 18, pp. 1819.
24. *Ibid.*, Foster, Sir Thomas Roe..., pp. XXXVIII-XLIX, 128-145.
25. *Ibid.*, Foster, Sir Thomas Roe..., pp. XXXVIIIXLIX, 128-145.
26 *LML*, cod. 11, fls. 42/83-84, 76/135-37; cod. 12, fls. 3/78; cod. 13, fl. 46/91; *India*, cx. 4, doc. 192.
27. Elphinistone, *The Rise of..*, p. 37; Danvers, *Portuguese..*, Vol. II, pp. 207-212.
28. *LML*, cod. 16, fls. 23/53-54; cod. 17, fls. 14/4, 173/43, 44, 218/67v.
29. *LML*, cod. 17, fls. 173/43.
30. *LML*, cod. 17, fls. 173/43, 218/67v, cod. 20, fl. 56/111.
31. *LML*, cod. 22, fls. 11/4.
32. *LML*, cod. 24, fls. 399/185; Danvers, *Portuguese..*, Vol. II, pp. 223-24; Pissurlenkar, 'Os Fragmentos'.., (passim)
33. *LML*, cod. 24, fls. 399/185; cod. 30, fls. 314/26364; Pissurlenkar, 'Os Fragmentos'.., (passim)
34. *LML*, cod. 32, fls. 36/11, 72; Biker, *Tratados...*, vol. II, pp. 50-60; Elphinistone, *The Rise of..*, p. 38-39
35. *ACF*, 1162, fls. 147148; *LML*, cod. 38, fls. 111/28989v.
36. *Ibid.*
37. *LML*, cod. 34, fls. 2/33v, 3/55v, 114/25-25v; cod. 44, fls. 180/426-427v.
38. *LML*, cod. 38, fls. 47/102-103, 110/285, 112/291-292v, 297-300
39. *LML*, cod. 40, fls. 57/116117v.
40. *LML*, cod. 40, fls. 57/116-117v, 64/138-39v, 90/189, 183/365, 187/373; cod. 42, fl. 58/41.
41. *LML*, cod. 44, fls. 19/35, 220.
42. *LML*, cod. 45, fls. 29/29-29v.
43. *LML*, cod. 44, fls. 74/152, 238-38v.
44. *ACF*, 1163, fls. 63v-64.
45. *ACF*, 1163, fls. 191-191v; LML, cod. 49, fls. 100/234-234$_v$.
46. *LML*, cod. 50, fls. 47/97v. 113; cod. 52, fl. 67/148.
47. *LML*, cod. 48, fls. 452/309v., 229/191-191v, 288/225-225v; cod. 54, fl. 35/69.

48. *LML*, cod. 43, fls. 65/100, 117; cod. 52, fl. 6/16; cod. 53, fls. 4/77v; cod. 54, fl. 34/67; cod. 55, fl. 30/31; cod. 56, fls. 61/123, 62/125, 213-13v; *India*, cx. 11, doc. 162; cx. 20, doc. 143; cx. 21, doc. 1; *ACF*, cod. 1164, fls. 59, 103, 147, 226v; cod. 1167, fl. 91.

49. *India*, cx. 25, docs. 54, 128, 142; Danvers, *Portuguese..*, Vol. II, pp. 331-332.

50. *India*, cx. 26, docs. 170; cx. 27, doc. 21, 87; cx. 28, doc. 180.

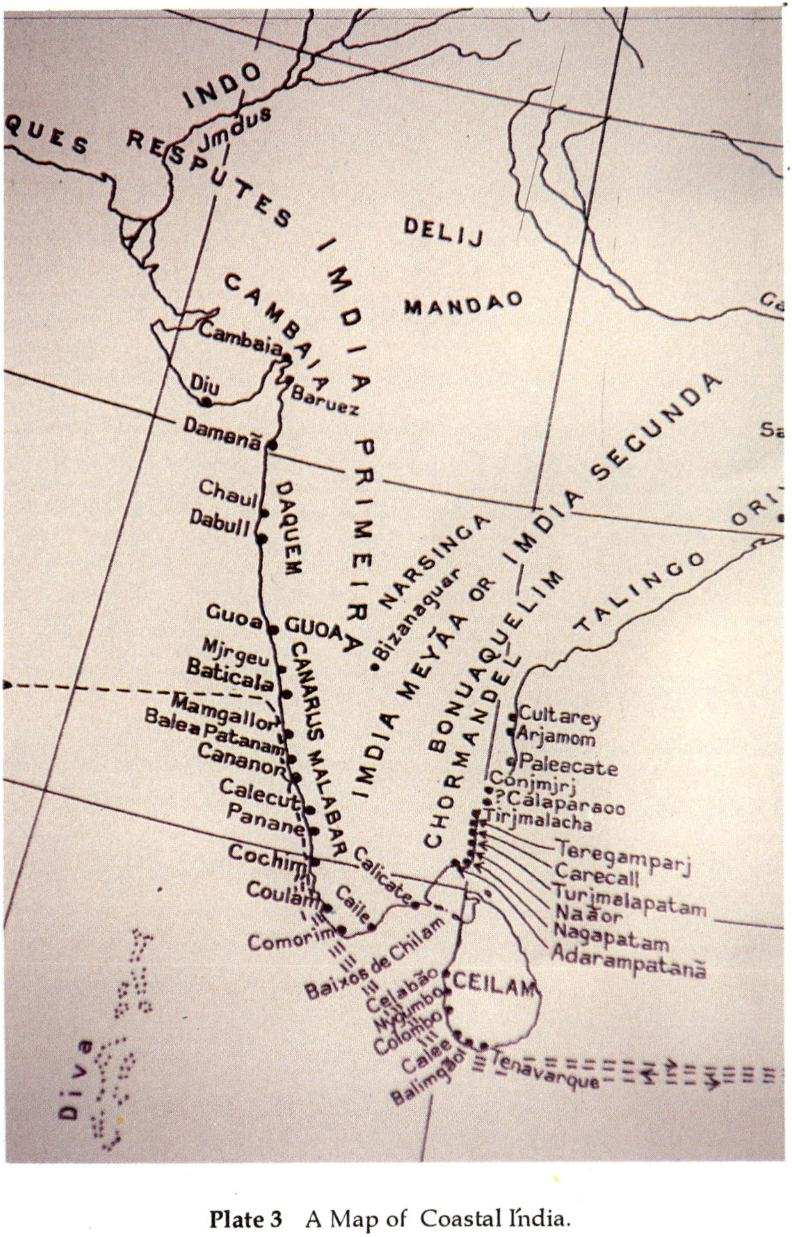

Plate 3 A Map of Coastal Índia.

Chapter - 3

Portuguese Export Trade in Pepper

Pepper was the backbone of the Portuguese Asian spice trade, even if its value per unit of weight was not high as that of the luxury spices. Due to its importance and value, King Dom Manuel I declared it as a prime commodity of royal monopoly.(1) As early as in 1509, the Portuguese first Viceroy, Dom Francisco de Almeida, while at Diu, was asked by its Governor, Malik Ayaz, about the reasons of the Portuguese presence in the Indian waters. To which he replied that he had been sent to serve his King by providing *Pimenta e Drogas*, (pepper and drugs).(2) No wonder, of course, for the Portuguese knew of the huge profit reaped by the Venetians and the Arabs who hitherto had provided this commodity to Europe. Thereafter, trading in this commodity was strictly prohibited, except by Portuguese officials on the royal account. In all the *Cartazes* issued, either to a king or a merchant, pepper was clearly forbidden as an item of trade.(3) Even the Portuguese officers were not permitted to have any transactions in it. Thus, among the exported goods to Portugal, pepper was always the first commodity stowed on board the carracks. Detailed standing orders were designed to ensure that this was accomplished with 'great care and diligent watch'. About two-third of the compartments of the ships were occupied by this commodity.(4)

In this chapter the varieties of pepper produced in various regions and brought to the Portuguese factories is the major subject of study. I have also given special attention to the import of *Cabedal da Pimenta* (pepper money) and the volume of pepper procured from various regions and dispatched to Portugal, as well as to the merchants, both native Indians and Portuguese settlers who supplied this commodity to the crown. And finally, I have treated the areas from which the Portuguese drew their supply.

There were three main varieties of pepper. Black pepper, which was in great demand and was used widely in Europe. Long pepper, which was traded in the whole of sixteenth century by the Portuguese but disappeared from the seventeenth century records, and finally, white pepper, specially used for medicinal purposes. Of these varieties, black pepper had the largest market in the seventeenth century.

Pepper, an item of international competition, was produced mainly in the south, in the stretch of territory from Cape Camorin, covering the whole region of Malabar (at present Kerala) to Kanara (the present Karnataka).(5) During most of the sixteenth, and more intermittently in the seventeenth, it was principal source for Portuguese pepper purchases in India. Malabar, during this period not seriously threatened by any invasion from the land or by the activities of any local power out to upset the existing political balance.(6)

Among the Malabar Kingdoms, Cannanore, Calicut, Cochin, Quilon were the largest and most powerful of those from which the Portuguese had to buy their pepper during the sixteenth and first half of the seventeenth centuries.

Cannanore was a flourishing trading port for the supply of pepper. The merchants dealing with the trade were mostly the Indianised descendants of Arab immigrants, locally known as Moplahs. They dominated the trade not only in Cannanore but also all over the Malabar towns. The Portuguese conducted most of their formal business in Cannanore with Ali Rajah, after about 1625 also the hereditary leader of the Cannanore Moplahs.(7)

The quality of the Cannanore pepper was reputedly the best in Malabar. Throughout the sixteenth century, the Portuguese purchased most of their pepper from here, except in the year between 1587-1605 (official purchase were, however, made in 1593) when they refused to buy due to the increased price demanded by Ali Rajah.(8) In 1606, when supplies from Kanara and other regions of Malabar became scarce, the Portuguese made an agreement on prices and resumed trade with Ali Rajah.(9) Though Cannanore supplies never rose to great volumes, they remained stable for the rest of the of the first half of the seventeenth century.

Calicut was well known for its bulk of pepper. But after the establishment of the Dutch in this region, the Portuguese withdrew their attention from here. This must be the main reason why the

Portuguese documents contain no indication of pepper purchase from this territory during the first half of the seventeenth century.

Cochin, one of the greatest pepper producing regions of Malabar and the most confident ally of the Portuguese in India, as has been discussed earlier in first and second chapters, was a major source of pepper supply next to Kanara. Cochin pepper was cheapest but of an inferior quality compared with Kanara. During most of the seventeenth century, the Portuguese exploited their friendship with the King to get it inexpensively. As the prices were uneconomical for the producers, this frequently led to the disappearance of pepper from the Portuguese controlled markets and they probably sold it to other merchants who supplied the Dutch or English at a comparatively higher price.

Quilon, was of lesser importance than Cochin. Pepper from this region was the same quality as of Cochin. Because of less intensive cultivation, pepper was generally brought from the neighbouring areas of Kayamkulam and other places to its factory and weighing house. However, in the seventeenth century they fetched most of the pepper from here especially at the time of natural calamity or scarcity in the northern regions.

In Kanara, the major pepper producing states were Onor, Barcelore and Mangalore, under the rule of the Nayakas of Ikkeri. The Portuguese occasionally entered into treaties with them and obtained rights to trade in his territories. During the sixteenth century as a whole, Portuguese transactions with the Kanara states, compared with other parts of western India, were unimportant. However, from the second decade of the seventeenth century, in the midst of an all round decline in Portuguese trade with India, Kanara acquired a relative importance.(10) The acquisition of parts of Kanara by the Portuguese had important implications for their official pepper trade. It widened the choice of sources available to them, allowing for greater flexibility in buying tactics.

The price of Kanara pepper was higher than all other regions but it is believed that its quality was far superior to that of Malabar.(11) Portuguese preference probably was due to this. But the circumstances prevailing in that period had played a vital role in it. However, supplies from Kanara were disrupted from time to time because of the expansionist wars of Venkatappa Nayak, the ruler of Ikkeri, though without leading to a complete breakdown. Both sides worked out suitable compromises.

Malacca, too, was important for the supply of pepper. The pepper from this region was doubt superior in quality to that of both Malabar and Kanara. Since this place was far away from the effective sway of Portuguese power, it was not very convenient for them to bring pepper from it safely. Moreover, the presence of the Dutch in the early seventeenth century, had very often disrupted the supply. However, even under these circumstances, the Portuguese, till the end of third decade of the seventeenth century, still brought pepper from Malacca to Goa and then reshipped it to Portugal.

Import of Cabedal da Pimenta (Pepper Money) in Goa

During the early sixteenth century, the Portuguese government used to send only one-fourth of the total sum needed for the purchase of its monopoly commodities with the rest to be made up in commodities or else to be provided to the Indian merchants and rulers on credit.(12) However, in the second decade of the century, most of the amount sent for the purchase of the Indian goods, especially pepper, was through the merchant-contractors.(13) As it has been discussed earlier, pepper was one of the most profitable and precious commodities and so the India House spent a great part of it's funds on this. During the seventeenth century, it was found that there was regular export of money under the *Cabedal da Pimenta*(14) provided by the government. The King of Portugal in order to maintain a full monopoly over this item, sent as much money as he could afford from his bankers and merchants.(15) Though the amount fluctuated every year, it was certainly related to the financial condition of the Portuguese government. The amount sent under this rubric, *Cabedal da Pimenta*, was to be utilised for the purchase of nothing but pepper.(16) From time to time strict orders were issued in this regard to reinforce it. It was, indeed, followed most of the time, except during the fifth and the sixth decades when some money was utilised for the purchase of saltpetre, only because of the very critical situation of the *Estado da India*, and that too when the required volume of pepper was not available at Cochin.(18) During the third decade, being helpless from the unbearable defence expenditure at home (expenditure on the war with the Dutch in the Netherlands) and in the colonies, the Portuguese government, with the aim of raising investments in the private sector, encouraged their merchant financiers to form a syndicate on the pattern of the Dutch and the English trading companies. Some times, when the government failed to send sufficient cash for the purchase of pepper, the king instructed the treasury of Goa to provide the money from the income of the *Estado da India*.(19) Following is the detail of the pepper money sent from Lisbon to Goa on the annual fleet during the first two decades:(20)

TABLE 3.1
PEPPER MONEY DURING
1601 - 1620

YEAR	AMOUNT IN ASHRAFIS[21]	SOURCES
1601-4	-	-
1605	3,40,000	*LML*, cod. I, fl. 11/35
1611	1,97,916	*LML*, cod. 13a, fl. 161-179;
1612	1,48,438	AHU, *India*, cx. 2,
1613	94,562	doc. 73, cx. 9, doc. 177.
1614	1,97,116	
1615	9,30,825 [22]	(The above mentioned sources have been utilised for all the years)
1616	79,166	
1617	3,97,812	
1618	2,37,500	
1619	1,60,000	
1620	1,61,772	
TOTAL	29,27,108 Ashrafis	

Total of second decade only 25,87,108 Ashrafis

Average for the second decade, 2,58,710 Ashrafis.

(-)means not available

During the second decade, the import of cash oscillated between 1,00,000 and 9,00,000 giving an average of 2,58,108 Ashrafis per year. However, the volume of pepper bought and sent to Portugal also fluctuated in the same manner.(23)

During the third decade, amidst all the problems, blockades, wars and the commercial rivalries(24), the Portuguese government managed to send more or less the same amount but much of it was utilised for the defence.(25)

It was during this period only that a Portuguese trading company was formed on the pattern of the English and the Dutch Companies. Though the company was formed in 1628 to solve the problems of the government and to uplift the diminishing trade, but the idea to formulate such company had been growing right from the end of the sixteenth century. Nevertheless, it could be formulated only on August 27, 1628. This step was taken when the government of Portugal realised her inability to provide sufficient funds for the purchase of necessary goods specially pepper. The expenditure on defence of the state went on increasing, trade started diminishing with the steady increase in prices, moreover, their relations with local contractors and rulers also deteriorated because of their debts which brought down the position of the Portuguese Crown in the East. The inquisition during the end of the sixteenth century worked as fuel on fire for the increasing crisis especially in the case of New Christians.(26) Furthermore, they felt threatened by the possibility of an alliance between the contractors and with the other Protestant European Companies. Thus, pressed by these circumstances, the Company was formed by a royal decree containing a sixty-eight clause Charter setting out its constitution, power and privileges.(27)

The charter provided for a board of directors to administer the Company's affairs in Lisbon, to formulate policies, and to supervise a subordinate board in Goa. The Lisbon board at least in theory, was to be fully independent of all organs of government in Portugal. The *Conselho do Estado* (Council of States) and the subordinate offices, were specially forbidden to interfere in Company's affairs. Besides, the board of the Directors was to be directly subordinated to the Crown through the *Conselho do Comércio* (Council of Commerce) in Madrid. But the ships themselves continued to be fitted out at the dockyard facilities of the *Armazem da India*, in Lisbon. The crews and the navigational instruments were to be supplied as before. However, the aim behind all the formalities was to improve and uplift the decreasing commerce of the East. All these efforts seem to have gone waste since they brought no satisfactory improvement comparing with the previous export.

TABLE 3.2

Pepper Money During

1621 - 1630

YEAR	AMOUNT IN ASHRAFIS(21)	SOURCES
1621	1,60,000	*LML* cod. 13a, fls. 161-179;
1622	2,84,000	*India,* cx .2, doc. 73, cx. 9, doc. 177
1623-24	5,39,165	*do*

1625	1,60,000	*do*
1626	3,06,743	*do*
1627	80,000	*do*
1628	1,46,000	*do*
1629	2,40,000	*do*
1630	1,07,590	*do*
Total -	20,75,908	
Average -	2,07,590	

After 1633 the Portuguese *Companhia da India Oriental* ceased to function. The frequent delays and losses at sea suffered during 1631-1632, led inexorably to its collapse. Other reasons were the poor financial and material resources caused by the reluctance of Iberian capitalists to invest, the strength of the Dutch and the English competition, and the deteriorating supply and market condition for pepper. Partly it was also caused by friction between the bureaucracies in Portugal and those in India. The operations of the board and Company at Lisbon and Goa, particularly Goa, were thereby seriously handicapped. So far as its India trade was concerned, Portugal was house divided against itself during the Company regime; the dispute between the government officials at Goa and the Company directors continued and became a prestige issue eventually leading to a paralysis of the Company.(28) With a period of three years the company's capital had dwindled from an original 24,000,000 Ashrafis (12,000,000 Cruzados) to 1,200,000 Ashrafis. Moreover, the account books of the India House and *Armazem* showed that far from improving the balance of trade as intended, the Company has spent more on the fleets and received less from pepper sales, freight charges, and duties than had the previous administration.(29) In 1633 the government of Portugal handed over the charge of the Company to the India House and the five year experiment was over.(30)

The fall of the company followed the siege of Malacca and blockade of Goa simultaneously, and later it was followed by the struggle for the independence of their country against the sixty years yoke of Spain. However, all these required a huge amount to meet the expenditure incurred or to be incurred on arms and munitions as well as the payment and provisions for the soldiers. The Portuguese government felt helpless in providing sufficient amounts for the purchase of pepper. For about three years no money could be sent from Portugal to India. Forced by the circumstances, the authorities at Goa, sent money for the purchase of pepper from the treasury of the state. The total amount brought from Portugal under both the Company control as well as that which was sent from the state treasury by the consent of the Ministers of the Council of Finance, are given below:

Table 3.3

Pepper Money During 1631 - 1640

YEAR	AMOUNT IN ASHRAFIS	SOURCES
1631	18,256	*India,* cx. 10, doc. 195
1632	95,536	*Ibid*
1633	2,05,196	*Ibid*
1634	64,000	*ACF,* cod. 1162, fl. 137
1635	2,00,000	*ACF,* cod. 1162, fls. 182-82v *India,* cx. 11, doc. 179
1636	2,00,000	*India,* cx. 11, doc. 191
1637	3,000	*ACF,* cod. 1162, fls. 195, 201v; cod. 1163, fl. 9v
1638	-	-
1639	40,000	*ACF,* cod. 1163, fls. 46v.
1640	60,000	*ACF,* cod. 1163, fls. 117-118
1640	60,000	*ACF,* cod. 1163, fls. 117-118

Total - 9,35,988 (Includes the money utilised from the treasury of Goa,1634-1640)

Average - 93,598.8

Thus, it is noted that the total investments for the purchase of pepper from all the sources could reach to maximum forty percent in comparison to the previous decades. The total amount as shown in the table 3.3 was 9,35,988 Ashrafis. The fourth decade was still worst. No money could be spared from the crown for the purchase of pepper. All the money was utilised from the income of the *Estado da India.* A total of only twenty percent could be invested from the treasury of Goa. Soon after the loss of Malacca, the Dutch had started their campaign in earnest against the territory of Ceylon. Under such conditions some cash could be sent from Portugal, but only for defence expenditures. Even the money dispatched by the treasury of Goa fluctuated between 14,000 Ashrafis and 60,000 Ashrafis, including 3,671 kgs. of opium. The exact wealth invested for the purchase of pepper in this fifth decade can be seen in the following table:

Table 3.4

Pepper Money During

1641 - 1650

YEAR	AMOUNT IN ASHRAFIS	SOURCES
1641	14,362	*ACF*, cod. 1163, fls. 130-30v, 150-53v, 160-61v, 175,180-182V.
1642	61,456	*ACF*, cod. 1163, fls. 202v, 219, 226.
1643	4,058	*ACF*, cod. 1163, fls. 58v, 274v
1644	-	
1645	30,000	*ACF*, cod. 1164, fls.101, 129v
1646	50,000	*ACF*, cod. 1164, fls. 155v, 159, 175v
1647	3,671 kgs. 0pium	*Ibid*. fl. 228v
1648	-	
1649	25,000	*ACF*, cod. 1166 fls. 27-28
1650	20,000	*ACF*, cod. 1166, fls. 56v.
Total	1,77,876. & 3,671 kgs. of Opium	
Average	17,786 Ashrafis.	

(-) Means not available.

The next decade was the period of turmoil and decline of the Portuguese commercial settlements. For about five years some amount was brought from Portugal, which is until 1656. After this the main Portuguese settlements came into the grip of war. But still the amount invested in pepper was in pepper was better than the previous decade. The real investment can be seen in the following table:

Table 3.5

Pepper Money During

1651- 1660

YEAR	AMOUNT INASHRAFIS	SOURCES
1651	91,500	*ACF*, cod. 1166, fls. 64, 73v. 86v; *India* cx. 21, doc. 49, 79
1652	70,015	*ACF*, cod. 1166, fls. 95v. 102, 113v.,128-129
1653	-	
1654	95,611	*India*, cx. 22, doc. 126
1655	18,000	*ACF*, cod. 1167, fls. 88v.
1656	45,000	*ACF*, cod. 1167, fls. 106, 133, 137.

Total	2,28,626 Ashrafis.
Average	53,354 Ashrafis.

Over all total for 56 Years from Portugal - 60,14,630

Over all total of money employed from Goa treasury 4,22,376

Thus out of total forty seven years investments, continuous import of money to thirty three years had been from Portugal, i.e. 60,14,630 Ashrafis and fourteen years or more had been employed from the treasury of Goa, i.e. 4,22,376 Ashrafis. Thus, average import from Portugal had been 1,82,226 Ashrafis per year and average investment from the Goa treasury was 30,169 per year.

Volume of Pepper Exported to Portugal From Goa

The volume of Portuguese export trade in pepper depended chiefly upon the demand of the European countries where it was to be supplied and secondly on the financial condition of the Portuguese government which sent money for the purchase of pepper. In practice, however, only a modest fraction of the pepper produced in South-west India was bought by the Portuguese. In the entire producing area from Onor in the north to Travancore in the south, the minimum annual pepper production in the first decade of the seventeenth century was estimated at 100,000 bahars (about 317,000 quintals)(31) of which not more than 20,000 to 30,000 quintals were dispatched on the carracks to Lisbon a mere ten percent of the total.(32) But in reality, during the first half of the seventeenth century even this could never be procured regularly.(33)

In the first decade of the seventeenth century, the Portuguese government suffered a setback as the authorities at Goa were unsuccessful in providing full demand of the Crown. The volume of export in this period decreased by 35 percent compared with that of the average export of the last decades of the sixteenth century. The total export of pepper during this period (table 3.6) was 71,950 quintals supplied rather intermittently because of the inability of pepper in Malabar and Malacca. This was due to the presence of the two northern European nations, the Dutch and the English in the Eastern Archipelago who bought all the pepper and spices from this region. During this period only the Dutch had concluded a peace treaty with the ruler of Calicut, which proved to be barrier for the Portuguese collection of pepper from Malabar. Nevertheless, during the period between 1603 and 1605, during the blockade of Goa and difficult years for the Portuguese supply of pepper from Cochin and other ports, the Portuguese officers were able to get their consignment, among other ways, through the efforts of the

Bishop of this region.(34) Even though the actual volume of the pepper from Malabar and Kanara is not known, it was somewhere between fifty and fifty-five percent from Malabar, around thirty percent from Kanara, and the rest from Malacca.(35) On the other hand, the Dutch and the English had so glutted the markets of the entire European continents by the Eastern pepper and spices(36) that there was less demand for what the Portuguese imported. Here, it will be quite suitable to mention that until the late sixteenth century, German and Italian merchants were supplying Portuguese pepper to all north and North-western Europe. But after the Dutch rose against the Portuguese commercial empire, it more or less blocked the whole north European market for the Portuguese pepper. Thus it was quite natural that the Portuguese enjoyed less demand for it. The total export of pepper from Goa to Lisbon, depicted in the documents are shown in the following table:

Table 3.6

Pepper Export from Goa to Lisbon in Quintals During 1601 - 1610

1	2	3	4	5	6	7
Year	**Kanara**	**Cranganore**	**Cochin**	**Quilon**	**Malacca**	**Total**
1601-7	-	-	-	-	-	25,590
1608-10	-	-	-	-	-	46,360

Over all total in ten years 71,950

Average per year 7,195

Sources: *BSGL*, India House; Res. Maço 4, N° 88, doc.18/13, 20/115, 21/14; Francisco da Costa, Clerk of the Cochin Factory, *Relatório sobre o trato da pimenta, Archivo General de Simancas, Secretaria provinciales*, (in *DUP*, III, ed. Silva Rego, Lisbon, 1960), cod. 1571, pp. 306-307, 311; Luis de Figueiredo Falcão, *Livro em que se...*, p. 5

During the second decade of seventeenth century pepper export fluctuated between 5,000 quintals to 11,500 quintals per year. The average export during this period was around 9,100 quintals per year, which meant the export increased by 15 percent when compared with the last decade. However, during this period Kanara pepper took on new importance in the trade. It was about 70.5 percent exported from Kanara and 29.5 percent of the total export from Malabar and Malacca.(37) However, Malabar merchants started taking much interest in the buyers who paid more profitable amounts than the Portuguese. The Portuguese, even after many pressures from the merchants to increase the price, tried to maintain the old and very lower ones. On the other hand they were helpless in Kanara to influence the prices. It was at least 20 percent more than the Malabar pepper price. In the following table the total export of pepper from Goa to Portugal has been shown:(38)

Table 3.7

Pepper Export From Goa to Lisbon in Qunitals During 1611 - 1620

1 Year	2 Kanara	3 Cranganore	4 Cochin	5 Quilon	6 Malacca	7 Total
1611	7,025	483	-	-	2,001	9,508
1612	4,237	518	-	585	2,583	8,002
1613	6,402	-	-	-	-	6,402
1614	2,950	-	7,722	-	-	10,355
1615	11,741	-	2,126	1,374	-	15,841
1616	4,374	-	1,341	-	-	5,715
1617	9,602	-	491	-	1,498	11,591
1618	10,078	-	814	-	-	10,892
1619	5,916	-	83	-	-	5,999
1620	3,266	-	4,320	-	-	7,586
Total			91,891 Quintals			

Average per year 9,189

Sources: *LMG*, No. 13a. fls. 164-179; *India*, cx. 4, doc. 25; cx. 9, doc. 177.

During the third decade the export was stable. Portuguese ships carried back home on an average of about 9,198 quintals every year with the exception of 21,373 quintals that was dispatched in 1624, since the ships could not leave Goa in 1623 due to the Dutch blockade of the port. However, this decade could be considered as a troublesome period for Portuguese trading activities on the whole, massive Dutch and English attacks on Bombay and Quilon hindered the shipping to Goa. However, Kanara pepper made up only 44,5 percent of the total because the Portuguese Venkatappa Nayak relations remained hostile during the last years of the decade.(39) But somehow, they resumed their supply from this region by 1630. During this time of disturbance, the Portuguese sought help from their oldest allies, Quilon and Cochin for their supply and thus they brought from them almost 45,5% of their Malabar pepper.(40) The remaining ten percent, most probably, was brought from Malacca. It was only at this time, incidentally, in 1628, that the Portuguese efforts to form their own *Companhia da India Oriental*, or East India Company of the merchants mostly new Christians, finally succeeded.

Table 3.8

Pepper Export From Goa to Lisbon in Quintals During 1621 - 1630

1 Year	2 Kanara	3 Cranganore	4 Cochin	5 Quilon	6 Malacca	7 Total
1621	5,478	-	394	-	-	5,872
1622	2,980	-	6,178	-	-	9,158
1623-24	17,577	-	3,794	-	-	21,373
1625	2,920	-	3,528	3,522	-	9,970
1626	5,150	-	9,680	-	-	14,830
1627-28	2,957	-	2,864	-	-	5,821
1628-29	1,790	-	3,715	-	-	5,505
1629-30	1,877	-	3,321	4,686	-	10,884
1630-31	-	-	-	-	-	9,061
Total			91,810 Quintals			
Average per year	9,181					

Table 3.9

Pepper Export From Goa to Lisbon in Quintals During 1631 - 1640

1 Year	2 Kanara	3 Cranganore	4 Cochin	5 Quilon	6 Malacca	7 Total
1631	-	-	1,855	3,663	-	5,518
1632-33	9,686	-	-	-	-	9,686
1633-34	6,152	-	2,893	-	-	9,045
1635	5,133	-	1,418	3,492	-	10,043
1636	2,628	1,000	3,100	-	-	6,725
1637	-	-	-	-	-	4,284
1638	1,000	-	-	-	-	1,000
1639	-	-	-	-	-	-
1640	1,623	-	2,000	-	-	2,623
Total		52,547.0				

Average including the blockade years 1637-1640 5,254.7

Sources: *India*, cx. 10, doc. 11, 23, 81, 203-204, 206; cx. 11, doc. 157, 184, 221; cx. 12, doc. 7, 19, 25, 144, 150; cx. 13, doc. 10, 24, 39, 119, 132, 149, 168, 170, 175, 176, 183, 188; cx. 14, doc. 20; *Lynch* cod. 14, pp. 57, 59, 62-64, 89, 227-28, 239, 250.

Till the end of the third decade pepper trade between India and Portugal was almost stable but from the beginning of the fourth decade it gradually declined. These were obviously the most difficult years for the Portuguese *Estado da India* commerce in the East. In a broader sense the whole Portuguese world was shaken. The Dutch invasion of Ceylon in 1638, the blockades of Malacca and Goa simultaneously from 1631-1642, the war of independence in Portugal, all these led to a heavy tax on Portuguese resources and a decline in commerce. In more normal times, the average fluctuation over the years of trade was not much, about ten percent. But if blockade years are included it goes down by sixty percent.(41) Since the supply from Kanara had resumed, the export trade reached to 57.5 percent. The Malabar pepper was only about 42.5 percent.

The continuous sieges of Goa, Malacca and Ceylon resulted in Goa's ruin and Malacca's loss. Commerce was brought to standstill because of their engagements in wars on different fronts.(42) Nevertheless, the total export during 1641-50, was merely 8,923 quintals. The maximum volume was derived from Malabar and eighteen percent from Kanara as brought to Goa and forwarded to Portugal during the total four years export.(43) During this period, in the year 1649, there were 79,769 sacks or bags of pepper (79,769 *sacos de Pimenta de Bantam a 50 catty cada saco*)(44). The weight of each bag is not clear. If determined by a Catty, which was probably a coin of Java and its neighbouring countries, it becomes more difficult to ascertain the reality. If one sac was one quintal, then in that case total export of Bantam pepper comes to about 79,769 quintals in 1649, which is an exaggerated volume.(45) Thus, the total export could be counted 88,892 quintal and average can be assumed around 8,800 quintals? if this is true, than it can be regarded as reflecting the most determined efforts of Portuguese officials even under such adverse circumstances and thus the calculation regarding the Portuguese trade has to be revised. The following table points out the possible exports.

The sixth decade saw still worse conditions. The maximum date that trade could be continued was 1656. Thereafter, the whole Portuguese settlements sank into the thick clouds of disaster. Ceylon was lost during 1655-58 (28): between 1659 and 1633, the major strongholds in the 'pepper land', Cranganore, Cochin and Quilon, had passed into the hands of the Dutch.(46) The maximum and final volume that could be drawn from the territories of Malabar was about 88.5 percent and Kanara had to part with 11.5 percent of the total export of 14,434 quintals with in six years. Here is detailed table of the export of pepper from Goa to Lisbon:

Table 3.10

Pepper Export From Goa to Lisbon in Qunitals During 1641 - 1650

1	2	3	4	5	6	7
Year	**Kanara**	**Cranganore**	**Cochin**	**Quilon**	**Malacca**	**Total**
1641	-	-	-	-	-	-
1642	0,490	-	2,500	-	-	2,990
1643	-	-	-	-	-	8,000
1644	-	-	-	-	-	-
1645	-	-	2,000	-	-	2,000
1646	-	-	2,808	-	-	2,808
1647	-	-	-	-	-	-
1648	-	-	-	-	-	1,125
1649	1,125	79,769 Bags	-	-	-	-
1650	-	-	-	-	-	-
Total	14,115.00 Quintals 79,769 Bags.					
Average	1,411.50 Quintal					

Sources: *India*, cx. 14, doc. 143, 149, 174, 18; cx. 20, doc. 120, also refer to the table 3.4

Table 3.11

Pepper Export from Goa to Lisbon in Quintals During 1651 - 1660-63

1	2	3	4	5	6	7
Year	**Kanara**	**Cranganore**	**Cochin**	**Quilon**	**Malacca**	**Total**
1651	0,750	-	5,000	-	-	5,750
1652	0,938	-	2,220	-	-	3,158
1653	-	-	-	-	-	-
1654	-	-	1,402	0,952	-	2,354
1655	-	-	0,842	-	-	0,840
1656	-	-	1,209	1,123	-	2,332
1657-1663	*Portuguese engagements in war with the Dutch and Local powers and their loss of Ceylon, Quilon, Cranganore and Cochin to the Dutch.*					
Total	14,434					
Average in six year	2,405					

Sources: See table 3.5

Purchase Prices of Pepper

There was a great difference in the prices of the Kanara pepper and that of Malabar. The prices of Kanara pepper had always been higher than that of either Malabar or Malacca. There were major fluctuations in prices during this period under review, especially that of Kanara. Till the second decade and most of the years of the third decade, prices of Malabar pepper had been stable, then it rose in the early 1630's from 10.5 Ashrafis to 14 Ashrafis per quintal. The price of pepper in Kanara in 1611 per quintal was 15.5 Ashrafis and by 1622 it rose to 19.5 Ashrafis, but in the same year it came down to 16.5 Ashrafis. Again it went on increasing and decreasing throughout the whole period of this study. The reason in brief behind this oscillation of prices can be considered mostly the trade rivalry between the other European nationals and the Portuguese. It is a truism that when the demand is much and supply is scarce the price goes up. Similarly, when production exceeds demand, the rate of sale and price come down. However, during this period, much of the prices also depended on the political condition. For instance, the Portuguese had to accept even the unacceptable demands of the Kanara ruler, Venkatappa Nayak, during their peace mission.(47) Whereas they were quite in a good position in the Kingdom of Cannanore, Cranganore, Cochin and Quilon and they could exploit their friendships either by force of arms or by tactics. The table of the pepper prices with its geographical production has been provided below and shows that fluctuation in the prices of pepper in those regions:

Table 3.12

Purchase Prices of Pepper on the Western Coast of India in Ashrafis

YEAR	KANARA	MALABAR	SOURCES
1601-10	14.75	10-10.1/2	*AGS.*, cod. 1571, fls. 30-57;
1611	15.50	10-14.00	*LML*, cod. 13a, fls. 16479;
1612	do	9.50	*INDIA*, cx. 3, doc. 38;
1613	16.50	-	*ACF*, cod. 1162, fls. 20-44v;
1614	16-18	12.00	cod. 1163, fls. 274v., 194;
1615	16.50-18.00	12.50	cod. 1166, fls. 102, 113v.;
1616	19-19.50	11.50	cod. 1167, fl. 173.
1617	19.50	-	do
1618	18.50	-	do
1619	18.00	12.00	do
1620	19.00	13.50	do
1621	19-20.50	15.50	do
1622	16-19.50	12.50	do
1623-1624	17.50	-	do
1625	16.00	-	do

1626	23.15	-	do
1627	24.50	-	do
1628	23.00	-	do
1629	15.50-22.00	-	do
1630-31	22.00	-	do
1632	23.00	-	do
1633	24.50	-	do
1634	23.50	-	do
1635	21.50	-	do
1636	17.00	-	do
1637	14.00	-	do
1638	14.00	-	do
1639	14.00	-	do
1640	17.00	-	do
1641	35.50	-	do
1642-1643	28.00	-	do
1649-1650	20.50	15.00	do
1651	22.00	15.00	do
1652	23-24	21.50	do
1653-55	15.50-21.50	-	do
1656	14.00-21.00	-	do
1657-1663	15.00	-	do

(-) Dash means data not available.

(*) All the prices are mentioned in the documents either in CRUZADOS, PAGODAS etc. but I have reduced them into Ashrafis (xerafins). For the equivalence of the coins see Appendix V.

Mode of Procurement and Medium of Payment

Normally, the pepper bought by the Portuguese for export to Portugal was acquired from middlemen at weighing houses and factories in Malabar and Kanara and later brought to Goa. The middlemen who bought the dried pepper from the cultivators transported it by cart, oxen or riverboat to the markets in land or on the coast, and sold it there to distributors and exporters. Most middlemen were independent operators, but some acted as agents for wealthy coastal merchants. The traders who served as middlemen in the pepper trade were apparently a heterogeneous group of Hindus, Muslims, Christian and new Christians.(48) But the Portuguese preferred, when possible, to deal with Christians especially the new Christian middlemen.(49)

In Malabar, the Portuguese bought from or through local Christians, sometimes utilising the influence of the church authorities to see that the supplies were forthcoming.(50) As Luis da Costa confirmed at the beginning of the seventeenth century, it is a well known fact that the Saint Thomas Christians brought in most of the pepper to Cochin and always had done so. Even in the difficult years 1603 -1605, when pepper was scarce on the Malabar coast due to the presence of the other Europeans, Christian merchants were persuaded, largely through the efforts of Bishop and Archdeacon of Angomale, to keep the Portuguese factory at Cochin supplied.(51) During the first half of the seventeenth century, Portuguese pepper at Cochin was supplied mostly through a big businessman, Manuel Ramos, probably a New Christian, and his family collaborators.(52) In Cannanore, despite all their dislike, the Portuguese authorities conducted trade with Ali Rajah, the hereditary leader of the Cannanore Moplahs, during the late sixteenth and the first half of the seventeenth centuries.(53)

In Kanara, conditions were somewhat different. Here, the Portuguese practice was to arrange contracts with individual merchants or syndicates, whether Portuguese, Eurasian or Indian, Christian or Hindu. For example, in 1602, a certain Mendes António, Mendes de Tomar and António Fernandes de Sampaio contracted to supply the Portuguese in Kanara pepper, and in 1603 an Indian goldsmith and his nephew agreed to supply 1,500 quintals at Onor and Barcelore. Later in the same decade, the Portuguese were buying pepper at Onor on contract from Brahmins.(54) Finally, with the rise of Venkatappa Nayak, the Portuguese bought most of their Kanara pepper on contract from the Nayakas of Ikkeri, though by force of circumstances rather than by preference. During the second and third decades, two prominent businessmen, Rama da Gama, and Pascoal Rodrigues, contracted and supplied Kanara pepper to the Portuguese.(55) Though the Portuguese, according to the contract promised to buy 3,000 Khandis (about 9,000 quintals) of pepper every year from them, they were hardly in a position to buy the full contracted volume at any time.(56) However, in 1628, the contractors stopped all supply of pepper on the ground that the Portuguese debt was not clear since long.(57) During the same time, a new contract was made with the ambassador of Venkatappa Nayak, Vitula Sinai, for the supply of Kanara pepper.(58) During the fourth decade, Narsina (probably Narsimha) Sinai, a resident of Barcelore, and his family contracted to provide with the Kanara pepper.(59) During the same period, another negotiation was made with Timappa Nayaka, brother of Sankara da Gama, a New Christian and one of the prominent textile merchant.(60) In 1637, the pepper contract with the ambassador of Virabhadra Nayak, the ruler of Ikkeri, and the Portuguese failed because of the Nayaka's demand of an exorbitant price.(61) In the beginning of the fifth decade, Santuji Sinai, another business magnate of this period, busied himself in settling the contract with the Portuguese at a very high price due to the presence of other prospective foreign buyers.(62) After 1643, contracts were normally made through diplomatic relations. Mangoji Sinai, a big businessman and the ambassador of Virabhadra Nayak, supplied most of the Portuguese requirement of pepper.(63) The Portuguese authorities in Kanara, as in Malabar, also tried to use the influence of Church and religious authorities to settle political as well as commercial matters.

During 1649, Fr. António Correia was sent as an ambassador to the court of Ikkeri, as an exchange for one Rama Chandra Sinai from the side of Nayak to settle the matter against the Dutch and regularise the supply of pepper.(64)

These various contractors acquired their stocks either through sending their own agents to buy in the fields, or else directly from the lesser middlemen.(65) It is, however, quite impossible to determine the profitable value of these middlemen.(66) Although the prices offered by the Portuguese buyers on the coast in the sixteenth and the seventeenth centuries are known in some instances, there appears to be no corresponding information about the rates at which the middlemen paid the producer, and this no way of calculating gross profit.

The economic subordination of the pepper cultivators, is suggested by the fact that they were frequently forced to pledge their pepper in advance to middlemen.(67) In the early sixteenth century the middlemen would each year acquired the next season's crop either for a cash advance or in exchange for cotton cloths, and other goods which they kept at the seaports.(68) More or less the same tactics was followed in the seventeenth century.

Usually the Portuguese authorities bought the pepper from middlemen or contractors after a small or a half payment of the total amount. The remaining amount was to be paid after the arrival of the ships with pepper money from Portugal. Many a time it differed according to the contract. Some times the contractors supplied half of the contracted volume of pepper and the rest only upon full payment. In 1636, Timappa Nayak refused to supply any amount at all until full payment was made in advance.(69) However, the Portuguese normally made payments in cash after the delivery.

Various Branches of the Portuguese Trade

Apart from the local merchants trading with the neighbouring principalities under the Portuguese *Cartaz* system, the Portuguese themselves maintained a regular trade with these areas in order to enforce their monopoly. Other than the volume of pepper they exported from Goa to Portugal, they sent their shiploads of pepper to Muscat and other countries to purchase goods they needed in return from these areas. Following are a few details of the Portuguese export of pepper to Muscat to meet the demands of the fortress.

Table 3.13

YEAR	VOLUME IN kgs.	DIRECTION	SOURCES
1628	20,980	Kanara-Muscat	*ACF*, 1161, fls. 39-39v.
1629	41,960	Kanara-Muscat	*LML*,cod. 26, fl.115 246
1641	66,096	Kanara-Muscat	*ACF*, 1161, fls. 64v.

Portuguese Pepper Distribution in Europe and in Africa

During the sixteenth and a few decades of the early seventeenth century, the German, the Italians and the Portuguese merchants used to deliver pepper brought from India via Cape route, to the various countries of northern Europe.(70) However, after the Portuguese commercial relation entangled with the Dutch and the English, it became quite difficult for these merchants to maintain trade relation with all these countries as before. The import of pepper during the first half of the seventeenth century has already been shown. The average import in Lisbon for the whole of the period under review including the most difficult years comes to between 4,000 and 6,000 quintals. But excluding the blockade years, it becomes to about 7,000 to 10,000 quintals per year.(71) The use of pepper in Portugal and its colonies was estimated by Konrad Rott during 1579-80 at a mere 1,500 quintals per year.(72) Thus on the basis of this, nevertheless, it can be assumed that the remaining volume must have been exported to other countries with which Portugal was at peace.

Thus, this study would suggest that the Portuguese followed a more systematic pattern of pepper trade when compared with that of the sixteenth century. They would have certainly profited by this trade in this century if the international situation had not interfered with it. Even in such circumstances they strove to maintain in volume of the export at least until the 1630's but it became quite intermittent in the remaining years of this study.

Notes

Portuguese Trade in Pepper

1. *APO-CR*, Fasciculo 5, parte I, pp. 10-11.
2. Gaspar Correa, *Lendas da India...*, vol. I, parte II, p. 94-8.
3. *HAG*, cod. 1043, fls. 59-60, Also see appendix I.
4. *India*, cx. 7, doc. 200a. See Appendix II, A Map of ship showing the space reserved for the loading of pepper.
5. Tomé Pires, *Suma Oriental*, Vol. I, pp. 60-62; Barbosa, *The Book of Duarte Barbosa...*, vol. II, pp. 99-102; Linschoten, *The Voyages of ...*, I, pp. 65-74; Vol. II, pp. 72-75.
6. Disney, *Twilight of the pepper...*, pp. 79; See Chapter 2, Part I.
7. Baldaeus, '*A True and Exact Description...*, vol. III, p. 8.
8. Disney, *Twilight of the pepper...*, p. 8.
9. *AGS*, cod. 1571, pp. 306; Mendes da Luz, *Livro das Cidades...*, p. 45v.
10. Disney, *Twilight of the pepper...*, pp. 14-16
11. *LMG*, cod. 13a, fls. 164-179; *India*, cx. 9, doc. 177.
12. Mathew, *Portuguese Trade..*, pp. 157.
13. See Chapter I, Volume of the Portuguese trade.
14. There were other heads also, vis, *compra das roupas* etc.
15. It is assumed that some of the merchants must have been advancing money on loan to the government, probably on a fixed contract. (See Chapter 8)
16. *LML*, cod. 2, fls. 10/33-38v, 18/65-67v; cod. 4, fls. 179/172 175; cod. 5, fls. 49/107-107v, 50/109, 51/111, 53/115-121v; cod. 6, p. 37/77; cod. 7, fls. 41/85; cod. 9, fls. 68/154, 150/326, 142/310-310v, 157/340-40v; cod. 10, fls. 131/384; cod. 11, fls. 291/462-63, 207/334-335; cod. 12, fls. 107/347 48; cod. 14, fl. 15/29; cod. 16, fls. 193/518, 295/748.
17. *Ibid.*
18. *LML*, cod. 25, fl. 155/308; *India*, cx. 12, doc. 144.
19. It is believed on the basis of the money utilised from the Council of the Finance of the States (Goa).
20. According to the export of pepper (Ref. table 3.6) it is believed that import of money was more than it is shown in Table 3.1.
21. Cash was received either in *Cruzados or Xerafins*, but it has been reduced to Ashrafis according to its exchange value. See Appendix V.

22. This amount included the money for the purchase of cloth also.
23. Only half of it was for the purchase of pepper.
24. See Chapter 2, part II and III.
25. See Table 3.7
26. *India*, cx. 12, docs. 10, 17; B. Aj. *Jesuitas na Asia*, 46 XIII30, pp. 21-24, 32-33; *LML*, cod. 16, fls. 80/183-84; cod. 17, fl. 20; cod. 23, fl. 301; cod. 26, p. 264; cod. 28, fl. 370; cod. 30, fl. 186-186v, 294v; cod. 52, fl. 182; cod. 55, fls. 182, 380v. *Lynch* cod. 14, fls. 55-70, 227, 239, 250.
27. B. Aj. *Jesuitas na Asia*, 50v-37, pp. 503-513; *LML*, cod. 27, fl. 507.
28. Disney, *Twilight of the pepper...*, pp. 137-41.
29. *LML*, cod. 28, fls. 18-26, 30-38, 46, 421, 425, 427; cod. 30, fls. 257v-258, 280-80v; cod. 31, fls. 309, 438; cod. 32, fl. 114; cod. 33, fl.s 111-112v.; cod. 35, fl. 152; cod. 36, fl. 193, 212-212v, 318; cod. 37, fl. 157; cod. 38, fl. 512.
30. *Ibid*. Disney, *Twilight of the pepper...*, pp. 146.
31. See Appendix VI.
32. *AGS*, cod. 1571, pp. 350-351.
33. See Table of exports below.
34. See Table 1.1
35. *DHM*, II, pp. 175, 353-54; AGS, cod. 1571, pp. 320-321, 379.
36. See documents used in 3.6
37. *APO-BP*, tomo IV, vol. II, part I, pp. 28-29; Danvers, *Letters received...*, vol. I, pp. 20-21
38. See documents used in Table 3.7
39. For area vise pepper export see appendix III.
40. See Chapter 2 part I, Portuguese Konkan Relations.
41. See Table 3.8
42. See Chapter 2 Part II.
43. See Table 3.10.
44. *India*, cx. 20, doc. 126.
45. I Cati=5,000 réis. *Diccionário Universal das Moedas, Pezos e Moedas*, Lisboa 1793.
46. See Chapter 2, part I & II.
47. See Chapter 2, part I.
48. *LML*, cod. 32, fl. 106; Barbosa, *The Book of Duarte Barbosa...*, vol. II, p. 56; Baldaeus, '*A True and Exact Description...*, vol. III, p. 622; Boyajian, *Portuguese Bankers...* (passim)
49. *Ibid*.
50. *DHM*, II, pp. 175, 353-54;

51. *DHM*, II, pp. 175, 35354; AGS, cod. 1571, pp. 320-321, 379. 52. *ACF*, cod. 1167, fls. 106v, 133, 137.

53. AGS, cod. 1571, pp. 306; Mendes da Luz, *Livro das Cidades...*, p. 45v; *LML*, cod. 15, fls. 183-183v; *ACF*, cod. 1162, fls. 213-213v, 225-225v.

54. AGS, cod. 1571, pp. 305.

55. *LMG*, cod. 13a, fls. 164-179; *India*, cx. 9, doc. 177.

56. *Ibid*.

57. *LMG*, cod. 13a, fls. 164-179; *India*, cx. 9, doc. 177; LML, cod. 16, fls. 183-84; See Chapter XVIII.

58. *ACF*, cod. 1161, fls. 40-43v.

59. *ACF*, cod. 1162, fls. 182-82v.

60. *ACF*, cod. 1162, fls. 186v87; *India*, cx. 11, docs. 11, 34.

61. *India*, cx. 12, doc 144.

62. *ACF*, cod. 1163, fls. 130-30v, 150-150v, 153, 155-56v, 160v-61, 175, 182-82v.

63. *Ibid*., fls. 58v, 274v.

64. *ACF*, cod. 1166, fls. 27-28, 73v.

65. Disney, *Twilight of the Pepper...*, pp. 37.

66. *LML*, cod. 32, fl. 106.

67. Disney, *Twilight of the Pepper...*, pp. 34.

68. Barbosa, *The Book of Duarte Barbosa...*, vol. II, p. 56

69. *India*, cx. 11, docs. 11, 34; ACF, cod. 1162, fls. 186v-87.

70. See Boyajian, *Portuguese Bankers*...(passim); Godinho, (First Edition), *Os Descobrimentos e a economia mundial*,...(passim); Fernando Braudel, *O Mundo Mediterrâneo e o Mundo Mediterrâneo na época do Filipe II*, (passim).

71. See Appendix IV.

72. Lach, *Asia in the Making of Europe...*, Vol. I, Book I, pp. 136-137.

51. Ibid. II, pp. 377, 380-84; ACE, cod. 1571, pp. 520-521, 379-82, 404; cod. 1107, fls. 10v, 13, 13[illegible]

53. ACE, cod. 1571, pp. 306; Mendes da Luz, Livro das Cidades, p. 159; [illegible] cod. 15, fls. 184-185v; [illegible] cod. 18, 210-211v, 218-219v

54. ACE, cod. 1571, pp. 563

55. [illegible] cod. 166, fls. 10-10v, 72; [illegible] 177

56. Ibid.

57. [illegible] fls. 164-179; [illegible] 1772 [illegible] cod. [illegible] 183-84; see Chapter XVIII

58. [illegible] cod. 1161, fls. 40-43v.

59. [illegible] cod. 1162, fls. 13v, 82v

60. [illegible] cod. 1162 [illegible] II, doc. II, 34

61. [illegible] 12, doc. 14.

62. ACE, cod. 1155, II, 230, 30, 130-135, 152-156, 162, 164-166, 107, 61, 125, 132-132v

63. Ibid. fls. 59v, 274v.

64. [illegible] cod. [illegible] 37-28 [illegible]

65. Disney, Twilight of the Pepper [illegible] pp. [illegible]

66. [illegible] vol. 32, fl. 110.

67. Disney, Twilight of the Pepper [illegible] pp. [illegible]

68. Boxer, The Portuguese [illegible] vol. II, p. 54

69. [illegible] II, 34 [illegible] cod. 1152, fls. [illegible]

70. [illegible] Portugues [illegible] Godinho [illegible] [illegible] Fernando [illegible] [illegible]

71. See Appendix [illegible]

72. [illegible] vol. I, book I, pp. 136, 137.

Plate 4 Portuguese Merchant-ships at the Cochin Harbour *(A.H.U)*

CHAPTER - 4

Portuguese Trade in Textiles

Indian textiles were another important commodity of the Portuguese trade during the seventeenth century. Although, these had been an item of trade in the sixteenth century, the Portuguese bought them mainly to exchange for pepper, spices and other commodities from South-east Asian countries as well as from the coastal regions of India.(1) A very negligible volume of textiles ever seems to have been exported to Portugal(2) except towards the end of the century between 1580 and 1590 cloth deliveries in Lisbon from Asia averaged between three and four millions of Cruzados and so on. However, a sudden change occurred in the seventeenth century when the Portuguese started trans-shipping this commodity in bulk to the metropolises at least till the end of the third decade when the volume and value in Lisbon began to decline. I believe, however, that much of the decline of textiles trade of the *carreira da India,* along with other reasons, represented a shift of preference by the merchants from investment in cloth to precious stones. Precious stones had the advantage of being concealable and thus paid little or no customs duties in Lisbon, and they required little space on vessels at a time when the tonnage of *carreira* shipping overall was declining rapidly. Official correspondence in Lisbon and Goa also reflects a preference among merchants in the period for precious stones, which naturally alarmed the crown, whose customs revenues were in decline in part because of the shift to precious stones.(3) Going back to the reasons of the sudden increase of trade in the Asian textiles it is proposed with the fact that the primary reason seems to have been the hostilities between the Dutch and the Portuguese. I believe that under force of circumstances, the Portuguese began trading more vigorously in this commodity when their trade declined in other commodities. If so, there was logic in the shift. Presumably, till the end of the third quarters of the sixteenth century, the Portuguese home demand for cloth was provided by the Dutch merchants, made or finished in the Lowland provinces. They, in return took back salt and Indian goods to their country.(4)

Eventually, the confiscation of the Dutch cargoes and their ships by King Philip II and closing of the Iberian ports in 1585, 1595, and 1597, brought the whole machinery to standstill. Thereafter the Portuguese began importing directly for their own internal markets. Another reason behind the rise of textiles as an important commodity during the seventeenth century seems to have been the demand by the African countries, especially from São Jorge da Mina, from which they obtained maximum number of slaves in exchange for Indian textiles and food grains. Due to frequent wars during this period, the Portuguese need for slaves increased to an urgent priority since they were employed as sailors on the ships and sometimes even were used as soldiers and artillerymen. Hence, the demand for textiles increased almost daily, while the shaky state of Portuguese finances kept them far from achieving their goal. But even such circumstances, they carried on their trade in this commodity with some degree of success. In this chapter I have attempted to study the various varieties, the area from where the Portuguese got their supplies, money imported from Portugal for the purchase of textiles and the mode of procurement. Special attention will be paid to the volume procured and different countries traded with. At the end of the chapter, the role of textiles will be discussed.

Kinds of Textiles

There were almost eighty to ninety varieties of cloths in all, exported by the Portuguese to Portugal as well as distributed to various other countries and ports for the exchange of necessary goods. Some of them were very expensive and bought for the royal use. Some were of medium quality and sent to South-East Asian countries as well as to Portugal. Inferior quality textiles were exported to African countries and used by the poorer classes of people. A brief description about some of the textiles is follows:

Among the expensive cloths, *Taftas* was most costly. Usually it was woven of silk amidst gold or silver threads. Plain and better quality silks were also to be found. In general these were printed with various colours and used for making dresses and curtains for doors and windows. They were exclusively for royal use or by the high nobility.

Another sort was Satin or Velvet. This was also combined with gold or silver threads, as in silk cloths, and was another expensive fabric used by royalty or the rich. The Satin from Italy, especially from Florence and Genoa was very famous, just as that from Lyon in France.(5) In India, Gujarat had been the prime centre for its production during this period. This quality was produced in two varieties. One was expensive, as was above mentioned, while other was imitation. Normally the imitation was yellow in colour.(6) *Roupas de Seda*, or silk cloth, was another costly fabric produced in various colours. Semiano, was a good quality printed cloth, normally known as *Chints*.(7) It was produced in Samana, in the neighbourhood of Delhi and Sirhind. *Tafecira* or *Taficira* was a striped cotton cloth produced in Sindh. *Salampuri* was another variety of cotton cloth produced in the Salampur district or, probably, at the Coromandel coast.(8) Sarja was produced of silk or woollen threads and concluded among the expensive cloths. *Percalços* was a very thin and tightly woven cotton cloth, commonly known as Cambric-Muslin. *Mermolanos* or *Malmal* was a very thin fabric from Bengal as well as from Gujarat. *Cutunias* a kind of silk scarf or costly handkerchief, was produced mostly in Bengal and Surat.(9) Apart from these species, costly carpets, socks, gowns and many other types of cloths for shirts were also exported.

Among the medium quality, *Arganizes* was the most famous. It was cotton fabric woven in both thin and coarse. Usually it was produced in two colours, blue and white. It was a product of Golconda and Bijapur, and brought to Goa mostly from the region of Balaghat.(10) *Beatilha*, or Golconda Muslin was a fine textile esteemed much in European countries. It was produced mostly in the areas of Balaghat and Burhanpur. Usually it was found in the coastal towns of Massulipattam. It was also near 1/3 miles south to St. Thomas, known as Palleacate, (11) or Pulicat. Then there was *Berame* or *Beirame*. This was printed cotton cloth known as Chints and produced in two qualities, fine and coarse. It was generally woven in Cambay.(12) Other good quality cotton cloth was *Bertangil* or Calico. It was produced in the vicinity of Daman, usually in blue, black and white colours and exported in bulk to the Southeast Asian countries.(13) *Bafta*, a calico of different quality, produced in the areas of Burhanpur and Machhiwara. Its blue and red colours were attractive features for this variety.(14) There were also another very well known variety among the Portuguese textile exports, *Cacha*. It, probably, was to be identified with the present *Gamcha* or *Cacha*, still commonly used in north India. It was almost

128 cm. long and 64 cm. broad (2 *Covados comprido e 1 covado largo*). Normally, this is the size of *Cacha* or *Gamcha*. It was a cotton product of Gujarat and exported both to the South-East Asian and African countries.(15) *Canequin*, a thin cotton fabric, was produced in Daman. It was another good quality *calico*. It was much in demand in the west European countries.(16) Among the Bengali products, *Cassa*, a very thin cotton fabric, stands second in quality compared with *Malemole*.(17) *Chandes* was produced in the vicinity of Gujarat and Balaghat and was exported by the Portuguese to various countries.(18) *Cajrauti* was a fine cotton textile and produced in Daman and nearby regions. It was produced in many colours.(19) *Chunni* or *Chunderi*. It's local name in the north India is *Dupatta*.(20) In Europe, women used it for scarves.(21) *Chita* or *Chint* was a very famous product of Massulipattam. Daman, Bassein, and Cambay also produced this variety. But the one from Massulipattam was in great demand by the Portuguese and later by the Dutch for export to Europe or for the exchange of Asian commodities.(22) *Daryabadi* and *Daryapuri* are also two names found in the Portuguese documents. It was a printed cloth much liked by the Europeans in this period.(23) *Mantagem Grande* and *Mantagem Pequeno*, were two other verities among the Portuguese exports. Actually both these varieties were the same but differed in size as indicated by name. They were products of Cambay.(24) *Panos*, a general term used to describe medium quality cloths, could be of linen, cotton, wool and silk. Its literal meaning is merely a piece of cloth. There were various qualities and sizes. Textiles *Dozeno* (having 1,200 threads) or woven by 1,200 threads; Sezeno (with 1,600 threads), *Dezocheno*, woven with 1,800 threads; *Vinteno*, woven with 2,000 threads; Vinte dozeno, having 2,200 threads and *Vintequatreno* had 2,400 threads etc. After the quality of *Dozeno*, the qualities were much more refined. It varied much; *Pano* very thin, medium quality (less thin), mixture (variety of colours). Inferior quality, spotted, printed very big piece, small Piece, coarse and thin etc. They also vary in names, like *Panos de Mocha, Panos de Cambaya* etc. In general one *Pano* means a piece of cloth with a breadth and length of a petticoat. There were *Panos* of different types printed, stripped, plain and spotted.(25) *Guingão* was Produced in two varieties, silk and cotton. It was produced in Cambay and Balaghat. It is assumed that silk *Guingão* was produced in Cambay and cotton was woven in Balaghat.(26) Apart from these medium quality cloths, silk and spun cotton threads were also taken to Portugal for multiple purposes.(27)

There were various types of cheap quality cotton and linen cloths produced in the regions of Gujarat and Balaghat. This was mainly used by poor people and a means of exchange for slaves and ivory from the African countries. During this period a huge volume was taken to African countries to exchange for commodities or for sale. There were about eight to ten varieties of cheap quality textiles taken to Africa, or used in the ships by lower class workers. Among such cloths, *Guiné Grosso*, or *Guiné* cloth was very famous.(28) There were two kinds of cloth in this variety, thin and coarse mainly in blue and black colours. A big volume was produced in the Balaghat and Golconda regions. In the Portuguese sources it is very often mentioned as *Roupas Pretas* (or black cloth). Among other cheap varieties, *Balaghate, Arganises, Bertangil, Cacha, Chandes, Despizes, Gandares, Ladrilhos, Mantagem grandes, and Pequenos, Panos, Roupas Sorteadas, Sagris,* and various others were exported to different countries.(29)

These textiles were sold to the Portuguese in corias (koris), which comprised twenty pieces of any size, depending the contract. Usually they were measured in *covados*.(30) Another means of supply was in bales.

Much adulteration was found in the textile industry, especially at the source of supply. For instance, silken varieties used to vary in breadths, length and quality. The length and breadth were ascertained by measurement, the quality depended upon whether the stuffs were uniformly woven, whether the weight was right or cotton threads coated, which was very common for the weavers in order to save some money.(31) Costly fabrics which were woven with silver and gold threads had to have those carefully counted to be sure that they contained the requisite quantity. Sometimes they used to use some foreign stuff to increase the weight of the fabrics. All these examinations required much practice and experience on the part of the buyer. This was one of the reasons why the Portuguese needed to employ middlemen or brokers for their purchase.

In cotton textiles, for instance, sellers used to mix inferior quality cloths in between the costly ones in batches of 50 to 60 pieces. Sometimes they loaded fewer pieces than the required quantity. To avoid all these malpractice, much care and attention was necessary.(32)

Area of Procurement

The major staple centres for the purchase of cotton and silk textiles were Broach, Cambay and Surat in Gujarat,(33) Balaghat in the territory of Bijapur(34), Massulipattam, in Golconda and finally, Bengal.

The ports of Gujarat had trade relations with various ports on the western coast of India especially with Chaul, Goa, Calicut, and Cochin. In the west, merchant ships sailed to the countries like Africa, Arabia and Persia, in the eastern regions, Malacca, Moluccas, Borneo and many other important places.(35) Tomé Pires has clearly indicated that, "it (Gujarati trade) chiefly stretches out two arms, with her right arms she reaches out towards Eden, and with the other towards Malacca, as the most important places for trade".(36) Barbosa found Gujarat very busy indeed in the early sixteenth century. Merchants from all over the world were found negotiating their business, importing much of their foreign goods to fetch textiles, indigo and other wares. Cambay had been famous for its white cotton fabrics, both fine and coarse, some of them printed in patterns. Other than these cloths coloured velvets of cheap quality, velvety satins, taffet cloths, and thick carpets were found worth exporting from Cambay.(37)

By the end of the sixteenth century, however, this port city had lost its importance as an entrepot because of silting of the sea. No big ship could reach it. Thereafter, the merchants somehow brought their goods on small boats to the big ships that anchored away from the port.(38) Due to this inconvenience, they started bringing their merchandise to the port city of Surat. Thus, in a very short span of time, Surat grew to a very important port for the textile trade and became a great centre of commercial activity in the early seventeenth century, just as Antwerp had grown rapidly a century earlier at the expense of Bruges. Another centre for the purchase of the textile was Balaghat in the territory of Bijapur. This place became prominent during the second decade of the seventeenth century, mainly because of the Portuguese conflict with the Dutch and the English off the ports of Gujarat. It was rather the safest place from which the Portuguese could obtain their supplies of textiles in abundance in order to send to African and South-east Asian countries for the exchange of necessary goods. Moreover, it was reported that textiles from this region were cheaper than that of Cambay but that the Banias and the contractors made much profit on its transactions with the Portuguese. Thus, it became more expensive to do business there than in Gujarat.(39) However, there was no alternative except to make the best of the situation.

Massulipattam, in the Kingdom of Golconda, was another important port town which produced different types of textiles during the seventeenth century. Here, the Portuguese maintained a factory till the Dutch expelled them in the second decade of the seventeenth century.(40) Nevertheless, they maintained their trade relations through contractors. Textiles, especially, Beatilha, from this region enjoyed a good demand in the overseas market.(41)

Tavernier mentions *Chints* or printed cloth namely *Calmendar*, probably a corrupt form of Kalamkari. It was fabricated in Burhanpur.(42) It is strange that he did not mention Beatilha, which was brought to Goa and exported to Portugal in huge volume.(43) Chints from Burhanpur and Sironj was also very much esteemed for export to Portugal.

Other than these varieties, various types of handkerchiefs were exported which were used as scarf material in the European countries.(44) It is apparent that Golconda textiles were of much importance in the Portuguese commercial world.

Bengal had been known for its silk fabrics. From here, merchants used to get woven as well as raw silk wares. Normally, they brought Bengal textiles to the port of Surat or Cambay or took it to the city of Ahmedabad for it's finishing. At all these places numerous artisans used to reside and they produced various types of designs, print them into various charming colours, which caught the sights of the European merchants. Apart from the silk fabrics, the Portuguese also purchased bundles of silk threads for their own use, probably for weaving cloths in Europe. Kasimbar, in the district of Murshidabad in Bengal, could provide more than 22,000 bales of silk annually. Each bale (approximately 26 on average, although some historians held as many as 35 Corjas) contained between 250 and 350 pieces of cloth. All these raw silks were brought to the kingdom of Gujarat, especially to Ahmedabad and Surat where they were woven into fabrics of various types.(45) Carpets of silk and gold , others of silk, gold and silver, others entirely of silk, were produced at Surat. Woollen carpets were made at Fatehpur Sikri, the city founded by the Mughal emperor Akbar during the second half of the sixteenth century. Satins, with bands of gold and silver, some with bands of different colours, and some uniform, were made at Ahmedabad and Surat respectively.(46)

There were many other places in the hinterlands where cotton stuffs were produced. The Baftas, or cotton cloths required to be dyed red, blue, or black were taken to Agra and Ahmedabad, where indigo was produced in abundance and used for dyeing the cloths. Such kinds of textiles are mentioned in the Portuguese documents as *Bofetas Pintados*, or simply *Bofetas*.(47) This was a simple and cheap type of cloth which was exported to the African countries like Melindi, Mina and Mozambique, where it was sold to the Kafirs.(48) Good quality Bafta was exported to South-east Asian countries like Philippines, Borneo, Java, Sumatra and other islands. Other ordinary qualities of cloth used for export were brought from Agra and the vicinity of Lahore, or else from Bengal, Baroda, Broach, Navsari and other places. Usually, these were brought in crude condition to Navsari and Broach, where they were bleached in large fields. Cotton textiles from Agra, Lahore and Bengal were comparatively of better quality than those from Navsari and Broach. Spun items were also an export commodity.(49)

Import of Money for the Purchase of Textiles

Due to the importance of textiles in the seventeenth century, the Portuguese government, just as in the case of pepper money, hold in reserve some amounts of cash for the purchase of textiles. In the early decades of the century, Portuguese authorities were much attentive towards the sending of money for the purchase of cloths. It should be remembered here that textile was a commodity, which had enjoyed royal patronage even before they became commercially important, and so, the government at Goa was used to providing for its acquisition. Nevertheless, after the fourth decade, the government of Portugal faced the same problem as was the case with pepper and other merchandises. However, more it depended upon the merchant-bankers on whose finances the set-up was depending. These merchants, as has been mentioned earlier, started taking more interest in the commodities more profitable, less voluminous and safe; the diamonds and precious stones. Since the risk of burning and drowning of the ships were too often, presumably, it was one of the major reasons why they stopped investing in this item so vigorously. However, since the demand was to be fulfilled, therefore, it is assumed that Portuguese authorities at Goa had to utilise some money from the treasury. But the exact amount utilised by the *Estado da India* is not clearly found. Here is a table which furnishes the details of money imported from Europe during the first half of the seventeenth century:

Table 4.1

Money Utilised for the Purchase of Textiles

YEAR	MONEY IN Xs.	SOURCES
1605	1,70,000	*LML*, cod. 1, fl. 35
1616	1,61,572	*India*, cx. 4, doc. 50
1617	80,000	*India*, cx. 4, doc. 142
1628	6,000	*LML*, 26, fl. 654.
1629	25,000	*ACF*, 1161, fl. 86v87.
1631	4,00,000	*Jesuitas Na Asia*, No. 46-XVII-30, fls. 37-37v
1633	1,09,000	*India*, cx. 10, doc. 195
1635	3,30,000	*India*, cx. 11, doc. 157.

Money for the Purchase and Payments

Normally, trade was handled by the Gujarati Banias who directly contacted the weavers according to the demands of the Portuguese authorities. Sometimes trade in this commodity was conducted through middlemen who acted as agents between the Portuguese authorities and the local merchants or weavers. In the early decades of the seventeenth century, Gassaras Parec (probably Dasrath Parekh), one of the biggest merchants from Cambay, settled in Goa and provided for the Portuguese demands through his agents.(50) Mangoji Sinai was another merchant contractor. He basically dealt in pepper trade, but from time to time supplied the Portuguese with their requirements of textiles from the regions of Balaghat and Golconda.(51) Among the other big merchants who dealt directly with the Portuguese, in supplying cloths, from different regions were Govinda and Pondia (Pandya), two prominent businessmen from the region of Gujarat. They had several business houses on various ports dealing in spices and textiles. They usually bought textiles mostly from the regions of Gujarat and supplied them to the Portuguese whenever required.(52) Giraji Bania (probably Goraji Bania) was among the others who supplied cloths from Cambay.(53) In other cases, the Portuguese authorities instructed the governors of Diu, Daman and Bassein to supply the demands of the crown by contacting directly with the weavers, but such occasion were rare and risky, since they were not very experienced in this field of commerce.(54) The Portuguese also had a trading factory on the port town of Massulipattam specially to deal in textiles. There, the Portuguese merchants contacted weavers through middlemen and settled the business for the *Carreira da India*.(55)

However, the actual nature of the transactions are not clear. In Bengal, the Portuguese had to negotiate their transactions through Muslim merchants. These merchants received certain commodities from the Portuguese in exchange for the textiles.(56)

There were various means of payment for cloth. Some times, the Portuguese supplied pepper, ginger, cinnamon and various sorts of spices to obtain textiles. Usually, merchants dealing in this business bought the necessary commodities and supplied them to the petty contractors. These brought the textiles, thus purchased, to Goa and sold them to the Portuguese. There were several private merchants as well as the officials also carrying on trade in this commodity. Portuguese payment for this particular merchandise was usually in cash.(57) During the period especially after the second decade of the seventeenth century, Portuguese authorities were very attentive in making payment for the textiles because of the presence of the Dutch and the English, who also needed this same merchandise for the supply of their own spices in South-East Asia.(58)

Volume of Trade

The Portuguese trade in Indian textiles, both with India and with other foreign countries passed through several vicissitude in the first half of the seventeenth century. The advent of the Dutch and the English during this period to share in the monopolistic trade of the Portuguese in Indian textiles and spices naturally had affected the volume. Nevertheless, the Portuguese officials still managed to carry on with their trade to a greater extent.

The Portuguese conducted their trade in Indian textiles on various levels. One can distinguish the official trade, the trade which the Portuguese officials and merchants carried on their individual capacity and finally, unofficial trade avoiding the Portuguese *Cartazes*. Even official trade had four different branches, namely the trade with parts of the Indian subcontinent, with the African countries, with the South-East Asian countries and finally the export to Portugal.

Portuguese needed much of the Gujarati textiles for the purchase of the spices from the Malabar Coast and the regions of Kanara, and vice-versa. In the early decades of the seventeenth century, attempts were made to modernise the port town of Daman by diverting the trade from Surat, which as previously mentioned, rose to prominence after the silting of the gulf of Cambay.(59) In this attempt, many of the merchants and contractors from these regions were forced to come to Daman, to and from which more than 500 ships and boats used to sail every year, loading textiles and indigo to various coastal towns and ports like, Surat, Bassein, Diu in the north, and to the southern ports like Goa, Cochin, Ceylon and finally, towards Malacca.(60) To achieve their target, they tightened their vigilance and forced the *Cartaz* system more vigorously than ever before. Even so, however, some two or three ships sailed every year in the name of the Portuguese officials and Fidalgos.(61)

Somehow, the measures for the diversion of trade from Surat to Daman by the Portuguese authorities were not crowned with success because of opposition from Muslim merchants of Gujarat and other unknown reasons. Forced by the circumstances, the Portuguese authorities were obliged to regularise their trade with Adil Shah of Bijapur through embassies from both sides for acquisition of Balaghat textiles. Since this was profitable for the both parties, it was not much difficult to mobilise the matter.

In 1615, many types of textiles, gunny bags and other materials were sent to buy pepper from Cochin and Quilon. They were together worth more than 1,000 Ashrafis. Following were the items sent on the ship.(62)

Name of the Fabrics

Table 4.2

NAME OF THE FABRICS	QUANTITY	PRICE PER Pc. IN Xs.
Velvet	4 pcs	50
Damasquilhos/Silk cloth	2 Coris	60
Cochinilha?	258 Coris	-
Silk scarf	2 Coris	-
Gunny bags for pepper	98 Coris	3
Packing materials	30 Coris	2.5

In 1616, Portuguese merchants exported a heavy load of textiles for Cochin, Bengal, and other places in exchange for various types of export goods for Portugal.(63) Sometimes, they bought some of the very expensive cloths for the exchange of courtesies with the local rulers. For instance, in 1625, The Portuguese viceroy sent some of the costly textiles, Golconda muslin, tuffet cloths and with many small and big sizes gold buttons for them, to the king of Cochin for the sake of goodwill.(64)

From the very beginning of the sixteenth century, when the Portuguese began their trade relations with India, they found that the African countries, especially Mozambique, Mombassa, Mina and other places on the west coast had great demands for the Indian textile.(65) These areas were known for their slave trade, and during this period, Portuguese officials used to carry a big volume of textiles produced in Cambay and Balaghat to Africa for the exchange for slaves, ivory, precious stones and metals. For example, in 1617, Guine cloths and various other varieties worth 15,000 to 20,000 Ashrafis were sent to the Castelo da Mina for the exchange with ivory and slaves.(66) During 1633-34, more than 7,048 pcs. of cloth were dispatched to there for exchange with slaves. There were three varieties of cloths on the ships, the Naos Capitania and Sacramento. They were valued at 5,300 Ashrafis.(67)

In 1643, two ships sailed towards Mozambique directly from Diu loading 40,000 pieces of cloths of different qualities and varieties. (68) Similarly in 1658, three ships left the port of Diu carrying textiles of various kinds for Mozambique. In all there were 80,000 pieces of cloths on the ships.(69)

Portuguese supplied textiles not only to the areas mentioned above but also to the neighbouring island of Ceylon. In 1614-15, a huge volume of cloths was supplied to Ceylon in order to buy 600 Bahars (about 1,800 quintals) of cinnamon. Similarly, much cinnamon was bought to purchase textiles from Gujarat, which were to be sent to Portugal the following year.(70) Apart from this, more than 17,000 Ashrafis out of the land revenue of the villages of Ceylon were used every year to purchase Cambay cloths.(71)

The Portuguese merchants had trade relations with the South-East Asian countries from the beginning of the sixteenth century. They carried Indian textiles collected from the different regions to the straits of Malacca, and brought back spices, especially pepper, cardamom, cloves, mace and nutmegs.(72) In 1616, they exported a huge volume of medium quality textiles to these islands to exchange for spices of various sorts and potteries from China.(73)

Besides all this trans-coastal trading Portuguese authorities exported a huge volume of cloths to their own country on the annual cargo ships as has been pointed out earlier.

In the early seventeenth century much fluctuation in the Indian market was found because of the presence of the Dutch and the English in that area. Even the export volume was affected by the fluctuation. However, there are documents that furnish some scattered information regarding the early seventeenth century trade. It is noted that in the first decade of this century, trade was conducted but details per year are lacking. There is scanty information regarding the contracts formulated by the Portuguese to procure Indian textiles. For instance, in 1605, 1,800,000 *Cruzados* were sent from Portugal for the purchase of pepper and cloths.(74) Another documents indicates the renewal of the treaties with the neighbouring states of Bijapur for the supply of pepper by the Portuguese. In 1613, along with the general exports, some very expensive cloth was also sent for royal use.(76) Detailed survey of the tables of the exports to Portugal will provide a complete picture of the export during 1613-1657.(77) Textiles exports reached to its peak in 1616, when more than 239,803 pieces of cloths of diverse quality and some big carpets were exported, chiefly for the sale in the countries neighbouring Portugal and for home use, besides, the *Liberdades* of the maritime officers which amounted to 200 big bundles, 72 big boxes, 35 small boxes, 9 half boxes and 120 pieces of cloths. Apart from the woven fabrics, there were more than 5,053 kgs. crude silk, 2,400 big rolls of silk threads and 76,120 kgs. of spun cotton which were loaded on the ships. In 1617, there had been very little export that is only 5,000 pieces. In 1618, the export again rose to higher volume. There were more than 31,620 pieces of Guine cloths, and 77,000 kgs. of ordinary cloths, packed in 70 boxes and 7 bundles, dispatched on the annual cargo ships. The second highest export of textiles was in the year 1630 when more than 256,000 pieces of cloth and 60 carpets of good quality were exported. After this only in 1649 was some considerable volume again exported.(78) Though there had been continuous trade between 1620-1629, 1631-1648, the details regarding varieties and volumes are lacking in the documents. It is better to have a glimpse of trade, which the documents provide for other years. For example, in 1623, 100 big boxes of fine cloths were exported to Portugal. Apart from this, Manguji Sinai and Krishna Chatim, some of the prominent business men of this period, gave more than 1,200 Ashrafis on credit to the Portuguese for the import of silk from Bengal to Goa.(79) The Portuguese merchants did bring silk to Goa but whether it was re-exported to Portugal is not known. In 1624, the king of Portugal instructed the officers in India to take great interest in the textiles trade, which he said was decreasing day by day and making it difficult to meet the requirements.(80) Moreover, the *Vedor da Fazenda* issued a prohibitary order for private merchants to trade in this commodity because of the decreasing volume more due to the participation of the North-west Europeans. It was further pointed out that the Dutch and the English had bought all the indigo and drugs from the regions of Gujarat; hence they should not be allowed to take any quantity of textiles from that region which was badly needed in Portugal for re-export to the fort of São Jorge de Mina.(81) By 1627, the stock of textiles at India House sent 6,000 Ashrafis in addition to the yearly dispatch of money.(83) In 1629, the *Vedor da Fazenda*, André Salema, sent a report of the financial condition of the *Estado da India* and requested cash for the purchase of textiles and pepper since the Portuguese government in India was too poor to meet the demand of the crown.(84) Accordingly the government of Portugal sent the money for the fulfilment of the orders. Thus, the volume of textiles could be improved by 1630.

After this, a remarkable change had been noted in the trade like that seen in the case of other commodities. But there is a difference in the nature of the reasons of the textiles and other commodities. For instance, the Portuguese government had sent more than 400,000 Ashrafis for the purchase of textiles, but it was not possible to obtain them because of the great famine in Gujarat between 1631-1633, which resulted in the loss of great property and many human lives. A majority of the artisan and cultivators of cotton were dead. Until the end of the fourth decade, this loss could not be recovered.(85) Therefore, Portuguese authorities diverted their attention towards Balaghat for the necessary items.(86) In 1633, they could procure only 7,046 pieces of textiles from this region. (87) Between 1634 and 1635, 12,300 pieces of cloths could be purchased for the cargo ships bound for Portugal.(88) Again in 1636, many letters were dispatched to the viceroy to send cloths to meet the demands of the kingdom.(89) However, no indication is traceable regarding the fulfilment of orders for this year. In 1638, the authorities were instructed to use the tobacco rent for the purchase of the textiles.(90) But it is difficult to say how much was the amount invested in this commodity. Though a close check on the movements of the Portuguese shipping was kept by the Dutch, the viceroy sent instructions to the *Armada* of the northern forts to collect rice and pepper from the Kanara forts and use that in buying textiles from the city of Cambay.(91) The continuous fight between the Dutch the Portuguese for the monopoly of cinnamon of Ceylon was intensified during this time and did not permit the officers to carry on with the trade, since they had been using much of the capital for pepper and textiles for the succour and provisioning of the soldiers. It was only in 1649 that the Portuguese authorities managed to send some of the very expensive qualities of cloths like, velvets, baftas, woven with silver and gold threads, various types of Gujarati textiles, both fine and coarse. The number of pieces exported was 40,011 other than 144 carpets from Surat and 2 carpets from Persia.(92) Between 1650 and 1656, for six years, there has been no trade. It was during this period that the island of Ceylon was lost. In 1657, a mere quantity of 1,440 pieces of cloths could be dispatched on the annual ships.(93) Though the decay of their power was being felt by the Portuguese in the southern areas of Malabar, they managed to load a ship with textiles at the port of Surat which unfortunately got wrecked off Chaul on her way to Goa. However, orders were issued by the viceroy to sell the cloths, which could be saved.

Thus with broad survey of the whole Portuguese trade in textiles, it can not only be demonstrated that such a trade in them existed, but that this commodity also enjoyed much importance in the crown's commercial dealings. The area from most of the time textiles were procured in the years of this study was Balaghat. This region took on much importance especially after the English-Portuguese war of the 1613-1615, and the increasing power of the English in the Gulf of Cambay forced the Portuguese authorities to search for some other alternatives. In the later period of the fourth decade onwards, the trade in textiles began diminishing in comparison with the previous decades. The reasons were no doubt many: the financial conditions of the Portuguese *Estado da India*, the corruption among the Portuguese officials dealing in the commodity, the diversion of the private investors in different commodities saving a lot of customs, the famine of Gujarat one of the severest calamities of the age, the blockade of Goa during 1637-1641, by the Dutch, the Luso Dutch war of 1644-1658. All these factors had been disastrous to progress the trade. 0n the other hand, this war and rivalry had great effect on the prices of cloths, which went on increasing as can be clearly seen by even a casual look at the price list attached.(95)

The rivalry with Dutch and the English also had completely different aspect than the ones just described. They increased the demand for the Indian textiles among the Portuguese, who needed them both for home consumption and for the exchange for slaves who were being employed on the ship. Therefore, the Portuguese had to depend upon various regions than Gujarat alone. They thus came in contact with many more regions of India and abroad then they did in the procurement of pepper, which was cultivated mainly in the vicinity of Kanara and Malabar. Textiles, on the contrary, were collected from the Kingdom of Cambay, the Coromandel Coast, Bengal, and especially from Balaghat. Thus the trade in textiles alone involved more regions than any other commodity. Since this item was not an item of royal monopoly, Portuguese officials as well as private merchants took more active part, though the details of such trade have not been found. The Portuguese supplied Indian textiles to markets of Southeast Asian countries, Ceylon, Africa and probably to the countries neighbouring Portugal. The increasing demand naturally led to a considerable growth in the rate of production of cotton, because of which the Dutch as well as the English could easily find the greater supply of cotton textiles. It may be said that they reaped the harvest sowed by the Portuguese, and that in due course they took more interest in cotton and other textiles than that in pepper and spices.

Notes

Portuguese Trade in Textiles

1. Barbosa, *The Book of Duarte Barbosa...*, vol. II, p. 182-84.
2. Mathew, *Portuguese Trade..*, pp. 133.
3. *India*, cx. 11, docs. 14, 63, 73; Kail, *The Dutch in India*, pp. 711.
4. *Ibid.*
5. Luis Lisanti Filho, *Negócios Coloniais...*, (Glossary) pp. LXVIII.
6. *India*, cx. 2, doc. 93.
7. Naqvi, *Urban Centres...*, pp. 135-39, 217-221; *E.F.*, 1618-21, pp. 59, 93, 161, 168, 178, 337; E.F., 1622- 23, pp. 9; *E.F.*, 1624-29, pp. 93-149.
8. *India*, cx. 20, doc. 126; See Appendix VII.
9. *India*, cx. 2, doc. 95, 147; cx. 3, doc. 152; cx. 4, doc. 25, 50, 93, 104, 136, 137, 177, 186; cx. 6, doc. 55; *LML*, cod. 17, fls. 32v, 83; *LMG*, cod. 13b, fls. 392-410.
10. *Ibid*.
11. *India*, cx. 2, doc. 95, 147; cx. 3, doc. 152; cx. 4, doc. 25, 50, 93, 104, 136, 137, 177, 86; cx. 6, doc. 55; *LML*, cod. 17, fls. 32v, 83; *LMG*, cod. 13b, fls. 392-410; *APO-BP*, tomo IV, vol. II, part I, pp. 89; *JBHS*, Vol. II, part 1 & 2, pp. 258 59.
12. *India*, cx. 2, doc. 95, 147; cx. 3, doc. 152; cx. 4, doc. 25, 50, 93, 104, 136, 137, 177, 186; cx. 6, doc. 55; *LML*, cod. 17, fls. 32v, 83; *LMG*, cod. 13b, fls. 392410.

13. *Ibid.*
14. *Ibid.*; *India*, cx. 20, doc. 126.
15. *Ibid.*
16. *Ibid.*; Filho, *Negócios Coloniais...*, (Glossary) pp. LVI.
17. *Ibid.*
18. *Ibid.*
19. *Ibid.*; *O Oriente Português...*, no. 3 & 4, Vol. XVII17, pp. 84-91.
20. *Ibid.*
21. *Ibid.*
22. Filho, *Negócios Coloniais...*, (Glossary) pp. LVII.
23. *India*, cx. 20, doc. 126.
24. *India*, cx. 2, doc. 95, 147; cx. 3, doc. 152; cx. 4, doc. 25, 50, 93, 104, 136, 137, 177, 186; cx. 6, doc. 55; *LML*, cod. 17, fls. 32v, 83; *LMG*, cod. 13b, fls. 392410.
25. Filho, *Negócios Coloniais...*, (Glossary) pp. LXV.
26. *India*, cx. 2, doc. 95, 147; cx. 3, doc. 152; cx. 4, doc. 25, 50, 93, 104, 136, 137, 177, 186; cx. 6, doc. 55; *LML*, cod. 17, fls. 32v, 83; *LMG*, cod. 13b, fls. 392-410.
27. *Ibid.*
28. *India*, cx. 10, docs. 122, 206; cx. 13, doc. 66; cx. 15, doc. 87; cx. 17, doc. 49; cx. 20, doc. 126; cx. 23, doc. 85; *LML*, cod. 32, fls. 17272v; *ACF*, cod. 1167, fl. 197.
29. *Ibid.*
30. 1 Covado = 64 cms. See *Diccionrio da Silva Morais*, vol. I.
31. Tavernier, *Tavernier's Travels...*, vol. II, pp. 2129.
32. *Ibid.*
33. Barbosa, *The Book of Duarte Barbosa...*, vol. II, p. 182-84; Tomé Pires, *Suma Oriental*, Vol. I, pp. 43.
34. Sen, *The Indian Travels...*, pp. 101-104.
35. Barbosa, *The Book of Duarte Barbosa...*, vol. II, p. 182-84;
36. Tomé Pires, *Suma Oriental*, Vol. I, pp. 42.
37. Pearson, *Merchants and Rulers...*, pp. 1012.
38. *Ibid.* pp. 78.
39. *India*, cx. 3, doc. 64.
40. Kail, *The Dutch in India...*, pp. 46-47.
41. Linschoten, *Itinerario...*, vol. I, pp. 90-92.
42. Tavernier, *Tavernier's Travels...*, vol. II, p. 45.
43. It was called as Golconda Muslin, *India*, Cxs. 17 (passim) See Ap

pendix VIII and IX; Vijaya Ramaswami, *Weavers in Mediaeval South India..*, IHR, Vol. VI, No. 12, pp. 125-126.

44. Tavernier, *Tavernier's Travels...*, vol. II, pp. 4.
45. *Ibid.*, pp. 23.
46. *Ibid.*, pp. 46.
47. See Appendix VII.
48. *Kafir* was used for African people. Literally it means Non-believers.
49. Tavernier, *Tavernier's Travels...*, vol. II, pp. 38.
50. *India*, cx. 4, doc. 50.
51. *India*, cx. 4, doc. 50; cx. 10, docs. 122, 206; cx. 13, doc. 66.
52. *India*, cx. 2, doc. 93; cx. 3, doc. 40.
53. *India*, cx. 4, doc. 25, 50, 93, 104, 136, 177, 186.
54. Tavernier, *Tavernier's Travels...*, vol. II, pp. 21-29.
55. Vijaya Ramaswami, *Weavers...*, IHR, Vol. VI, No. 12, pp. 125-30.
56. *Ibid.*
57. *LML*, cod. 1, fls. 35; cod. 26, fl. 654; 167, fl. 197; *India*, cx. 4, doc. 50, 177; cx. 10, doc. 195. cx. 11, doc. 157.
58. Om Prakash, *The Dutch Factories...*, p. 118; Kail, *The Dutch in India...*, pp. 15-28.
59. *India*, cx. 2, doc. 119.
60. *Ibid.*
61. *Ibid.*
62. *India*, cx. 3, doc. 1.
63. *India*, cx. 4, doc. 107.
64. *India*, cx. 8, doc. 88.
65. Barbosa, *The Book of Duarte Barbosa...*, vol. II, p. 182-84; Tomé Pires, *Suma Oriental*, Vol. I, pp. 40-45.
66. *India*, cx. 4, doc. 159.
67. *India*, cx. 10, docs. 122, 206.
68. *India*, cx. 17, doc. 49.
69. *ACF*, cod. 1167, fl. 197v.
70. *India*, cx. 3, doc.144.
71. *India*, cx. 2, doc. 133.
72. *Cartas...*, tomo I, pp. 52, 83, 269; tomo VII, p. 78; tomo VIII, pp. 41, 42, 132.
73. *India*, cx. 4, doc. 107.
74. *LML*, cod. 1, fls. 35.
75. *LML*, cod. 1, fls. 35, 75, 183v, 185v.

76. See Appendix VIII & IX.
77. *Ibid.*
78. See Appendix - IX.
79. *LML*, cod. 17, fls. 32v. 83; *ACF*, cod. 1160, fl. 192-93; cod. 1161, p. 191.
80. *LML*, cod. 20, fl. 245.
81. *LML*, cod. 17, fls. 82; cod. 22, fls. 163-166.
82. *LML*, cod. 24, fls. 8283.
83. *LML*, cod. 26, fl. 654.
84. *LML*, cod. 26, fl. 268.
85. B. Aj. *Jesuitas na Asia*, 46-XIII-30, pp. 37-37v.
86. *LML*, cod. 30, fls. 232-232v.
87. *India*, cx. 10, docs. 122, 202.
88. *India*, cx. 13, doc. 66; *LML*, cod. 32, fls. 172-172v.
89. *LML*, cod. 36, fls. 218, 252-53; cod. 37, fls. 55v, 171-172.
90. *LML*, cod. 44, fls. 228-238v.
91. *LML*, cod. 47, fls. 40-40v
92. *India*, cx. 20, doc. 126.
93. *ACF*, cod. 1167, fl. 197v; For the conversion of Bars see *India*, cx. 17, doc. 49; 1 Bar = 20 Cori
94. *ACF*, cod. 1168, fl. 105v.
95. See Appendix X.

Plate 5 Canarian bringing wheat on oxen packs to Goa from Balaghat for selling. Facsimilie XXXIV, *Imagens do Oriente*.

CHAPTER - 5

Trade in Cinnamon, Rice and Tobacco

All three of these commodities occupied different places in the Portuguese commercial operations. Cinnamon was one of the most profitable commodities during this period and was exported to Portugal in additions to being supplied to the various coastal regions. Rice took on great importance during the second decade of the seventeenth century and was supplied to the Portuguese settlements only in order to meet the demands of population as well as the needs of the soldiers fighting against Protestant Europeans. Tobacco, which the Portuguese probably introduced from the new world in the sixteenth century,(1) was not exactly exported but it is believed that it produced considerable revenue for the Portuguese treasury from the areas where it was cultivated. Thus for the sake of convenience, this chapter has been divided into three main parts:

(i) Cinnamon Trade

Throughout the sixteenth century cinnamon was declared as one of the restricted items for the local merchants(2) but when it rose to great importance in the early seventeenth century and generated much profit, it was declared as a commodity of royal monopoly.(3) The crown should, there fore, have gained mightily from the royal monopoly in this spice, but in actual practice the chief profit were reaped by the governors and officials who traded in cinnamon despite all the legislation enacted at Goa and Lisbon to prevent such mal-practices.(4) In this section, the qualities of cinnamon produced in various countries, and its volume procured by the various contractors and merchants will be examined thoroughly. Special attention will be paid to focus on the volume supplied to the various neighbouring countries and, finally, that taken to Portugal.

(a) Qualities and Areas of Production

Cinnamon was produced chiefly in Ceylon, especially in the regions of Kandy, Jaffna, and Colombo. The Portuguese as in their other colonies, here too maintained fortresses and factories from the second decade of the sixteenth century. Some inferior quality was also grown in Malabar and in Mindanao. But as Linschoten observed in 1596, "the cinnamon of Ceylon is the best and finest in the world, and at least three times dearer in price!."(5) Thus generally cinnamon was brought from Ceylon and exported to Portugal. No evidence has been found that it was ever exported from Malabar.

(b) Mode of Procurement and Payment

Mainly the Portuguese officials through Portuguese merchants handled the trade in cinnamon from Ceylon only. These merchants who dealt in this trade were settled either in Ceylon itself or in vicinities of Cochin and Quilon. Jerónimo da Costa was one of the prominent merchants during the third and fourth decades of the seventeenth century.(6) He not only provided cinnamon on cash payment but also on credit. For instances, during 1624-26.

Portuguese authorities still had to pay him an amount of 78,000 Ashrafis.(7) It is, however, not clear when and how he supplied cinnamon on credit. Another important business man who collected cinnamon from the interiors of Kandy and Jaffna and provided the Portuguese authorities were Dom Diogo Coutinho and António Pinto.(8) João Serrão was one of the richest merchants during the Portuguese regime in Ceylon, who once provided cinnamon on credit, the biggest consignments being worth 235,000 Ashrafis, as the Portuguese were not in Position to buy all by cash(9). It is, however, certain through one of his letters, which he wrote to the King of Portugal in 1635, demanding his debt. He proposed to the King to pay the amount by allowing him to carry 150 quintals of cinnamon every year on the account of the crown.(10) Marcel Macedo and Jerónimo de Macedo were the businessmen who were engaged for supplying cinnamon to the Portuguese government after 1640.(11)

Cinnamon was bought by the Portuguese authorities through payment of cash as well as by supplying textiles or other commodities as demanded by the contractors. It was only the contractors who visited the farms and negotiated with the peasants or with middlemen. Normally the Sinhalese people had demand for textiles in exchange for cinnamon, but how the values were determined is not clear. It seems to have been an occasional, rather than a regular process. For instance, in 1622, cinnamon was bought in exchange for textiles.(12) There were also other occasions when the Portuguese were bound to supply textiles for buying their stock of cinnamon. This system, however, was very profitable as it helped increasing the production of textile as well.

During this period, the purchase price of cinnamon fluctuated widely, as can be seen in the table 5.1. Prices fixed for the purchase for the stock for the annual ships differed in accordance with which the officer bought this commodity on account of their *Liberdades*.(13) During the early years of the seventeenth century, official purchases were made at the rate of 6 Ashrafis per quintal and for the navy officials it was fixed between 21 and 23 Ashrafis. The *Liberdades* price was always fixed at Goa as per rule.(14) During the third decade, the purchase rate for the crown rose by 100 percent that is between 10 and 12 Ashrafis. The reason was said to be short supply.(15) At this time official purchases were made at the rate of 33 to 34 Ashrafis per quintal. Thus the price oscillated during this period considerably. The maximum price paid by the Portuguese for the stock of the state was around 25 Ashrafis per quintal. The Dutch interference in this territory had much effect on the prices of cinnamon especially during the fourth and fifth decades. In the island, the war that followed, the Dutch openly challenged the Portuguese mariners and pre-empted the supply for their own ships. Thus it decreased the Portuguese share and pushed up the prices of cinnamon.

Table 5.1

Purchase Price of Cinnamon in Ceylon

YEAR	RATE PER QUINTAL IN Xs.	SOURCES
1611	21-23 for officers	*India*, cx. 2, doc. 73.
1612	6 for government	*Ibid*, doc. 82
1623-24	10-12 for government	*Ibid*, cx. 8, docs. 101, 192
1625	10 for government	*ACF*, cod. 1162, fls. 238v.
1634	33.5 for officers	*Ibid*, fol. 123
1637	6 for government	*Ibid*, cod. 1163, fl. 5
1638	34 for officers	*India*, cx. 12, doc. 140
1646-47	12.5 for government	*ACF*, cod. 1166, fls. 24-25
1649	25 for government	*ACF*, 1165, fls. 62, 84, 87
1649	33 for officers	Ibid.

(c) Volume of Trade

Portuguese authorities, in spite of all the barriers and problems, were in a position at least during the first four decades to carry on with their trade successfully in parts of the world. They not only took a big volume of cinnamon to their homeland but also supplied to other destinations in India and beyond China in the East; and Muscat, in the west, mainly in exchange for local commodities. Though this was not a regular trade but occurred frequently it is believed, and involved exchange rather than outright sale. However, since more detail is not found than is indicated in table 5.2, nothing can be said precisely.

Table 5.2

Export of Cinnamon to the Various Countries

YEAR	VOLUME IN kgs.	COUNTRIES	SOURCES
1612	46,186	China	*India*, cx. 2, doc. 82
1623-24	13,007	Muscat	*India*, cx. 8, doc. 101
1631	82,900	Cochin	*LML*, 28, fl. 139/276
1640		Muscat	*ACF*, 1163, fls. 93,101
1648	10,594	Muscat	*ACF*, 1165, fl. 50.
1651	524	Muscat	*ACF*, 1166, fl. 57
1652		Muscat	*ACF*, 1166, fl. 96
Total	1,53,211 kgs.		

Thus, in the table it can be clearly seen that Muscat obtained a fairly regular supply of cinnamon though less in volume than that to Cochin.

(d) Cinnamon Export to Portugal

In this merchandise too, much fluctuation can be found during the period under review. Though a total of 3,000 quintals was supposed to be exported yearly,(16) practically it was not feasible for the Portuguese authorities to provide regularly to the fleets for a variety of reasons such as lack of funds, non-availability of cinnamon and so on. However, in order to maintain a regular supply, the King of Portugal issued orders to keep on hand a stock of at least 3,000 quintals so that ships would not return without the necessary volume. The table 5.3, suggests that during the first decade of the seventeenth century, trade in cinnamon may have been conducted only in 1603, and that to a mere volume of 105 kgs.. However, the real trade started during the second decade, in 1611 and grew to maximum in 1615 when the Portuguese exported 270,642 kgs. of cinnamon. If available figures are correct, they would indicate that fluctuations were considerable throughout the second decade.

Table 5.3

Export of Cinnamon to Portugal 1603 - 1620

YEAR	VOLUME IN kgs.	SOURCES
1603	105	*India*, cod. 36, fls. 137-38
1611	2,600	*India*, cx. 2, doc. 73
1614	166,300	*India*, cx. 3, doc. 144
1615	270,642	*India*, cx. 2, docs. 6, 123, 133; cod. 31, fls. 39-43
1616	178,004	*India*, cx. 4, docs. 25, 145, 177
1617-18	55,175	*India*, cx. 5, doc. 164; cod. 34, fls. 42-42v; *LML*, cod. 11, fl. 275
1620	9,441	*ACF*, cod. 1160, fls. 71-72
Total	683,267 kgs.	
Average per year	85,408 kgs.	

During the third decade, the cinnamon trade diminished considerably, fluctuating between 104,900 kgs.. and 160.654, with the average hardly fifty percent of the previous decade. The reason for this fall was said to be the blockade of Goa and Ceylon ports simultaneously during 1620-1621. Corruption among officials is another possible reason for this decline. Even after repeated instructions by the King of Portugal, the stock was not maintained for the crown. On the contrary, cinnamon continued to be unloaded in the name of *Quintaladas* or *Liberdades*.(19) Moreover, the officers increased their *Liberdades* more than the allowed quantity, some times reaching higher than 200 to 300 percent of the originally allowed to each worker on the ship.(20) Thus situation became the reason for the issuing the prohibitary orders to stop the *Liberdades* in this commodity and declared it as an item of royal monopoly.(21) Instead of cinnamon the "liberty" was thereafter given in textiles or indigo. But even through repeated orders, it could not be stopped.(22)

Not only that, two Fidalgos, Dom Diogo Coutinho and António Pinto, went two steps further and bought more than 34,877 quintals of cinnamon from the Jaffna and Colombo factories and were about to sail off when the Viceroy got word of it and forced them to cede to the fleet bound for Portugal.(23) Such abuses, of course, belonged to the Portuguese officialdom and variously found.

Table 5.4

Export of Cinnamon to Portugal 1621 - 1630

YEAR	VOLUME IN kgs.	SOURCES
1622	123,782	*LML*, cod. 15, p. 264/181v; cod. 16, p. 206/7,; *India*, cod. 34, fls. 42-42v., 108; *ACF*, cod. 1162, fls. 58v-59v
1623	99,780	*India*, cod. 35, fls. 24-24v.
1624	209,800	*India*, cx. 8, doc. 192.
1624-25	160,654	*ACF*, cod. 1167, fls. 58-59, 238-38v; *India*, cx. 8, doc. 198; *LML*, 27, fl. 179/367.
1629	104,900	*LML*, cod. 27, fl. 179/367
Total	698,916 kgs.	
Average	139,782 kgs.	
Average for ten years	69,891 kgs.	

During the fourth decade, cinnamon export reached to its height comparing with all the previous decades. The total export was about 800,753 kgs. or 15,266 quintals. Although trade was conducted only five years, it was considerable. Out of these five years, for almost three, ships sailed to Portugal directly from Colombo (between 1637-40) because of the Dutch blockade of Goa. The money utilised for the purchase of cinnamon during this period was pepper money diverted from Cochin because crown's Factors were unable to obtain any quantity of pepper from there.(24) Moreover, because of the Dutch danger, cash could not be brought from Goa for the purchase of cinnamon. The year 1640's payment for the purchase of cinnamon was made in gold bullion by two big businessmen from Cochin, Jerónimo de Macedo and Marçal de Macedo mentioned before.(25)

Table 5.5

Export of Cinnamon to Portugal 1631 - 1640

YEAR	VOLUME IN kgs.	SOURCES
1632	33,830	*ACF*, Cod. 1162, fls. 58v-59v
1633	332,533	*LML*, cod. 30, fls. 317/264v.
1637	349,631	*ACF*, cod. 1163, fl. 5
1638	62,940	*India*, cx. 12, doc. 140
1640	21,819	*ACF*, cod. 1163, fls. 105-106
Total	800,753 kgs.	
Average	160,151 kgs.	
Average for ten years	80,475 kgs.	

The fifth and sixth decades were the periods of decay of Portuguese power in the Kingdom of Ceylon. The Dutch Portuguese war that followed right from 1634 onwards, ended with the loss of their southern cinnamon producing settlements to the Dutch in 1656. Almost fifty to sixty percent of the income of the Portuguese *Estado da India* was utilised to save this territory, but all in vain.(26) The steady opposition of the Dutch, however, rendered their position both hazardous and insecure, especially during this period. However, even in such condition, they managed to handle some trade. The export, as it is shown in table 5.6 between 1646 and 1652 was a maximum of 379,916 kgs., but the average did not reach more than 75,983 kgs. per year, accounting only when the trade was conducted.(27)

Table 5.6

Export of Cinnamon to Portugal 1641 - 1652

YEAR	VOLUME IN kgs.	SOURCES
1646	106,882	*LML*, cod. 55, fl. 183/216
1647	117,750	*LML*, 59, fl. 27;ACF, cod. 1166, fls. 34-35
1649	134,042	*ACF*, 1165, fls. 62, 84v, 85-87; *LML*, 59, fl. 27; *India*, cx. 20, doc. 126.
1652	21,242	*ACF*, 1167, fls. 99v, 108
Total	379,916 kgs.	
Average	75,983 kgs.	
Average for ten years		31,659 kgs.
Over all total	2,253,272 kgs. /	42,960 Quintals
Average for 19 years	118,593	
Average for 43 years	52,401	

Thus, if one refers to the tables, it becomes evident that the volume of cinnamon was quite considerable, at least when compared with the early sixteenth century data.(28) It was around 2,253,593 kgs. or 42,960 quintals in all nineteenth years when the trade was conducted. The average for years when it was conducted was about 118,593 kgs. or 2,261 quintals, but if we include other years also which was almost 43 years, then the average comes down to 52,401 kgs. or 1,000 quintal only. However, considering the importance of the commodity it was too little, but if the circumstances are taken into account, is remarkable that the Portuguese could manage to trade this much.

Portuguese Trade in Rice

Rice was another important commodity in this period. Never before the third decade of the seventeenth century was this item bought by the Portuguese in such abundançe. This increase in the demand for rice by the Portuguese was due mainly to the prevailing circumstances rather than to its profitability. It was never an item of export to Portugal. Normally, the Portuguese bought it for the provisioning of fortresses and factories on the western coast of India as well as to the neighbouring places to the Persian Gulf ports of Muscat, to the Swahili states, to Ceylon, Malacca, and so forth. Hence, I hope to indicate here just how this trade operated in regard to its varieties, the areas from which they were purchased, who the merchants were and the way they procured, together with prices, and the modes of payment. I have paid special attention on its volume as supplied to Indian and foreign ports and to its impact on the Indian merchant and the cultivators.

(a) Varieties and the Direction of the Trade

There are three kinds of rice, which the Portuguese trade, as mentioned in sources. They are categorised as *Fino* (high quality), *Meão* (medium quality), and Somenos (ordinary). The high quality was as *girasol* (mentioned as giracal), the medium quality as chambasol (Chamacal) and the ordinary was called as paddy rice or Amateur (*Cultor*).(29) Usually the first and the last were traded briskly. High quality rice was produced in bulk in the regions of Barcelore, Mangalore, Onor (Honawar) and a little in Bassein. Medium quality rice was cultivated in the vicinity of Goa, Bardez and Salssete. The third quality was produced in the regions mentioned above besides Chaul and Goa. This third quality was locally known Bhat and the Portuguese documents refer it to as *Bate*.

The Merchants, Mode of Procurement, Prices and the Payment

One of the most important contractors who provided for the Portuguese demand from the region of Kanara was Vitula Nayak who was also known for his reputation as a trader in the pepper and textile markets.(30) During 1628 and 1629, he was the one who provided rice from Barcelore. In 1628, his agents brought rice worth 21,462 Ashrafis to the Goa port from Kanara.(31) Manuel Ramos and Francisco Marques were the main contractors who collected rice from the cultivators of Goa.(32) Another important merchant Marçal Macedo, who actively participated in textiles trade from Balaghat, was also involved in the rice commerce during this period.(33) From Cochin, António de Pinto da Costa, married and settled there, was another big merchant dealing in rice and who provided for the Portuguese demand. In Mangalore, Rama Queny had good reputation among the rice contractors.

Usually these merchants got their supplies from the peasants through their agents. Some times the agents or the producers themselves brought their rice to the big merchants and sold them at agreed prices. It is difficult to say just how profitable this business was for the cultivators, but it seem that the merchant class people fleeced the producers because of their week financial position as was the case in the pepper trade. But it is certain that the increasing demand by the Portuguese and dependence of the merchants on the peasants did improve the position of cultivators who could bargain because of the short supply. Thus the production did improve in order to meet the demand. The longer the war continued, the higher the demand grew. But as the pricing table for rice indicates, it had less effect on it. For instance at the end of the third decade, a quintal of rice *girasol* cost one and a half Ashrafis, but it rose to 2.4 Ashrafis by the middle of the fourth decade and in 1639 it came down to 1.98 Ashrafis.

Table 5.7
Prices of Rice

YEAR	PRICE PER QUINTAL GERASOL IN Xs.	SOURCES
1628	1.50	*ACF*, cod. 1162, fl. 24v
1631	1.75	*ACF*, cod. 1162, fls. 42, 165; *India*, cx. 9, doc. 26.
1635	2.40	*ACF*, cod. 1162, fl. 170
1639	1.98	*ACF*, cod. 1163, fl. 50v

Normally, the contractors in this business required cash, but some times rice was paid in other commodities too. Since there was no regular fund for the purchase of rice, Portuguese authorities had to use cash from the treasury of Goa. Some times the taxes from a particular commodity were also assigned for the purchase of rice. For instance, during 1636-37, tobacco and food grains taxes from the fortress of Onor were used for the purchase of rice from the dealers.(34) Ships of the merchants were frequently employed in fetching of rice or for sending the cash for rice. For example, in 1630, 4,000 São Tomés in gold were sent to Barcelore in a *naveta mourisca* (a ship belonging to a Muslim merchant), accompanied by another ship owned by António Carreira Salema. In return they were to bring rice from there.(35) It is presumed that often it was done to avoid the clash with the Dutch and the English.

Volume of Rice in Coastal and Trans-Coastal Trade

Among the commodity for which the Portuguese dealt in their coastal trade, such as pepper, spices, textiles, rice, ivory and various other things, rice acquired a dominant position. Doubtlessly it was an item yielding no profit to them. They bought it mainly from the survival of their crews and the soldiers residing in their settlements during the time of war. The Portuguese exported rice to the different ports on the western coast of India, to the Persian gulf, to Mozambique, to Ceylon and finally to Malacca. Exports to all these areas and countries had been exposed in the following tables.

Volume of Rice Brought from the Various Regions to Goa Port

Apart from the rice produced in Goa and its surroundings, a substantial volume was brought from other parts of the western coast of India. It should be remembered here that Goa was the biggest European colony in Asia, and great number of people were living in it. Thus it is obvious that from the time of the siege of Goa from the beginning of the third decade up through the end of the fourth, Portuguese authorities had to bring some of their supplies from other regions. The details of imports made from the various areas are given in the following table:

Table 5.8

Rice Import Into Goa

YEAR	VOLUME IN kgs. Girasol	DIRECTIONS from	SOURCES
1629	2,64,243	Bassein	*ACF*, 1161, fls. 86-87, 94
1629	4,99,481	Barcelore	*Ibid*, fls. 95-95v.
1629	5,24,500	Diu	*Ibid*, fl. 96v,
1630	2,80,607	Barcelore	*Ibid*, fl. 117v, 122v, 123
1630	2,77,985	Mangalore	*Ibid*,
1630	55,072	Salssete	*Ibid*,
1636	1,04,500	Onor	*Ibid*, 1162, fl. 202v
1643	66,087	Chaul	*Ibid*, 1164, fl. 14v.
1661	1,57,350	Barcelore/Diu	*Ibid*, 1168, fl. 37
Total	27,54,325 kgs./52,513 Quintals		

Thus it becomes evident that the majority of the purchases were made from the regions of Kanara and to a lesser extent from

Bassein. The total import from all the regions mentioned in the above table was about 42,513 quintals, out of which 59.19 percent alone was from Kanara, about 23.5 percent was from Diu and rest from other regions.

Export of Rice from Various Regions to Muscat

Loss of Hormuz in the third decade was considerable jolt for Portuguese power in the Persian Gulf. The English and the Persian forces had shaken the every existence of the Portuguese in that region. The Portuguese authorities were found to keep their interest safe at least by saving their settlement at Muscat against the Oman's, who were emerging as a sea power during this period of hostilities, the Portuguese had lost almost all the means of getting a food supply or any provision from this region. Probably, this was the main reason why they were forced to supply food grains to their soldiers and their subject residing there. However, the nip and tuck battle (though with not much loss of life) ended in January, 1650. The Portuguese could not resist any longer and finally the Oman's were successful in capturing the fort of Muscat together with a number of Portuguese ships in the Harbour.(36) Following was the export of rice to Muscat:

Table 5.9

Rice Export to Muscat

YEAR	VOLUME IN kgs.	DIRECTIONS From	SOURCES
1629	2,83,230	Bassein	*ACF*, 1162, fl. 89v.
1629	5,95,569	Barcelore	*Ibid*, fls. 88v-89
1630	39,652	Goa	*Ibid*, fls. 124, 131v.
1631	4,72,052	Barcelore	*Ibid*, fls. 131-131v; 1162, fl. 7v.
1632	3,13,500	Goa	*Ibid*, 1162, fl. 22v
1632-33	8,36,000	Barcelore	*Ibid*, fls.50v51.
1633	4,19,862	Goa	*Ibid*, fl. 64.
1633	8,36,050	Barcelore	*Ibid*, fl. 64.
1641	66,180	Goa	*Ibid*, 1163, fl. 178
1646	Paddy	Goa	*Ibid*, 1164, fl. 156
1652	Paddy	Goa	*Ibid*, 1164, fl. 96.
Total	51,15,955 kgs. / 97,576 Quintals		

This was the maximum export during this period under review. Once gain, more rice obtained from the region of Kanara than from any other. It was about 53 percent from there alone. The rest was from Goa. However, total export, as can be seen in the table, was 97,576 quintals and the average for the years it was exported came to about 10,841 quintals.

Export of Rice to Mozambique

Mozambique, to some extent had different position during this period. Though there had been frequent interventions and warfare between the Dutch and the Portuguese but they were less effective than the other places. Nevertheless, rice was exported to this country also but less regularly for the sake of consumption by the people residing over there and occasionally for the exchange with the slaves and other goods. Yet, clear evidences are not available to prove that any slave was bought out of this item and on what amount. The total export within four years was 8,72,185 kgs. or 16,628 quintals a mere 17.5 percent of the aggregate of the export to Muscat. Following was the export of rice to Mozambique:

Table 5.10

Rice Export to Mozambique from Goa

YEAR	VOLUME IN kgs. Girasol	SOURCES
1633	4,02,000	ACF, *1162, fl. 62v.*
1634	2,01,000	ACF, *1162, fl. 88v*
1652	2,01,000	ACF, *1166, fl. 91.*
1657	68,185	ACF, *1167, fl. 157.*
Total	8,72,185 kgs./ 16,628 Quintals	

Export of Rice to Malacca

Malacca was captured by Albuquerque in 1511 and remained under the Portuguese control until 1641, when they were forced to surrender the island to the Dutch.(37) Although massive Dutch attacks had already started by the beginning of the seventeenth century, they could not gain any success against this island until the end of the fourth decade. This place, in reality, had been one of the important centres for controlling the Indonesian spice trade and served as a naval base, which stoppered the bottle neck between the Indian Ocean, the Java sea and the south China sea, for the alternative route via the Straits of Sunda was rarely used.(38) The Dutch attacks early in the century began by capturing Tidore and Amboina in 1605.(39) The Portuguese, realising the immediate danger for their island, Malacca, immediately undertook safety measures to buttress it. Among others they sent all sorts of provisions for their garrison there in response to the Dutch attacks from

Batavia (Jakarta). Rice, certainly was one of the items supplied in abundance at the critical hours. The Dutch blockade of the Straits of Malacca during 1634-41 required much provisioning for the soldiers. The year 1640 was the last time when the Portuguese authorities managed to send any amount of aid to the citadel and, finally in 1641, it fell into the hands of the Dutch.(40) But the course of the war was illustrated by their purchase of rice from the Indian subcontinent. The purchase and exports are given below:

Table 5.11

Rice Export to Malacca from Various Regions

YEAR	VOLUME IN kgs.	DIRECTIONS From	SOURCES
1628	1,10,145	Barcelore	*ACF*, 1161, fls. 4v, 24
1628	1,75,707	Chaul	*ACF*, 1161, fls. 29v, 35
1636	1,76,232	Goa	*ACF*, 1162, fls. 197, 211
1638	-	Goa	*ACF*, 1163, fls. 28
1639	6,60,977	Goa	*ACF*, 1163, fls. 50v.
1640	47,677	Goa	*ACF*, 1163, fls. 111v-112
Total	11,70,683 kgs. / 22,319 Quintals.		

(-) Dash means data not available.

Total export to Malacca was only 22,319 quintals, in which a major share was from Goa and the rest from Kanara and Chaul.

Rice Export to Ceylon

Export of rice to Ceylon was the second highest during the whole period in the comparison with export to the other areas. Like the other Kingdoms, Ceylon was also in the grip of war. After getting their foothold at Malacca, the Dutch war-ships sailed towards Ceylon and continued their most fierce attack on this island until they were able to capture Colombo from the Portuguese in 1655 and ousted them from Jaffna in 1658. The Portuguese settlements in this island had a significant impact on the *Estado da India's* whole economy. Being one of the most profitable items of trade, Portuguese rice merchants earned a lot in this commodity. However, in order to save their trade settlements, the Portuguese had to direct much of their manpower, economy and grain there. Apart from other things rice was one of the major items sent to Ceylon. The details are depicted in the following tables:

Table 5.12
Rice Export to Ceylon from Various Regions

YEAR	VOLUME IN kgs.	DIRECTIONS From	SOURCES
1629	1,32,360	Goa	*ACF*, 1160, fl. 116
1630	28,532	Cranganore	*ACF*, 1161,fl.104,114,116
1631	83,920	Mangalore	*ACF*, 1161, fl.135, 171v
1631	89,	Cochin	*ACF*, 1161, fl.133v-34
1632	1,31,125	Barcelore	*ACF*, 1162, fl. 58v.
1634	7,29,055	Barcelore	*ACF*, 1162, fl. 90v
1636	2,20,290	Kanara	*ACF*, 1162, fl. 193
1638	5,64,300	Kanara	*ACF*, 1163, fl. 28
1643	800 Muras	Goa	*Ibid*, 1164, fl. 38
1644	2,42,330 Paddy	Goa	*Ibid*, 1164, fl. 60, 81
1644	11,014 Girasol	Goa	*Ibid*,
1655	41,960	Bassein	*Ibid*, 1167, fls. 85v-86v.
Total	22,74,051 kgs. / 43,356 Quintal 800 Muras		

Thus after an overall survey of export of rice to these particular areas of the world, it becomes evident that there was a specific period in which this commodity took an important position. It was, therefore, never before, that a need for rice appears to have existed in connection with the island, or at least no such information can be found. It was almost certainly because of the continuous wars that took place during the same period, when the Portuguese commercial empire was threatened from without. The Portuguese then needed more and more provisions especially rice, from the areas, which were not threatened at the time. During the war, food supplies from the affected areas were stopped. Thus it was necessary to arrange their requirements from elsewhere.

The total export from all the regions - the northern ports, Goa, Kanara and Malabar - was about 116,61,649 kgs. or 2,22,392 quintals which gives an average for 21 years of exports about 10,587 quintals and for 33 years, about 6,737 quintals. The maximum rice was from the Kanara region, about fifty percent; in the second place was Goa from which about 31.74 percent was exported. The northern ports of Bassein, Chaul, and Diu, had a share of 9.19 percent, Malabar and some unidentified places had eight percent of the total export to contribute.(41)

Tobacco Trade

In India, tobacco was first introduced by the Portuguese sometimes in the sixteenth century.(42) During the seventeenth century, it was produced only in the Portuguese territories on the western coast of India. However, it was not before the eighteenth century that it became an important and lucrative item of trade.(43) The assumption that its trade was flourishing is based on the facts of its cultivation and some revenue derived from it. This chapter's subsection will study the area where it was produced, those contractors who collected the rent from each place, and the volume of trade during the seventeenth century.

(a) Area of Tobacco Cultivation

Tobacco was cultivated mainly in Bassein, Daman and Chaul, in the northern areas of the Portuguese settlements, with Goa in the centre, and Kanara especially Barcelore, in the south. Normally, the landlords under the jurisdiction of the Portuguese authorities were encouraged to cultivate tobacco in their fields. Tobacco was grown in the open field. The plant consisted of green leaves, almost one foot in length and about six to eight inches in breadth. These were plucked and dried in the hot sun and exported. It is very strange to find that none of the sixteenth century historians or travellers has described the growing of tobacco. Although Moreland had agreed to its cultivation in the statement that "the crop had been acclimatised in Gujarat towards the end of the sixteenth century",(44) he also fails to point out who had been the first to introduced it into India.

(b) Volume of Trade

It appears initially that the trade in tobacco leaves was mainly handled by local merchants or by way of private trade.(45) But the growing demand and the profit derived by the merchants in tobacco alerted the Portuguese authorities to restrict such trade by issuing prohibitary order in 1641.(46) Further, it was enforced that a stock of tobacco worth 100.000 Ashrafis should be built up and stored every year.(47) However, it is difficult to ascertain the volume, because the price of tobacco is not traceable in the documents. Dr. Miguel Silva de Pereira was deputed to look into the matter and ascertain it if the orders were strictly observed.(48) The preventive order of 1641 leads one to believe that there had been some extent of trade conducted by the Portuguese and local merchants, but details regarding its volume and direction have yet to be uncovered. The only information that could be found in this regard is for the year 1644, when 7 pipas(49) of tobacco was brought from Barcelore to Goa in the galleon São Bento.(50) Again in 1651, 2,328 kgs. of tobacco were sent to Portugal along with the other more usual goods.(51)

(c) Merchant-Contractors involved in the Tobacco Trade

Usually, the Portuguese authorities had a practice of collecting taxes from lands where tobacco was cultivated. The collection of tax from tobacco producing areas was mainly exercised by the local merchants. The task was handled by way of contracts assigned every three years. In fact, auctions were made for each area and the contractors paying the greatest amount were preferred. Evidences of such collections are found from 1630 onwards. In the beginning of 1630's, one tax collector, Gesu Sinai, son of Aria Sinai, agreed to pay a sum of 12,800 Ashrafis on revenues (*rendas*) collected from Bassein per year.(52) But the next contract which was auctioned in 1632 from Bassein rose to 27,200 Ashrafis, an increase of 212 percent of the previous contract.(53) From the territory of Daman, the contractors yielded between 7,000 and 7,500 Ashrafis per year.(54) During the end of the period under review it rose to 8,000 Ashrafis.(55) From Bardez and Salssete, 60,000 Ashrafis were collected towards the end of 1662.(56) Chaul and Barcelore were also among the tobacco producing areas, but the revenue collected from them is not known in detail.(57) Under this system, it is however, not clear whether these collections were made on the accounts of the contractors dealing in tobacco trade or they were simply derived on behalf of the Portuguese authorities. Nevertheless, in either case the Portuguese treasury was receiving a substantial amount from tobacco cultivation or trade.

The contract assigned to one particular contractor could always be cancelled and handed over to the other merchant if it was found unsatisfactory for any cause. For instance, in 1640, when Manuel Fialho and Krishna Prabhu, contractors from Bardez failed to pay the stipulated amount in time to the treasury of Goa, the contract was given to Manguji Sinai, who at the same time was contractor of Chaul rent too.(58)

A second contract of Bassein territory tobacco rent was given to Asiba Camitim Sinai and Azu Nayak. Samana Sinai and Vituba Camitim Sinai were appointed as purveyors, (*Provedores*) on a high contract rate of 27,200 Ashrafis per year.(59) The rent collection of the Bardez area had been given to Ganoba Rano (Rane) nephew of Krishna Rane with the rent of 11,630 Ashrafis every year, which was to expire by 1640.(60) In the early months of 1640, it was handed over to Manuel Fialho and Krishna Prabhu. Muizelho Boralho and António Borges Pato were middlemen between the authorities and the contractors through whom this contract was made. Goa's taxation contract of tobacco was then given to a certain Norna Nayakat was taken over by Malada Kashi and Ponda Nayak.(62) In 1661, Renaga Sinai was found negotiating with the Portuguese authorities for the *Renda* of Daman. He had promised to pay 8,000 pardaos per year.(63)

In this type of contract system, if it was profitable for the Portuguese government, it certainly had drawbacks for the contractors as well as for the peasants.(64) Again, since the contractors were bound to deposit the amount once decided in the contract, they had to resort to the severest means while collecting the dues from the cultivators, irrespective of the problems and their inabilities to pay in the loan years.(65) Often it was a profitless business for the contractors. For example, between 1652-55 it was observed in Bassein that the contractors were unable to derive a gain of even ten percent per annum.(66) This was, however, brought to the knowledge of authorities, who in 1656 and 1661, repeatedly issued orders to remove the taxes on the payments.(67)

Thus, this brief section suggests that in one way or another, tobacco was produced in some abundance, though the details regarding its volume could not be traced. The Portuguese state derived substantial income out of its cultivation. However, it is not clear whether or not these merchant contractors were involved in the tobacco trade, and if so, on what level and volume?

Notes

Trace in Cinnamon, Rice and Tobacco

1. Panikkar, *A History of Kerala*, pp. 179.
2. HAG. cod. 1043, fls. 59-62; See Appendix I.
3. *India*, cx. 3, doc. 6; *LML*, cod. 5, fls. 29-30; Godinho, *Os Descobrimentos...*, vol. I, pp. 192-93; Boxer, *Portuguese Seaborne...*, pp. 62-63.
4. *India*, cx. 9, docs. 20, 85; *LML*, cod. 23, fls. 285; cod. 25, fl. 321.
5. Linschoten, *Itinerario...*, vol. I, pp. 80; Vol. II, pp. 76-78.
6. *India*, cx. 9, docs. 20, 85; *LML*, cod. 23, fls. 285; cod. 25, fl. 321.
7. *Ibid.*
8. *LML*, cod. 27, fl. 367.
9. AHU. cod. 40, fls. 146v-147; *LML*, cod. 36, fls. 300, 313.

10. *Ibid.*
11. *ACF*, cod. 1162, fl. 105v-6.
12. *LML*, cod. 15, fl. 181; cod. 16, fls. 7, 28; AHU, cod. 34, fls. 42-42v, 108-109; *ACF*, cod. 1162, fls. 58-59v.
13. See table 5.1 for the difference and documents.
14. See documents used in the table 5.1
15. *Ibid.*
16. *India*, cx. 3, doc. 60.
17. *LML*, cod. 5, fls. 29-31; *India*, cx. 2, doc. 6.
18. *LML*, cod. 16, fl. 728; AHU, cod. 34, fls. 42-42v, 108-109.
19. *India*, cx. 8, doc. 198; *LML*, cod. 20, fls. 293; *ACF*, cod. 1162, fls. 58-59v.
20. *LML*, cod. 21, fl. 131, 159, 265; cod. 22, fl. 83v.
21. *India*, cx. 3, doc. 6; *LML*, cod. 5, fl. 29-30; Godinho, *Os Descobrimentos...*, vol. II, pp. 192-93; Boxer, *Portuguese Seaborne...*, pp. 62-63.
22. *India*, cx. 9, docs. 20, 85; *LML*, cod. 23, fl. 285.
23. *ACF*, cod. 1162, fls. 105v-106.
24. *ACF*, cod. 1163, fls. 105v-106.
25. *Ibid.*
26. See Chapter VIII.
27. See Table 5.5.
28. Mathew, *Portuguese Trade..*, pp. 127.
29. *APO-BP*, tomo IV, vol. II, part I, pp. 317.
30. *ACF*, cod. 1161, fls. 88v-89.
31. *Ibid.*
32. *Ibid.*, fls. 118, 122v-123.
33. *Ibid.*, fls. 117v, 122v-123.
34. *ACF*, cod. 1162, fl. 202v.
35. *ACF*, cod. 1161, fls. 130v.
36. Boxer, *Portuguese Seaborne...*, pp. 133-35.
37. Boxer, *Portuguese Seaborne...*, pp. 46-47.
38. *Ibid.*
39. *Ibid.*, p. 110.
40. *Ibid.*
41. See Appendix XI.
42. Panikkar, *A History of Kerala*, pp. 179.
43. Boxer, *Portuguese Seaborne...*, pp. 321.

44. Moreland, *From Akbar to Aurangzeb...*, pp. 80-81.
45. *Ibid.*
46. *ACF*, cod. 1163, fls. 194v-195.
47. *Ibid.*
48. *ACF*, cod. 1163, fls. 194v-195.
49. It differed in size in various places. It was usually between 25 and 27 Almudes = 1 Pipa. See Append VI.
50. *ACF*, cod. 1164, fl. 69.
51. *India*, cx. 21, doc. 121.
52. *ACF*, cod. 1161, fls. 129-130.
53. *ACF*, cod. 1162, fls. 61v.62..
54. *ACF*, cod. 1166, fl. 106.
55. *ACF*, cod. 1168, fl. 38.
56. *India*, cx. 25, doc. 34.
57. *ACF*, cod. 1164, fl. 69.
58. *ACF*, cod. 1163, fls. 120-120v.
59. *ACF*, cod. 1162, fls. 61-62.
60. *ACF*, cod. 1163, fls. 66-66v.
61. *ACF*, cod. 1163, fls. 66-66v, 241-245v.
62. *ACF*, cod. 1164. fl. 61v.
63. *ACF*, cod. 1167. fl. 110.
64. *Ibid.*
65. *Ibid.*
66. *Ibid.*
67. *Ibid.*

Plate 6 A Hindu businessman from Cambay. Facsimilie XXXVIII, *Imagens do Oriente*.

Chapter - 6

Saltpetre, Precious Stones and Sundry Items of Export

This chapter has been divided into three main parts. The first has been devoted to the study of the saltpetre export, the second deals with the precious stones which became much important and lucrative commodity of trade at least for the private merchants avoiding the customs and, the third part will deal with various other items, comparatively less regularly exported, but were of considerable importance

Saltpetre Trade

Saltpetre was one of the major items of the Portuguese trade during the first half of the seventeenth century especially after the second decade. As with textiles, the saltpetre trade also took an important shape during this period mostly due to the international rivalries. This was used mainly in preparation of gunpowder. So long as the war continued, demand for it went on increasing accordingly. This is one of the reasons why in the sixteenth century very little has been mentioned about its trade. The demand for the Portuguese gunpowder was locally fulfilled by the *Casa da Polvora* (gunpowder magazine or factory). But since the demand for gunpowder increased constantly, and the factory at Goa failed to produce as much quantity as was needed, the requirement had to be filled by the crown from gunpowder factory at Lisbon. However, because gunpowder for India was to be produced in Portugal, the Portuguese authorities at Goa sent much saltpetre to Portugal on the annual carracks. In this present chapter I propose to study the means of production, and processing, the area of procurement and the merchants who provided the Portuguese demand. I have also emphasised the means of payment, prices and the volume of export, as I have in other chapters throughout this study.

Mode of Production, Processing and Use

Saltpetre was produced mainly through natural processes.

Normally, it was mined in the form of brown-black dust and washed in the factories by using water and some chemicals. Saltpetre, which was washed only once or twice, was supposed to be inferior quality. The Portuguese normally had it washed again in their factory at Goa before sending it to Portugal or using in the gunpowder factory in India. This type of saltpetre lost much of its weight while being so processed in the factory. Saltpetre, which was washed thrice, was of medium quality and those, which were washed four times, were considered to be the best. In these qualities, less loss of weight has been noted.(1)

Saltpetre, besides its role in making gunpowder, was used for preserving food, and as a medicine. But these other applications were minor when compared to its martial ones.

Area of Procurement and the Merchants

During the early years of the seventeenth century, Portuguese official obtained their supplies from the regions of Sindh, Balaghat, Cranganore and Tuticorim but as the demand increased due to the heavy pressures of war, other areas like Madurai, Jaffnapattam and Bengal were also tapped for its supply. It is believed that saltpetre from Madurai was better than other regions just mentioned.(2) It required only two washes for purification before it could be used for preparation of gunpowder whereas saltpetre from other regions required at least three to four washes before it could be dispatched to the factory.(3)

Among the merchant contractors who supplied the Portuguese demand for saltpetre, Vitula Nayak (or Vithal Nayak) stands first. Vitula Nayak was one of the biggest merchants of his time, as noted earlier in the cases of the pepper and textiles trades. He sent his agents to all regions of Kanara, such as to Mangalore and other places in the interior. Balaghat was also one of the main areas for his purchases. In march 1626, Portuguese authorities under pressure of events, made a contract with him for a period of two years.(4) After completion of this period, they did not renew the contract in 1628, but once again in 1631 they ordered a large quantity of saltpetre from him, which was refused on the ground that the contractual period was over. Moreover, the Nayak demanded a new price to be fixed for the new supply and contract.(5) Initially, the Portuguese were reluctant to accept it but later, as they failed to find any other solution to the problem, agreed to his demands.(6) On the other hand, Vitula Nayak promised to be punctual. Thus in 1632, when he could not procure the required quantity from Balaghat, he sent his agents to Mangalore to obtain it.(7)

In 1634, renewal of this contract was solicited by Vitula Nayak, who sent his representative to Goa with proposals for a new price since, as he professed, had lost much of his wealth due to the inflation of gold coins after the previous contract. He demanded an increase of two Ashrafis per quintal. His demands were agreed to, seeing that requirements for saltpetre had vastly increased and that the Portuguese feared a scarcity of this item.(8) Thereafter, not only did their need for saltpetre increase during the same period, but also the volume contracted with Vitula Nayak was inadequate. Then they made another contract with Pallu Nayak, an inhabitant of Goa.(9) According to the contract, he was obliged to supply 2,000 quintals of saltpetre every year. He was to be paid half in cash, with the other half to be paid after arrival of the ships from Portugal. For this cause two guarantors, Rama Queny and Vishnu das Sinai, brother of Nagarca Sinai were employed from the Portuguese side to ascertain the supply arrived in time.(10)

The King of Madurai was also approached for the supply of saltpetre from his territories, Tuticorim and Paliacate. This commodity was brought from Paliacate to the Cochin factory where it was refined and sent to Goa, either for reshipment to Portugal or consumption in Goa.(11) Elsewhere in Bengal, some Muslim merchants were enlisted in the service of the Portuguese for the purchase of saltpetre.(12) These merchants supplied this item to the port of Jaffnapattam in exchange for other goods.(13) Though the quality of Bengal Saltpetre was not good, but the circumstances under which the Portuguese were forced to buy were insurmountable.

Even though such attempts were made at the centre of the empire to ensure an adequate supply, sometimes, local officials in threatened areas had to supplement what Goa could spare them with their own procurement. From Jaffnapattam, for instances the Portuguese *Provedor*, Domingo Rodrigues, was forced from time to time to contact with the local merchants for its supply to make up for what he lacked.(14)

Thus during the whole period it is noted that two contractors Vitula Nayak and Paulo Nayak had been the major suppliers of this commodity to the Portuguese state apart from Rama Queny and Vishnu das Sinai. Vitula Nayak and probably his family associates were found supplying the Portuguese requirements as late as 1652. During this period he alone provided about 4,000 quintals of saltpetre. Even in 1656, and later in 1661, he was the one who supplied the major needs of the Portuguese for saltpetre.(15) Paulo Nayak was also found supplying this commodity to the Portuguese officials till the end of 1662-1663.(16)

Mode of Payment and Prices

Usually, payments to the contractors were made in cash in gold or silver coins.(17) Sometimes, they were paid half in advance and half after the arrival of the annual ships with money. This pre-payment (or else the payment in full) was made from the treasury of Goa. In case of Paulo Nayak, he was paid 9,000 Ashrafis out of 18,000 in advance before he supplied the goods. The remaining amount was paid by the guarantators, Rama Queny and Vishnu das Sinai on behalf of the Portuguese government as money from Goa did not arrive in time for the payment.(18) As per the conditions of the contract, Portuguese authorities were sometimes also obliged to pay in certain commodities. For example, they promised the King of Madurai to supply elephants in exchange for 1,000 quintals of saltpetre.(19) But it seems that due to unknown reasons, they failed to fulfil the promise and therefore, they had to supply some piece goods and costly fabrics meant for royal use in 1635.(20) Similar was the case of the Bengali Muslim merchants for whom the Portuguese promised to provide some elephants at the port of Jaffnapattam in exchange with 500 quintals of saltpetre but neither did they supply the elephants nor were able to pay for the saltpetre in cash. They complained the King of Portugal about it and the King issued orders in this regard.(21)

The table of prices (table 6.1) suggests that there was much fluctuation in the prices of saltpetre during the first half of the seventeenth century. Prices also, differed according to the area. For instance, in the early years of the third decade a quintal of saltpetre from Balaghat cost three and half Ashrafis, but in the beginning of the fourth decade it rose to ten and half Ashrafis per quintal, an increase of 300 percent. It can safely be assumed that inflation and short supply are the explanation for this situation.(22) Later, this price again fell in the same decade. It thus oscillated during the whole period of the study. Prices of saltpetre from Tuticorim fluctuated between seven and ten and a half Ashrafis per quintal. Prices of saltpetre from other regions are not to found in the documents.

Table 6.1

Purchase Price of Saltpetre in India in Qunitals

YEAR	AREA	PRICE IN Xs.	SOURCES
1625	Balaghat	3.50	*India*, cx. doc. 186
1631-34	Balaghat/Kanara	10.50	*ACF*, 1162, fls. 166-66v
1634	do	12.50	*Ibid*, fl. 144
1636	do	9.00	*Ibid*, fl. 212
1638	Tuticorim	7-10.50	*ACF*, 1163, fl. 48v-49v
1652	Balaghat	8.00	*ACF*, 1166, fl. 117v
1656	Balaghat	7.50	*Ibid*, fl. 128
1661	Balaghat	8.00	*Ibid*, fl. 119
1662-63	Balaghat	12.00	*India*, Cx. 26, doc. 64
1662-63	Balaghat	8.00 crude	*Ibid*,

Volume of Trade

It is noteworthy that during the period under review, all the profitable goods like pepper, cinnamon and textiles were gradually on the decline soon after the end of the third decade by margins of 25, 50 and 90 percent. On the contrary, saltpetre, increased in the forties by 500 percent, but in the fifth decade came down by 25 percent and remained the same in the sixth. No wonder, as this was an essential commodity, the Portuguese needed it for preparation of gunpowder. After all, their main aim was to save their settlements. The decline in the export of saltpetre can be the cause of the deteriorating financial condition. With a close look into the tables provided below, the exact, but not the complete, volume of trade can be realised under the specific circumstances which have already been discussed several times in the previous chapters.

During the first decade of the seventeenth century, it is observed that there was no trade conducted in saltpetre from any part of the country or at least no mention has been found in any document. In the second decade, only in 1616 was a negligible amount of 419.6 kgs. exported from Goa to Lisbon even though the Portuguese had already had many confrontations with the Dutch and the English.(23) Probably their demand for gunpowder could be met by stock already on hand. But during the third decade, the total export of saltpetre was about 2,105 quintals purchased from the region of Balaghat. The reason behind this increase can be understood the severe fighting in the Persian Gulf, blockade of Goa and sack of Bombay. All these actions consumed gunpowder at a furious rate. Following are the details of saltpetre exported only from Balaghat:

Table 6.2

Export of Saltpetre to Portugal During 1621-1630

YEAR	VOLUME IN kgs.	DIRECTIONS From	SOURCES
1623	5,450	Balaghat-Goa	*LML*, 17, fls. 24-25v
1625-26	1,04,900	Balaghat-Goa	*India*, Cx. 9, doc. 186
Total	1,10,350 kgs. / 2,103 Quintals		

During the fourth decade, the Dutch-Portuguese fighting on several fronts became very common: the blockade of Malacca and Goa by the Dutch with the help of Sultans on the western coast of India dealt a severe blow to the Portuguese power. Thus, to keep weapons, the necessity of saltpetre for making gunpowder increased. To illustrate this, table provided below showing the increased demand and export will be suffice:

Table 6.3

Export of Saltpetre to Portugal During 1631-1640

YEAR	VOLUME IN Kgs.	DIRECTIONS From	SOURCES
1631	-	Sindh-Goa	*ACF*, 1161, fls. 166-66v.
1633	4,353	Bengal-Goa	*India*, cx. 12, doc. 3
1635	8,130	Tuticorim-Goa	*India* cx. 11, doc. 44
1636	3,14,700	Tuticorim-Goa	*India*, Cx. 12, doc. 42
1636	1,04,900	Balaghat-Goa	*ACF*, 1162, fl. 212
1637	2,09,800	Tuticorim-Goa	*ACF*, 1163, fl. 16
1640	26,225	Bengal-Goa	*ACF*, 1163, fl. 116v.
Total	6,68,108 kgs. /12,737 Quintals.		
Average	1,11,351 kgs. / 2,122 Quintals		

Thus, as indicated in the above table of exports in the fourth decade, it is believed that the demand and the supply of saltpetre from the various regions increased from 400 to 500 percent when compared with the demand and export during the previous decades. The total expenditure of saltpetre was about 12,737 quintals in all the seven years of export mentioned, which gives as average of 2,212 quintals. Here one thing can be noted about the export years. As has already been mentioned that during the years between 1637 and 1641, a severe blockade of Goa was carried out by the Dutch. Under such conditions, plying of ships was too risky, but somehow, the Portuguese authorities managed to get their consignments dispatched from other ports not mentioned in the documents.

In the fifth decade, purchases made from the various regions of India was less than by 21.5%. In all about 5,23,656 kgs. total saltpetre was exported. During this period, a slight change in condition of the Portuguese *Estado da India* has been noted. Malacca was already lost to the Dutch in 1641, but still two major fronts were to be dealt with, the port of Muscat and the island of Ceylon. However, on the loss of Malacca, a major decline in financial condition of the Portuguese *Estado* was felt. The helplessness of the Portuguese crown to meet the demand of the Asian colonies only increased after 1640-1641. Until this time, the Portuguese had to fight the Dutch East India Company and the English in the Indian Ocean, and the Dutch West India Company in Brazil, but now they had to face a new enmity from Spain itself after their restoration during 1640-41.(24) Henceforth, for twenty years the Portuguese had to fight the Spaniards on the home front and the Dutch on the overseas.(25)

Table 6.4

Export of Saltpetre to Portugal During 1641-1650

YEAR	VOLUME IN kgs.	DIRECTIONS From	SOURCES
1644	78,675	Bengal-Goa	*ACF*, 1164, fl. 80v
1649	3,66,306	- -	*ACF*, 1164, fl. 2; *India*, cx. 20, Doc. 126.
1650	78,675	Bengal-Goa	*ACF*,1166, fl. 41
Total	5,23,656 kgs. / 9,983.50 Quintals		

During the next ten years, the export of saltpetre increased by seventeen percent in comparison to that of fourth decade. The total volume of saltpetre procured from the various regions was about 6,12,983 kgs., but only 5,69,239 kgs. were exported, some nine percent more than the last decade. Export of saltpetre has been depicted in the following table:

Table 6.5

Export of Saltpetre to Portugal During 1651-1660

YEAR	VOLUME IN kgs.	DIRECTIONS From	SOURCES
1651	3,06,989	Bengal-Goa	*ACF*, 1166, fls.54v, 58, 65.
1652	2,09,600	Balaghat-Goa	*ACF*, 1166, fls. 111
1656	52,450	Bengal-Goa	*ACF*, 1167, fl. 120
Total	5,69,239 kgs. / 10,853 Quintals		

During this decade, there had been several very important encounters between the Dutch and the Portuguese on the island of Ceylon and in Malabar. Colombo was handed over to the Dutch in 1656 and the Portuguese were expelled from Jaffna, their last stronghold in Ceylon, in 1658. Quilon was lost but recaptured in 1659. Usually, however, in all the battles, which ensued during this period in Asia, Portuguese attempts to regain their lost empire, proved unsuccessful.

Still worst conditions were to come in the seventh decade. The Portuguese were losing battles on all the fronts on the Malabar Coast. By 1663, with the loss of Cochin and Cannanore, the whole Portuguese fight with the Dutch came to an end. The entire Portuguese efforts, from both- the East and the West were utilised to revive their territories and trade but in vain. In a period of three years of the seventh decade, a mere volume of 436.5 quintal of saltpetre could be sent to Portugal for the manufacture of gunpowder.

Table 6.6

Export of Saltpetre to Portugal During 1661-1664

YEAR	VOLUME IN kgs.	DIRECTIONS From	SOURCES
1661	17,046	- -	*ACF*, 1167, fls. 120
1662	4,196	Chaul-Portugal	*ACF*, 1168, fls. 119v.
1663-64	1,678	Balaghat-Goa	*India*, Cx. 26, Doc. 64
Total	22,920 kgs. / 436.5 Quintals		

Thus with an over all survey of the export of saltpetre, it can easily be seen that within a period of 63 years, only twenty years successive trade was conducted.(25) During these twenty years, only 18,946,92.6 kgs. or 36,123.5 quintals of saltpetre was exported from Goa to Lisbon, an item which was uniquely in demand during this period of turmoil. However, the average export during the twenty years comes to 1,806 quintals per year, and for 43 years, starting from 1616, it come to only 840 quintals. As marked at the beginning of this chapter, it turned no profit for the Portuguese except for the merchants and producers.

During the whole period, the maximum trade was conducted from the regions of Tuticorim. It was almost 28,12% of the total saltpetre bought from this region. From Bengal and Balaghat each had share of 26.12% or a total of 52.24 percent. From unidentified regions there was 19.64 percent among the export. Apart from above mentioned exports, more than 1,26,596.5 kgs. of saltpetre was sent to Cochin and Quilon in 1652 for the preparation of gunpowder.(26)

Precious Stones (Diamonds)

One of the most important, valuable and profitable items of trade was the precious stones. This commodity rose to its prominence during the second decade of the seventeenth century. As it has been pointed out in the fourth chapter that much of the decline of textile trade of the *Carreira da India* was due to the preference by the merchants, who used to invest in cloth, to the precious stones. Precious stones had the advantage of being concealable and thus paid little or no customs duties in Lisbon, and they required little space on vessels at a time when the tonnage of *carreira* shipping overall started declining rapidly. Official correspondence in Lisbon and Goa also reflects a preference among merchants in the period for precious stones, which naturally alarmed the crown, whose customs revenues were in decline in part because of the shift of precious stones.

Precious stone cargoes of the *Carreira da India* presented the great problem to evaluate, both in terms of volume and value. First of all, what is the precise size and capacity of a *Bizalho* or a *Boceta*, the most common containers of precious stones shipments. Official correspondence about 1598 indicated that one *Bizalho* ordered for the crown carried almost 300 stones ranging from quarter carat to a few diamonds of 10 carats. A treatise on precious tones available in Lisbon dated 1600 and the testimony of merchants themselves convinces that a *Bizalho* of diamonds was worth between 5,000 and 10,000 Cruzados delivered in Lisbon. An average has been calculated of 7,000 Cruzados. Then, the number of *Bizalhos* carried around the Cape to Lisbon each year presents another problem, since much of the precious stone cargoes were unregistered contraband. The new manifests indicate that merchants delivered between sixty and eighty *Bizalhos* for customs each year in Lisbon, which at 7,000 Cruzados works out to 400,000 to 600,000 Cruzados. There is at least one slide indication that unregistered volume was exceeded several times than the present figure. The Archbishop of Lisbon and officials of the India House reported that the carracks of 1615 delivered at least 300 *Bizalhos* to Lisbon(27) That figure was much more than any of the officials of India House could recall receiving. The deliveries in 1615 were so much exceptional because by accident they included most of the unregistered as well as the registered shipments of that year. The India House officials got hold of the unregistered shipments because one of the carracks had been wrecked in the Azores (at Faial) and its cargo had washed up on the beaches, where the officials picked them up.(28)

It was the diamond trade, however, that drew Simão Dias Vaaz (born in Lisbon about 1580), the son of Duarte Dias, o Feio, ("the ugly") and Branca Nunes, into the circle of Lisbon's greatest private merchants and financiers, a relationship that carried over to the *asientos* a few years later. Although Simão never traded directly with India or the Far East, he specialised in the diamond traffic from Lisbon, Antwerp and Amsterdam and in the insurance of cargoes from Goa to Lisbon and Lisbon to Antwerp or Amsterdam. Valentim and Ginés de Barona, André Lopes Pinto, and Simão's cousins in Lisbon supplied the diamonds, which they in turn had received from Manuel de Paz, Francisco Tinoco de Carvalho, Jorge Ribeiro Coresma, or other merchants in Goa. In 1620 Simão Dias Vaaz and Diogo Teixeira de Sampaio were the principal suppliers of diamonds and other precious stones for the Briers Diamond and jewellery firm of Frankfurt, which supplied princely and courtly customers in central Europe. Simão eventually brought Ginés de Barona, said to be the foremost diamond and lapidary expert in Europe, from Lisbon to Antwerp to work at his side. Ginés de Barona de Lacerda, meanwhile, represented the firm in Madrid and Simão's brother Manuel Dias Henriques was entrenched in Amsterdam's trade in 1626. João Mendes Henriques was already representing the family in Naples.(29) This broad family network encompassing the Iberian ports, Amsterdam, London, Hamburg, Naples, Rouen, Paris and the Baltic ports, recommended Simão to the *asientistas* as an especially valuable correspondent.(30)

Thus, the brief venture into the diamond trade from Goa to Lisbon under the Portuguese merchants' agents did show the amount of wealth employed in it and its profitable yield to them. Though it derived no profit to the Portuguese revenues but it did enriched the merchants who were constantly in contact with the governments' affairs and financing.

It is, however, generally noted that the transaction in this item always lacked with the type of diamond or stones carried in each *Bizalho* but there are scattered information about their types. For instance Missang, Bazares. In general the export of diamonds are as follows:

Table 6.7

Export of Daimonds to Portugal During

YEAR	VOLUME IN	SOURCES
1615	108 Bizalhos	*India*, Cx. 3, doc. 168
1616	2 Bocetas	*India*, Cx. 4, doc. 25
1618	71 Bizalhos	*India*, Cx. 5, doc. 164
1635	3 Bizalho	*India*, Cx. 11, doc. 193

Sundry Items of Export

Apart from the commodities mentioned earlier, there were more than forty other items in which Portuguese traded in this period. Although they were less traded, less regularly, they had relatively great importance in European countries. All these commodities and their volume, which they carried on the cargo ships, are discussed separately in the following manner.

Cardamom (Cardamomo)

Among the Indian goods, cardamom was in great demand, both in Europe and in Asia.(31) It grew mostly in the area between Cannanore and Chale near Calicut.(32) There were more than 2,884.5 kgs. of cardamom on the cargo ships bound for Portugal in 1616.(33) In 1618, there were about 3,672 kgs. of cardamom among the exported goods to Portugal.(34)

Clove (Cravo)

Clove and clove oil were both exported by the Portuguese and utilised in preparation of food as well as for medicinal purposes. This was produced mainly in the South-East Asian countries, especially grew in Moluccas.(35) Usually, all the products of this region were brought to the port of Malacca and then shipped to Goa. In due course, were exported to Portugal on the homeward bound ships. Apart from its origin and the volume exported, no other information is found in the documents.

Table 6.8

Export of Cloves to Portugal

YEAR	VOLUME IN	SOURCES
1616	6,137 kgs.	*India*, Cx. 4, Docs. 25, 188
1635	4,720	*India*, Cx. 11, Doc. 193.
1649	6,10,165	*India*, Cx. 20, Doc. 126.
Total	6,21,022 / 11,840 Quintals	

Ginger

This was another item of daily use in food and, believed to have medicinal value too. There were two varieties of ginger exported to Portugal.(36) Barbosa and Tomé Pires have describe them as Beledi and Dely ginger.(37) Beledi ginger grew in the vicinity of Calicut and in the interior, while the other one was produced in the area between Mount Deli and Cannanore. The former also grew in Bengal and considered better than the other one.(38) In the seventeenth century they were mentioned as *Conservas* and *Gengivre secco*.(39) *Conserva*, made of ginger and sugar was an item of delicacy for the Portuguese and was brought from Bengal to the Malabar coast in the sixteenth century for re-export to Portugal.(40) But in the seventeenth century it was brought to the port of Goa for the export to Lisbon.(41) The export of ginger had been made in the following manner:

Table 6.9

Ginger Export to Portugal

YEAR	VOLUME IN kgs.	SOURCES
1616	9,441	*India*, Cx. 4, Docs. 25,
1618	11,015 (conserva)	*India*, Cx. 5, Doc. 164.
1618	11,171(seco)	*Ibid*.
1649	86,114	*India*, Cx. 20, Doc. 126.
Total	1,17,741 kgs. / 2,264 Quintals	

Mace and Nutmeg (Maça e Nozmoscada)

Mace and nutmeg were the product of Banda and used as spices in the preparation of meat dishes.(42) From Banda it was brought to the port of Malacca, stored there and later sent to Goa. Nutmeg used to come in two forms, in flowers and in nuts. In 1616, the export from Goa to Lisbon included 2,230 kgs. of nutmeg.(43) In 1649, there were about 1,87,459 kgs. of nutmegs in nuts, and 89,180 kgs. in flower among the goods taken to Portugal.(44)

Seed Pearls (Aljofar)

Among the Portuguese exports, vast varieties of seed pearls, both for boutique and medicinal use were included. In 1616, more than 36 bags of Aljofar were sent to Portugal.(45) They were of highly expensive quality. Again in 1635, ten bags of pearls were dispatched on the annual carracks that left port of Goa for Portugal.(46)

Musk (Almiskar)

Musk was brought from north-west part of China, Tibet and Pegu.(47) There were 75 pots(Boiois) or 6,750 ounces of Almiskar in the cargo ships left Goa in 1616.(48) Only nine pots or 810 ounces of musk were sent to Portugal in 1618. Again in 1635 about 10 pots of musk were among the exported cargo to Portugal.(49)

Amber (Ambergris)

It was used in medicine by the physicians and also used as perfume during this period. It was product of Physeter Macrophalus, probably from intestines of whales and found floating in tropical seas.(50) This was brought from Maldives, Ceylon and other islands.(51) In 1616 there were seven pots(52) and in 1635 about ten pots of musk among goods exported.(53)

Saffron (Açafrão)

There were two varieties of saffron. One was called saffron of India generally used in preparation of food and in India known as Haldi. Second was an item of luxury. It was used for delicacy in the sweets. It was of deep orange-yellow colour and known as Zafran.(54) In 1618, there were about 209 kgs. of saffron of India among the exported merchandises to Portugal.(55)

Aloes Wood or Agallohchum (Aguilha Brava)

It grew mostly in the region of Cape Camorin and Ceylon. It is an incense wood, which smells like Sandal.(56) In 1618, about 525 kgs. of aloes woods were taken to Portugal.(57)

Sandalwood (Pao de Sandalo)

Garcia de Orta gives three varieties of sandal wood, namely red, white and yellow, which was brought to India from various parts of world especially from Timor, Tenassarim and Coromandel coasts and exported to Portugal.(58) In the seventeenth century only two varieties, red and white, were found among the exported goods of the Portuguese. In 1616, about 3,617 kgs. of red Sandal, and 394 kgs. of white sandal wood, were exported to Portugal.(59)

China Wood (Pao da China)

This was also like sandalwood but not of the same quality. As it is clear by its name, it was brought from China in exchange for spices and textiles by the Portuguese to Goa and thence exported to Portugal. During 1616-1618, about 2,098 kgs. of China wood was exported to Lisbon from Goa.(60)

Cowrie Shells (Búzios)

Búzios were small white colour shell especially which the Portuguese preferred to carry to Portugal or to their other settlements in the world. This was fished on the coastal regions of Africa and India. During this period it was used, chiefly in west Africa, as small coins.(61) In 1609 it was decreed that about 52,540 kgs. of Búzios should be sent to Portugal regularly.(62) It's export was as follows:

Table 6.10

Export of Shells to Portugal

YEAR	VOLUME IN kgs.	SOURCES
1609	52,450	*India*, cx. 4, docs. 25,
1616	52,400	*Ibid.*
1618	22,448	*India*, cx. 5, doc. 164.
1619	5,245	*India*, Cx. 5, Doc. 193.
Total	1,32,543 kgs. / 2,548 Quintals	

Benzoim (Benjoim, Beizoim)

There were two kinds of benzoim- white and black-, which were obtained from the region of Pegu. It grew mostly in Sumatra and Siam.(63) Some of the details regarding its export and volume have been given in the following table:

Table 6.11

Export of Benzoim to Portugal

YEAR	VOLUME IN kgs.	SOURCES
1616	786	*India*, Cx. 4, Docs. 25,
1618	1,574	*India*, Cx. 5, Doc. 164.
1635	59,868	*India*, Cx. 11, Doc. 193.
Total	62,228 kgs. / 1,196.5 Quintals	

Coca (Drug)

This was, probably brought from Pegu. It was not really an item of importance among the Portuguese export. In 1616 about 60 kgs. and in 1618, 630 kgs. were exported to Lisbon from Goa.(67)

Cotou (Unidentified)

There were about 315 kgs. of this variety among the exported goods of the Portuguese shipping to Portugal.(68)

Incense

Incense was brought from Arabia and Cambay in exchange for spices and pepper that the Portuguese officials provided for it, to Goa.(69) It was used mainly in churches during religious ceremonies.(70) There were about 787 kgs. of incense loaded on the fleet that left for Portugal in 1616.(71)

Iron

Among the exported goods, iron from Vijaynagar had played an important role for the building of ships, anchors, canon balls, cannons and divers types of materials. It had been commodity of regular trade and export but there is great dearth of information such as who were the merchants dealing in this item, and what was its volume etc. There was a big iron deposit existing in the vicinity of Goa, then in the lands of Adil Shah, but in what later became part of *Conquistas Novas*. The only considerable amount of information could be found in the documents are for the year 1632-33. There were 1,04,900 kgs. of iron exported from Goa to Lisbon.(72)

Indigo

Indigo was produced in the territories of Gujarat especially in Sarkhej, and Ahmadabad; Agra and Sindh. From these areas, indigo was brought to the ports of Cambay and Surat and sent to the port of Goa for the export to Portugal. This was an item of high profit in the later part of the seventeenth century. Even the Portuguese officials, in order to increase its trade gave many *liberdades* to the naval officials in 1624.(73) Because of the profit involved in the indigo trade, the Dutch took much interest in this items and also carried it to Europe.(74) Indigo was used mostly in dyeing cloths etc. During 1616-1618, about 37,002 kgs. of indigo collected from Sarkhej and other regions were exported to Portugal.(75)

Sealing Wax

It was produced in Malabar, Bengal, Sumatra and other places in the South-East Asian countries.(76) It was used for sealing letters, packets and especially official correspondence. Gunny bags, large and small, with goods, precious metals and stones sealed and only then loaded on the ships. If the seal was found broken, a thorough check was carried out.(77) Besides the official needs, one Dom Manuel Coutinho and afterwards (probably) his son, Dom Jerónimo Coutinho, were given a regular liberty of 100 quintals or 5,245 kgs. of sealing wax to carry on the ships bound to Portugal.(78) Between 1616 and 1618, Portuguese correspondence reports an export of about 7,474 kgs. of sealing wax to Portugal.(79) The biggest consignment was sent in 1649. About 51,053 kgs. of sealing wax was among the exported items to Portugal.(80)

Tincal and Camphor

These items were also among the Portuguese exported goods but no details could be extracted except for tincal, which was exported during 1616-18, about 7,500 kgs. As in the case of sealing wax, these items were also given as liberty to Dom Manuel Coutinho and, later to D. Jerónimo Coutinho. They were permitted to carry 30 quintals of each item mentioned above as part of their liberty.(81)

Mirabolan

This was found in the forests of Malabar, Dabhol, Cambay, Vijaynagar and other parts of Deccan.(76) It was mainly used by the doctors as medicine. There were about 1,416,15 kgs. of mirabolan exported between 1616 and 1618 to Portugal.(82)

Agate

In Arabic it is called Al-aquique, meaning Agate. It was found in place called Limadura in Gujarat.(83) It was said to have had the power to stop bleeding from any cut. It was in great demand by the Portuguese doctors. There were 1,101,45 kgs. of agate exported by them to Portugal during 1616-1618.(84)

Tamarind (Tamarinho)

Tamarind was collected from the regions of Malabar and Gujarat and was used in medicine in Portugal although in India it is used to give a taste to different dishes. In the sixteenth century, a substantial quantity was exported to Portugal.(85) But in the seventeenth century very little mention has been found. For instance in 1618, Portuguese factors acquired only 787 kgs. tamarind.(86)

Tutia

Tutia was brought from Arabian countries and exported to Portugal. It was used mainly by pharmacist and for the finishing of copper and zinc.(87) Very little volume was exported in the seventeenth century. Only 420 kgs. of tutia were dispatched by the Portuguese factor at Goa on the homeward bound carracks in 1616.(88)

Opium (Amfião / Opio)

This drug was brought from Malabar and Gujarat to the port of Goa and used by the chemists.(89) Some times people used it for intoxication too. It was, however, only a minor item in the trade to Europe. During 1622-23, there were only 70 balls of opium among the Portuguese export to Portugal.(90)

Areca Nuts

It was produced in Malabar and sent to many coastal regions of India.(91) It was used with pan (betel leaves) and also chewed for pleasure. Among the Portuguese export to Portugal during 1622-23, there were 1,680 kgs. of areca nuts on the ships.(92)

It can thus be seen that the Portuguese traded in about thirty varieties of items. Although they were far less important than the major spices they had their own choice and demand.

Therefore, when all the things in this chapter are considered, it can be said that saltpetre and precious stones, an unusual items of trade increased to a considerable volume while the interest of the merchants in other items were on decline. The third part has focussed on commodities used for multiple purposes. Though no one item was of great economic importance, cumulatively the minor commodities did assume considerable economic importance.

Notes

Saltpetre, Precious Stones and Sundry Items of Export

1. *India*, cx. 9, doc. 186; cx. 26, doc. 64; ACF, cod. 1163. fls. 48-49v.
2. *ACF*, cod. 1166. fls. 58, 65.
3. *Ibid.*
4. *ACF*, cod. 1161. fls. 166.
5. *Ibid.*
6. *Ibid.*
7. *Ibid.*
8. *ACF*, cod. 1162. fls. 144.
9. *ACF*, cod. 1162. fls. 212.
10. *Ibid.*
11. *ACF*, cod. 1162. fls. 144; *India*, cx. 11, doc. 44.
12. *Ibid.*
13. *ACF*, cod. 1163. fl. 116v.
14. *ACF*, cod. 1164. fl. 80.
15. *ACF*, cod. 1166. fl. 111v; cod. 1167, fl. 120.
16. *ACF*, cod. 1168. fl. 119v.
17. *ACF*, cod. 1161. fl. 166.
18. *ACF*, cod. 1162. fl. 212.
19. *India*, cx. 11, doc. 44.
20. See Appendix XII.
21. *ACF*, cod. 1163. fl. 116v.
22. *ACF*, cod. 1162. fl. 144.
23. See Chapter II, part II and III.
24. Winius, *The Fatal History*... pp. 51-54; Boxer, *Portuguese Seaborne*...,pp. 110-111.
25. *Ibid.*
26. See Appendix XIII; *ACF*, cod. 1166. fl. 128.
27. Boyajian, *Portuguese Bankers*..., p. 75; *India*, cx. 3, doc. 168; cx. 4, Doc. 25; cx. 5, doc. 164; cx. 9, doc. 73; cx. 11, 193.

28. *India*, cx. 11, doc. 193; cx. 12, doc. 19, Document no 9 shows the exact details about each bizalho and the owners name etc.
29. *Ibid.*; See Boyajian, *Portuguese Bankers...*, p. 141, 75.
30. *Ibid.*
31. Garcia de Orta, *Coloquios dos simples...*Vol. I, pp. 173-74.
32. *Ibid.*, p. 174.
33. *India*, cx. 4, docs. 25, 136.
34. *India*, cx. 5, docs. 164.
35. Barbosa, *The Book of Duarte Barbosa...*, vol. II, p. 228.
36. *India*, cx. 4, dos. 25; cx. 5, doc. 164; cx. 20, doc. 126; Garcia de Orta, *Coloquios dos simples...*Vol. II, pp. 5-6.
37. Barbosa, *The Book of Duarte Barbosa...*, vol. II, p. 228.
38. Tomé Pires, *Suma Oriental...*, vol. I, p. 83.
39. *India*, cx. 4, dos. 25; cx. 5, doc. 164.
40. Barbosa, *The Book of Duarte Barbosa...*, vol. II, p. 229.
41. See table 6.8.
42. Garcia de Orta, *Coloquios dos Simples...*Vol. II, pp. 81-83.
43. *India*, cx. 4, dos. 25.
44. *India*, cx. 20, dos. 126.
45. *India*, cx. 4, dos. 25; It is difficult to ascertain the size of a *Bizalho* or a *Saco* (Containers of the precious stones and diamonds).
46. *India*, cx. 11, dos. 41, 193.
47. Garcia de Orta, *Coloquios dos Simples...*Vol. II, pp. 42-43.
48. *India*, cx. 4, dos. 25.
49. *India*, cx. 11, docs. 41. 193.
50. Garcia de Orta, *Coloquios dos Simples...*Vol. I, pp. 54-55.
51. *Ibid.*
52. *India*, cx. 4 doc. 25.
53. *India*, cx. 11, docs. 193.
54. Garcia de Orta, *Coloquios dos Simples...*Vol. I, pp. 48-51.
55. *India*, cx. 5, doc. 164.
56. Garcia de Orta, *Coloquios dos Simples...*Vol. II, pp. 281-83.
57. *India*, cx. 5, doc. 164.
58. Garcia de Orta, *Coloquios dos Simples...*Vol. 1I, pp. 281-83.
59. *India*, cx. 4, docs. 25, 136.
60. *India*, cx. 5, docs. 164.
61. Garcia de Orta, *Coloquios dos Simples...*Vol. II, pp. 123, 131.

62. *India*, cx. 4, docs. 25, 136.
63. Garcia de Orta, *Coloquios dos Simples*...Vol. I, p. 84; Vol. II, pp. 34-36.
64. *India*, cx. 4, docs. 25.
65. Garcia de Orta, *Coloquios dos Simples*...Vol. I, p. 194.
66. *India*, cx. 12, doc. 3.
67. *India*, cx. 4, doc. 25; cx. 5, doc. 164.
68. *India*, cx. 5, doc. 164.
69. Garcia de Orta, *Coloquios dos Simples*...Vol. II, pp. 48, 351-57.
70. *Ibid.*
71. *India*, cx. 4, doc. 25
72. *India*, cx. 10, doc. 195.
73. *India*, cx. 8, doc. 192.
74. Moreland, From Akbar to..., (passim); Omprakash, *The Dutch Factories...*, pp. 1-21; Kail, *The Dutch...*, pp. 66-68.
75. *India*, cx. 4, doc. 25; cx. 5, doc, 164.
76. Garcia de Orta, *Coloquios dos Simples*...Vol. II, pp. 29-31.
77. See Chapter 1.
78. *India*, cx. 3, doc. 52; cx. 11, doc, 145.
79. *India*, cx. 20, doc. 126.
80. *India*, cx. 4, doc. 136; cx. 5, doc. 164.
81. *India*, cx. 3, doc. 52; cx. 11, doc. 145.
82. Garcia de Orta, *Coloquios dos Simples*...Vol. II, p. 154.
83. *India*, cx. 4, doc. 136; cx. 5, doc. 164.
84. Garcia de Orta, *Coloquios dos Simples*...Vol. II, p. 222-230.
85. *India*, cx. 4, doc. 136; cx. 5, doc. 164.
86. Garcia de Orta, *Coloquios dos Simples*...Vol. II, p. 319-20
87. *India*, cx. 5, doc. 164.
88. Garcia de Orta, *Coloquios dos Simples*...Vol. II, p. 301, 307, 359-61; António de Moraes Silva, *Diccionário*, vol. II, p. 948.
89. *India*, cod. 35, fls. 24-24v.
90. Tomé Pires, *Suma Oriental...*, vol. I, p. 83.
91. *India*, cod. 35, fls. 24v.

Plate 7 A Parsi from Bombay

Chapter - 7

Portuguese Imports into India

In order to buy Oriental goods, the king of Portugal, as already have been mentioned in previous chapters, dispatched regular funds under various heads. Still, when the authorities in India faced trouble in meeting the royal demands with the fixed amount of money, they imported certain precious things in exchange for the Indian goods. For instance, pepper and other spices could easily be bought with gold and silver bullion. These could be brought by supplying textiles and food grains. In this exchange of goods, the Portuguese officials imported various precious metals, stones, elephants, ivory, horses and so on, items which served their purposes during the seventeenth century. In his chapter I shall examine this practice including the imports of cash, precious metals, stones, elephants, ivory and other things keeping in view their origin, mode of procurements, the contractors or merchants who supplied them, their prices (if possible) and finally the details regarding their volume.

Import of Cash from Portugal

Although the import of cash under different rubrics has been discussed in previous chapters, it may be appropriate to give a summary of it here, too. In the beginning of the century, Portuguese officials imported cash ranging between 1,00,000 and 1,50,000 Ashrafis.(1) In the second decade this amount oscillated between 400,000 and 600,000 Ashrafis, and from the third decade onwards, it gradually declined because of the financial crisis of the King of Portugal, the rulers of Hapsburg dynasty who invested a lot of funds in his wars with Netherlands. During the third decade, as a lot of money was utilised to protect the Spanish crown from England, France and Holland's wars, the amount could remain to only around two to three hundreds of thousands of Ashrafis, and in the fourth, it was still short by around half of its former magnitude. The fifth and sixth decades indicate only 20 to 30% of the previous imports for the purchases of Indian commodities.(2) This timing coincides with the decisive battle for the future of the Asian colonies.

Import of Bullion (Gold)

The wealth brought Portugal was insufficient to buy the desired quota of Indian goods. For this reason, the Portuguese had to exploit various means to achieve the needed cash. They imported gold and silver from the various parts of the world by exchanging other commodities brought from Europe or purchase from India. Thus they brought with them from Europe a substantial volume of bullion in gold. This was quite profitable for the Portuguese. Usually the gold brought from the world market was minted at Goa. This process of minting fetched them more than 100% of profit. For example, if 5 paes of gold cost 10 Ashrafis, it was valued at 20 Ashrafis after minting. Usually, gold was brought from Mozambique, Monomotapa, China, besides that was brought from Portugal every now and then. It is believed that from African countries, especially from Monomotapa, there was regular import of gold every year.(3) Mozambique was also one of the countries from which they derived considerable imports. The gold business was handled by the agents of Vitula Sinai and Marca Sinai who set customarily Indian goods for exchange with gold during this period. It is very difficult to ascertain much about the prices of gold and the exact profits reaped by these businessmen. For instance, in 1660 a huge quantity of gold was imported from Mozambique to Goa at the rate of 315 Ashrafis per mark. But it is difficult if not impossible to know the exact weight of a mark. However, the following were the imports of gold during the first half of the seventeenth century:

Table 7.1

Import of Gold in Goa

YEAR	VOLUME	DIRECTION	SOURCES
1631	3 Bags	Monomotapa	*LML*, 15, fls. 45v-46v
1637	30 Paes	China	*ACF*, 1163, fl. 11
1639	100 Paes	China	*Ibid*, fl. 60
1640	141 Mark	Mozambique	*Ibid*, fl. 115
1641	11 Mark	Chaul	*Ibid*, fl. 173v.
1659	1,900 Matica	Mozambique	*ACF*, 1167, fl. 262
1663	1 Box	Portugal	*ACF*, 1168, fl. 130

Thus, having gone through the table of imports of gold bullion into Goa, one can assess that considerable gold was obtained and imported by means of exchange though it is not an exact figure. However, apart from these exports, there is scattered information regarding the traffic of gold during this period, but volume is not clear. For example, one of the Portuguese Viceroy, Conde de Linhares, suggests that there had been continuous import of valuable metals every monsoon from Monomotapa.(4) Again in 1631, in a letter to the captain of the fort of Monomotapa from the said Viceroy, it was instructed that at least 3 Pastas(5) of gold should be sent to Goa every year.(6) In 1637, it was decided by the Portuguese authorities at Macao that a continuous supply of gold should be sent to Goa and Cochin every year.(7) In the same year, out of 54 paes, 24 paes of gold was sold to a merchant in the city of Malacca to meet the expenditure of the defensive arms for the soldiers. This gold came from China to Goa via Malacca. It was during this time that the Dutch had systematically blockaded the ports of Goa and Malacca. Thus, all these details and the letters of the Viceroy indicate the fact a regular import of gold did exist during this period.

Import of Bullion (Silver)

Silver was another valuable metal, which, the Portuguese imported for the purposes of minting coins during the period under review. Generally, silver was imported from Mozambique Philippines and China. However, it is not evident through what method they procured it and the merchants who dealt in this transaction in this precious metal, but there are evidences that provide information regarding its trade. As late as 1650, it is reported that a large volume of silver was imported from Mozambique but the exact volume is ambiguous.(8) In 1653, there were 900,000 pesos in silver imported from China.(9)

Import of Copper

In the sixteenth century, copper was brought mainly for the minting of coins *Bazarucos* and *Reis* which was very profitable business.(10) But during the seventeenth century, apart from minting coins, it was also used when alloyed with tin for the founding of artillery to fight the enemy.(11) The exact situation during the seventeenth century as has already been discussed earlier, it is mentioned here to stress on the fact that this casting of cannon was only due to the pressure of war. However, it is reported that copper was brought from China, Japan and some unknown places during the great part of the seventeenth century, although it is not clear who the merchants or contractors dealing in this commodity were. Some inferences are found that during fourth decade, the Portuguese utilised the English merchants and their cargo ships for carrying copper from China.(12) Unlike the sixteenth century, prices of copper in this century were considerably higher. It was valued about 61 Ashrafis per quintal after incurring all expenditure at Goa.(13) Following were the imports during the first half of the seventeenth century:

Table 7.2

Import of Copper in Goa

YEAR	VOLUME in kgs.	DIRECTION	SOURCES
1617	52,450	China-Goa	*India*, 31, fl. 37v.
1623	157,350	China-Goa	*India*, 35, fl. 55-56v.
1624	52,450	China-Goa	*India*, 35, fl. 138-45.
1638	308,203	China-Goa	*India*, Cx. 12, doc. 51

Apart from these exports listed above, there were other imports. Since they are given in the original prices of China, it was difficult to convert them into normal rate and weights. Hence, my description has been made in the same form. For instance, in 1632, copper worth 3,000 *picos* was imported to Goa from China which later sent to Bassein shipyard for casting of artillery.(14) Similarly, in 1634, the import of copper from China was valued 15,000 *picos*(15) In 1639, it is reported that a huge quantity of copper was brought from China and Japan to Goa, but its quantitative details are missing in the document. This copper was brought to Goa via Bardes, which may be because of the blockade of the ports of Goa by the Dutch.(16)

Quicksilver and Leather Bags

Among the other imported goods, quick silver and leather bags can also be named. Usually they were brought from Mozambique to Goa. Although few details are found but scattered information could be obtained from some of the available sources. For example, in 1646, there was some consignment of quicksilver and leather bags kept ready for the cargo ships from Goa to Portugal.(17)

Precious Stones, Musk and Amber

The Portuguese imported some precious stones, pearl, musk and Amber also which were very much needed in the Indian empire and states by the Emperors and princes. They were brought mainly from Mozambique, Mombassa, and Hormuz by the merchants. Following were the imports of all these items in the seventeenth century:

Table 7.3

Import of Copper in Goa

YEAR	VOLUME	DIRECTION	SOURCES
1637	4 Mutras Aljofar	Hormuz	*ACF*, 1163, fls. 17-17v.
1649	7 Bags-Musk and Amber	Mozambique	*ACF*, 1165, fl. 77v.
1649	56 Bags Stones Bazares	Mozambique	*Ibid.*
1650	356 Ounces Amber	Mombassa	*ACF*, 1166, fl. 59v.

Import of Ivory into India

Ivory was also one of the profitable commodities during the period of this study. Every year the Portuguese merchants imported a considerable volume of this item into Goa. After the official formalities for the payment of duty were over, it was generally dispatched to Cambay or Surat, according to the contract. There were a number of noted artisans residing in these places who were experts in ivory work.

Contractors of Ivory

Import of ivory by the Portuguese was generally made through the private merchants under the Portuguese banner. Merchant contractors usually brought this item exclusively on their own risk and always had to pay duty. The most important businessman of this commodity during the first half of the century was Dom Estevão de Ataide, Captain-in-chief of Mozambique too participated in this trade by sending 80 bahars (about 13,304 kgs.) of ivory to Goa through his representative in August 1613.(18) Another contractor was Francisco Dias Barão, who brought more than 6,818 kgs. ivory and handed over to the *Alcaide-mor* of Goa, the official in charge of imports at the port f Goa, as per the rules.(19) António Coutinho was another ivory importer during this period.(20) Dr. Pedro Alves Pereira, one of the prominent men in Goa also participated in this trade. He was, probably, one of the privileged men of Goa who had been exempted from duty to be levied upon the goods he imported.(21) Besides all these contractors, Portuguese officials also participated in this trans-oceanic trade. For instance, the factor of the Mozambique fort was one of the officials who took part. In 1614, he sent about 23,282 kgs. of ivory to Goa at his own expense and paid the duty as other merchants did.(22) Martim Fernão de Castelo Branco, another official also took part in this trade during the third decade of the century.(23)

The merchants involved in the ivory trade obtained their consignment through some of their agents who collected ivory from the local hunters. Among such intermediaries, one Sebastião Fernandes can be named as a supplier to António Coutinho during the second decade of the seventeenth century.(24) Nuno Fernandes and Rui de Melo were the other middlemen who arranged cargoes for Dr. Alves Pereira during the second and third decades.(25)

During the second decade the prices paid by Dom Ataide for one kg. of ivory was about four and a half Ashrafis.(26) But later it can be ascertain that this rate went down to one and a half Ashrafis per kg.(27) This price of ivory remained stable until the end of the period under review.

Usually these merchants paid partially in Ashrafis or *Cruzados* and partly in gold bullion. Dom Ataide for example, paid in bullion worth 40,000 *Ashrafis* (6 mols) out of 56,500 Ashrafis to his men and agents during 1613-14.(23) Another mode of payment was through exchange for textiles from Cambay, where all ivory was consumed. Frequently, the entire ivory coming from Mozambique was re-shipped from Goa to Cambay or Surat for the purchase of textiles, which were then sent to Melindi through the Hindu merchants of Cambay, Balaghat or those of *Comlugo* or *Comliego.* This triangular arrangement save the merchants some outgoing duty levied by the *Estado da India.* For this reason the king of Portugal decreed to put a check on the practice, though to what effect, is unknown.

Volume of Ivory Import

Probably the demand of textiles from Mozambique and other African countries led to an increase in the volume of ivory imports. No doubt this became an important medium of exchange for the Gujarati commodities especially textiles and also provided heavy duties to the Portuguese state of India. It is found that in the seventeenth century, the latest year for which the information of import is available was 1613, though it continued intermittently till the third decade. Later, after 1626, trade was conducted only in 1644, after a pause of about eighteen years. Thereafter, it continued on until 1661 with some gaps. Details of the ivory imports into India especially on the port of Goa have been furnished here below:

Table 7.4

Imports of Ivory in India

YEAR	VOLUME IN kgs.	AMOUNT INVESTED IN Xs.	AREAS
1613	26,691	79,332	Mozambique
1614	23,282	69,246	Mozambique
1619	11,641	17,695	Mozambique
1620	2,308	3,476	Mozambique
1621	2,622	3,985	Mozambique
1625	1,232	1,870	Mozambique
1626	1,311	1,993	Mozambique
1644	944	1,432	Mozambique-Lisbon
1646	44,834	72,996	Mozambique-Diu
1650	1,229	1,846	Mombassa
1661	55,884 ?	84,944 ?	Mozambique
1661	34,642 ?	52,655?	Mozambique
Total	174,979	338-816	

Average for 11 years 15,907 kgs.

Thus, after having surveyed the table, it becomes evident that more than 50% of ivory was imported from Mozambique alone. It is not apparent how much was from Mombassa. The bulk of ivory imported from these African countries was stored at first at the house of Manuel Moraes in Goa and in due course it was sent to Cambay or Surat as per the contract. The reason for the dispatch of all the ivory to Cambay or other places in Gujarat was that the Indian artisans concentrated in this region were more skilled than any other that they enjoyed a de facto monopoly on producing ivory goods and therefore, no one could compete with them. The Portuguese, on account of their own monopolistic mentality frequently resorted to harassment and boycott to break the (counter) monopoly of the artisans though without success. In return, the Baniyas, especially from Diu, who had been supplying goods to foreign markets, lodged complaints with the king of Portugal as well as with the Viceroy at Goa. The king, probably being realistic enough to see the futility of attempts to break their monopoly, decreed that these artisans and Baniyas should not be harassed.(31)

Import of Elephants

Elephants were also imported into India by the Portuguese in order to exchange for certain goods. This was, in practice, assumed as royal transport. The pachyderms were sometimes brought for presentation to the local rulers mainly from Ceylon, as per their contract with the supplier of goods. According to one of the documents, each elephant cost about 2,166 Ashrafis.(32)

In the year 1633, three elephants were brought from the region of Manar in Ceylon to the port of Cochin, probably for presentation.(33) It is also reported that they were usually brought to the port of Cochin and only later sent to Goa. In addition, a few elephants were occasionally sent to Madurai from Ceylon for the purchase of saltpetre.(34) Similarly, it has been noticed that the Portuguese officials promised some merchants of Bengal who dealt in saltpetre, to provide elephants in return for their cargo.(35) In 1648, five elephants were sent as a present, three to the Nayak of Tanjore and two to the Nayak of Madurai, both for their services against the Dutch.(36) However, this never proved to be an item of regular import, at least during the period under discussion.

Import of Horses

In addition to the commodities listed above, occasionally horses were also imported into India by the local merchants with the permission of the Portuguese authorities. They were mainly needed by the soldiers and for royal use. For this reason the Portuguese authorities encouraged the local businessmen to import these animals. In fact, the Portuguese used to supply to local rulers with horses in order to insure continuity of their supply of various commodities.

Usually, Arabian and Persian horses were preferred and were considered to be of the best quality. However, in Kutch and Cambay, both of them in Gujarat, local merchants were also busy developing fine breeds, though they seem to have been less capable for working long hours without tiring. It is noted that there had been much import and few documents could be cited, but there seems to be a lack of sources in this regard. Generally, the merchants residing in Bassein handled this business. They usually brought horses and thence re-shipped to Goa. During this transaction, they had to pay duty twice on each consignment.

During the early decades of the seventeenth century about eighty horses were brought regularly to the port town of Bassein from Hormuz and the Arabian countries. But because of the duty, in 1616, they requested the Viceroy at Goa for an exemption on at least on eighty horses every year.(37) This request, however, was not considered as it would mean a loss of 12,000 Ashrafis per year.(38) But after a long discussion, the viceroy allowed them to import twenty-five horses free of duty every year as they were mainly brought for the use by the Portuguese soldiery.(39) Out of these twenty five, ten horses were permitted to be taken to the other region of India but remaining fifty five were to be imported only upon payment of duty.(40) But it seems that the merchants were not satisfied with decision and went on requesting more exemptions at least until 1622.(41)

In the same year, the Portuguese viceroy instructed the captain and the inhabitants of Daman to check carefully into the quality of the horses acquired while buying and supplying them.(42) Probably, there were hybrid as well as Arabian horses brought to the port of Goa. It is to be assumed that the merchants had developed the practice of keeping a stock of horses in the territories of Daman and Bassein. Since at the time of the great famine of Gujarat they died in great number, because of this reason, probably, the viceroy ordered them to desist from the practice.(43) In 1663, eighty horses were brought from Congo to the port of Bassein.(44)

Import of Slaves

Last but hardly least, slaves were of considerable importance in the Portuguese trade. The Portugese not only brought slaves to India but also took them to Portugal besides to Brazil, either captured from the ships in the ocean or purchased from Mozambique, Angola, São Jorge da Mina and other places.(45) During the sixteenth century, slaves were used for loading and unloading of the ships as well as for menial works in the hospitals.(46) But in the seventeenth century, besides being employed for carrying loads, they were trained to fight the Portuguese enemies at the time of shortage of soldiers, particularly when the Dutch-Portuguese wars reached their zenith.(47) To obtain slaves, they required a sufficient volume of textiles from India. As it has been seen earlier, the factor of India House sent cash for the purchase of Guiné cloths to exchange in *São Jorge da Mina*.(48) Though not much volume was found in the slave imported into India, but they did import a considerable number of them.

Though not extensive prices are found, it is believed that each male slave was valued to more than 100 to 105 Ashrafis during the third decade of the seventeenth century.(49) But as per the duty paid on each slave, i.e., forty Ashrafis, it becomes rather difficult to believe the cost of slave could have been so little.(50) Besides no detail exists regarding the mode of obtaining them or who the merchants were except that is dealt in Angola to be sent to Brazil throughout the whole century(51) and that other for one reference to the factor of Mina, Manuel Cunha, who sent some slaves on his own risk to Portugal in 1628.(52)

As reported, during the second half of the sixteenth century, the Portuguese trade in the African slaves reached a number 5,000 and 6,000.(53) However, it is quite surprising to note the number of slaves diminishing all of a sudden in the seventeenth century. Could be various reasons. Usually the age of the slaves or either sexes, male or female was limited to eighteen years only. But references are found that they were brought even below of the age limit.(54) This practice of the traders led to a heavy loss of life among the slaves while transporting them to India. When this was reported to the king of Portugal, he took appropriate measures in this regards.(55) Import of slaves below 18 years of age was declared a breach of law *(contra regimento)* and those involved in, were liable to be punished.(56)

In 1628, it was reported that a certain Turkish ship, which had slaves on board, attempted to enter the port of Diu without paying the necessary customs. The owners were penalised by 760 Ashrafis.(57) Besides, Manuel da Cunha, the factor of Mina sent twenty slaves to Portugal in the same year.(58)

After 1629, the only information regarding the import or trade in slaves is found for the year 1661, when some duty was paid at the customs house of Chaul as consequence of importing of some slaves, but the exact number is not ascertainable in the document.(59)

Thus, from this brief discussion it is clear enough that trade in slaves did exist, but the details regarding its real volume have yet to be unearthed.

Notes

Portuguese Imports Into India

1. For the first decade's import of money we can only depend upon the value of exported goods; Boyajian, in his book Portuguese *Bank ers at the Court of Spain*, p. 15, points out that about 500,000 cruzados of the proceeds of pepper was diverted by the King Philip II of Spain

to finance the wars in Flanders, thereby depriving the Goa-Lisbon trade.

2. See chapter 3 & 4 for the details of money imported and its decline.
3. *LML*, cod. 15, fls. 45v-46v.
4. *LML*, cod. 15, fls. 45v-46v.
5. It literally means a bag but how much it contained in weights are not known.
6. *LML*, cod. 28. fl. 280.
7. *LML*, cod. 41. fl. 174.
8. *ACF*, cod. 1166. fl. 57v.
9. *India*, cx. 22, doc. 6.
10. *Cartas*, tomo I, p. 413.
11. *ACF*, cod. 1162. fl. 42v-43.
12. *AHU*, cod. 35, fls. 55-56v.
13. *AHU*, cod. 35, fls. 55-56v.
14. *ACF*, cod. 1162. fls. 42-43.
15. *Ibid.*
16. *ACF*, cod. 1163. fls. 66-66v.
17. *ACF*, cod. 1164, fls. 66-66v.
18. *India*, cx. 2, doc. 93.
19. *India*, cx. 2, doc. 93.
20. *India*, cx. 2, doc. 93.
21. *LML*, cod. 8. fl. 33.
22. *India*, cx. 2, doc. 93.
23. *India*, cx. 9, doc. 43.
24. *India*, cx. 2, doc. 93.
25. *India*, cx. 9, doc. 43.
26. *India*, cx. 2, doc. 93.
27. *LML*, cod. 8. fl. 158.
28. *India*, cx. 2, doc. 93.
29. Probably name of a place from where the Portuguese had trade re lations. AHU, cod. 31, fls. 94-95; *LML*, cod. 9. fl. 158.
30. AHU, cod. 31, fls. 94-95; *LML*, cod. 9. fl. 158.
31. *LML*, cod. 31. fl. 263.
32. *ACF*, cod. 1162. fl. 65.
33. *ACF*, cod. 1162. fl. 65.
34. *India*, cx. 11, doc. 44

35. *ACF*, cod. 1164. fl. 116v.
36. *ACF*, cod. 1165. fl. 19.
37. *India*, cx. 4, doc. 117.
38. *India*, cx. 4, doc. 117.
39. AHU, cod. 31, fls. 82-83.
40. AHU, cod. 31, fls. 82-83.
41. *LML*, cod. 11. fls. 352-53.
42. *LML*, cod. 14. fl. 88; cod. 16, fl. 542.
43. *LML*, cod. 45, fls. 117-118; cod. 44, fl. 128.
44. *ACF*, cod. 1168. fl. 128v.
45. Boxer, *Portuguese Seaborne...*, pp. 84-105; Disney, *Twilight of the pepper...*, pp. 114-15.
46. Mathew, *Portuguese Trade...*, pp. 137-38; Godinho, *Os descobrimentos e a economia mundial...*, vol. II, pp. 547- 48.
47. See Chapter IV.
48. See Chapter IV.
49. AHU, cod. 38, fls. 107-8.
50. AHU, cod. 38, fls. 88.
51. AHU, cod. 38, fls. 107-8.
52. Godinho, *Os descobrimentos e a economia mundial...*, vol. II, pp. 547-48.
53. *LML*, cod. 12, fl. 546; cod. 13, fl. 207v; cod. 15, fls. 32v, 33v,
54. *LML*, cod. 12, fl. 546; cod. 13, fl. 207v; cod. 15, fls. 32v, 33v,
55. *LML*, cod. 12, fl. 546; cod. 13, fl. 207v; cod. 15, fls. 32v, 33v,
56. AHU, cod. 38, fl. 88.
57. AHU, cod. 38, fls. 107-108
58. *ACF*, cod. 1168. fl. 50.

Plate 8 An Indo-Portuguese Barber.

CHAPTER - 8

Finances and Financiers of the Portuguese Trade

The international turbulence dealt a severe blow to the Portuguese Crown's financial situation. Although, it was the main concern of the Spanish king to preserve the Portuguese territories in Asia was a main concern of the Spanish king besides all his preoccupation of the wars in the lowland countries, it affected the Portuguese resources also. Nevertheless, the foreign merchant contractors and bankers found it too risky to direct money at any kind of interest to the Portuguese as the enemies of Spain had turned out to be the enemy of Portugal and its colonial settlements. Though the king of Spain was in possession of some of the leading business magnates of the period, mostly the New Christians such as Manuel de Paz, Francisco Tinoco de Carvalho, Jorge Ribeiro Ciresma, Pero Gonçalves Brandão, and Rui Lopes da Silva had lived many years in India before settling in Madrid as Financiers, most of their wealth was utilised in order to maintain his own possession and resources in Europe than of the Portuguese *Estado da India*. All these bankers had lived and traded with Asia. It is impressive to note by what these merchants achieved in European finances- a realignment of European international payments from Mediterranean to an Atlantic network of exchange- and the importance of Asian enterprises as a source of their banking capital, mostly investing money in their own private trade than into the Portuguese official trade. And that is where the whole picture changes. One may have idea that the Portuguese international commerce was diminishing but in fact the official trade was transferred to unofficial one if not exclusively.(1) Besides all the direct involvement of the Portuguese bankers into the court of Spain, there were a few contractors showed some interest directly in the official trade, but it was too meagre to meet the requirements of Eastern colonies. Therefore, Lisbon had to scrape up funds for the purchase of the most profitable items of trade such as pepper, textiles, cinnamon and other goods. True, there was intermittent participation on the part of some European contractors who invested their wealth to obtain a supply. Still, the amounts sent from Portugal to Goa under various heads (see chapters 3 & 4) were not sufficient to provide for the desired procurements in the westbound fleets. Therefore, more funds had to be found in India itself. Here, some of the Portuguese merchants especially new Christians as well as the local merchants who had good financial bases were persuaded to take active interest in their maritime trade by providing cash on loan, commodities on credit and so on. Many of them indeed came forward with their cash and property. Moreover, the Portuguese relations with the Indian merchants and rulers had improved substantially during the one century old contacts. Quite a number of wealthy merchants joined hands with the Portuguese government and co-operated with their treasure and goods. Besides, when the expenditure on war-fare mounted and the demand for saltpetre increased, the state government put the income of the *Estado da India* at the disposal of the council of finance, for the fulfilment of the necessity. In this chapter I have intended to highlight the Portuguese financing of the maritime trade in the seventeenth century, their attempt to increase their financial resources by founding a new Portuguese commercial organisation. Special attention has been paid to shed some light on the Portuguese merchants who married and settled in India, and the Indian merchant financiers. Portuguese income for the Indian state through various sources together with its expenditure for the purchase of trading commodities- and in the end, the profit and loss on these commodities in the oceanic trade- will be thoroughly examined.

Import of Cash from Portugal

Seeing the dissension of the period and their inability to provide sufficient funds for the purchase of Indian goods, agents of the crown had categorised into rubrics the financing of *Estado da India*. This systematisation was made according to the importance and the value of the commodities. As has been earlier the case, pepper and textiles were among those that enjoyed special royal preference on the basis of their importance. The maximum amount during the first half of the seventeenth century was imported under the name *cabedal da pimenta*. There was about 60,14,630 Ashrafis imported from Portugal to India for the purchase of pepper.(2) In addition to it, about 9,84,572 Ashrafis were brought for the purchase of textiles.(3) And there were 84,000 Ashrafis sent from there for the maintenance of the *Estado da India*. Although these are only rough figures from the available source materials, they do establish a rough relationship. If so, the total import of money from Portugal was about 70,79,202 Ashrafis for the purchase of commodities as well as for the maintenance of the state. In fact this amount is little enough if employed for such a huge enterprise that the Portuguese purported to carry on. But it was a great deal if the situation and the troubles, which hindered their trading activities, are taken into consideration. However, the crown's grasp of the international turbulence can be noted by their effort to organise a *Companhia da India Oriental* on the pattern of the other European companies, in order to tap extra funds for the purchase of eastern goods and to meet the heavy expenditures for defence by raising 24,000,000 Ashrafis.(4) But all this ended in fiasco when the total balance decrease to 12,000,000 Ashrafis within a period of five years.(5) However, the troubles could not be remedied by any measure because the enemies were far united and powerful than the resources of the Portuguese crown.

European Financiers and the Portuguese Trade

From the very beginning of the sixteenth century, the king of Portugal had realised the financial inability of his nation to handle alone such a huge commercial enterprise. For this reason, even at the outset of the century he decreed and welcomed Portuguese as well as foreign merchants as participants in the overseas trade of Portugal with the East Indian sub-continent.(6) Throughout the sixteenth century, the Portuguese, German and Italian merchants took a very active part in the maritime trade of India by directing money on loan or outfitting their own ships under the Portuguese banner.(7) But by the end of the same century they kept away from Lisbon because of the increasing danger of war in both the Atlantic and Mediterranean except with the exception of few Germans and Italians group of merchants. (see chapter 1) Thus after the expiry of the Fuggers contract by 1621, they did not bother to renew it. Nevertheless, during the first half of the seventeenth century, very few foreign merchants could be found who were interested enough in the Portuguese Indian goods to loan money for its procurement. Here, therefore, I have tried to suggest the nature of the Portuguese involvement as well as that of foreign merchants in the Portuguese India trade where advancement of cash on loan or on the basis of contract was concerned.

Portuguese Merchant Financiers

Portuguese merchants had long been engaged in the royal activities with the eastern countries. But, as the risk or transportation due to burning and looting of ships increased, very few were willing to invest their cash, even at an exorbitant rate of interest.

In 1607, one anonymous Portuguese merchant alone invested 1,84,008 Ashrafis for the purchase of pepper.(8) In 1626, there was a group of 99 shareholders from Portugal collectively advanced 50,133 Ashrafis to buy pepper for the next year.(9) In the following year, the king of Portugal decreed for extra privileges for the bankers directing money to the crown and thus he could managed to get 400,000 Ashrafis from the Portuguese merchants alone.(10) This was the same year that the king of Portugal attempted to implement the idea of a Portuguese India Company. Therefore, it was probably in anticipation of such impending arrangement that the money was forthcoming. During the fourth decade, one big merchant, Jorge Lopes Henrique, provided the needs of the crown by subscribing more than 60,000 Ashrafis in cash, with a promise to buy his pepper in return.(11) Another banker who had previously given loan of about 10,000 *Cruzados* to the Portuguese government was contracted to purchase the whole stock of pepper from the India House during 1636-37.(12)

Thus, in brief, it can be said that this was far from satisfactory participation by the Portuguese bankers in the Portuguese trade as compared with that of sixteenth century.(13)

Italian Merchant Financiers

In the sixteenth century, Italian merchants, especially the Florentines, had played a vital role in shaping the Portuguese economy.(14) But during the seventeenth century, very nominal investment has been noticed by them, and it is certain that they began taking an increasing interest instead in the Indian commodities provided either by the north-west European or by the Arabs who in their attempt of revival of old caravan trade provided these goods to them.(15)

In 1610, António Fernandes Lucas Italiano along with twenty partners had contracted 11,523 quintals of Indian pepper and provided cash in advance. Among his twenty sharers, he alone had a fifty percent share, with the rest divided among others.(16)

In 1625, eight Genoese merchants signed a contract for indigo and pepper. The total amount invested in this deal was 171,000

Ashrafis. The first two Octavio Centevion and Carlos Estrata, had the biggest share of 28,500 Ashrafis each. The other six merchants, Vicencioses Coreafigo, I. Licimirca, Estevão Espinola, Pablo Agostimano, António Balbi, and Bartholomeu Espinola, each had a share of 19,000 Ashrafis.(17)

Another Italian, Francisco Bresaus, is found negotiating with the government during the fourth decade.(18) Henceforth, the name of the foreign merchants is not to be found in the documents. No wonder if they also feared a total loss because of the Portuguese war of independence from Spain.(19)

Merchant Financiers in India

Cash provided by the Portuguese crown together with the participation of private merchants in Portugal and southern Europe proved to be insufficient to meet the increasing demand of more funds during the first half of the seventeenth century. The general instability following the succession crisis had played havoc with the financial situation of the Portuguese government and few chose to invest in such a risky business. Presumably, the Portuguese officials then found adequate reasons for approaching the merchants and financiers in Asia, both among Portuguese settlers on credit from them. More over, the king of Portugal instructed the officials in India to extend all facilities to those interested in allocating funds to the Portuguese crown.(20) A number of Portuguese and Indian merchants residing on the western coast set forth to finance the crown with all possible means. In the following passage I have attempted to describe first the co-operation of the Portuguese financiers settled in Indian and then that of Indian merchants bankers both New Christian and non-Christians.

Portuguese Merchant financiers in India

There were two kinds of Portuguese financiers, the *castiços* and *mestiços* settled in the Portuguese colonies besides of the New Christians who actively helped the Portuguese government whenever it was required. But, normally as Pearson has pointed out, "it is difficult or impossible to make out difference between the local converts and the *castiços* and *mestiços*- João de Souza for example could be either".(21) But somehow I have tried to differentiate between the local converts or the New Christians and the Portuguese blood as far as it could be possible. For example, Sancara da Gama, who was the brother of Timappa Nayak, was obviously a New Christians. Though it is clear through sources that these businessmen were regular suppliers of merchandises and allocating funds for the Portuguese maritime commerce, it has been quite difficult to find the participation of each merchant banker's share per year, I bring the maximum information available in the Portuguese sources.

Garcia de Melo

He was one of the biggest merchants dealing in the pepper trade in India during the early seventeenth century. He was a resident of Cochin. In 1606, he assisted the *Estado da India* by tiding it over with a loan of 1,25,000 Ashrafis for the purchase of pepper pending the arrival of ships from Portugal with the cash.(22) The percentage of interest was stipulated at about 13.5 percent.

Pascoal Rodrigues & Rama da Gama

They were some of the leading businessmen of pepper from Kanara. For years, they were associated with Portuguese. Very often furnished the demands of the pepper from Kanara on credit. But once in 1618, the Portuguese authorities, however, could not clear up their dues of 12,000 Ashrafis till 1642.(23) Because of this reason, nevertheless, after completing their contract with the Portuguese in 1628, refused to supply any amount of pepper to them. There complaints to both the King of Portugal and the local authorities were not attended in due course of time.(24)

Manuel da Fonseca

He was one of the *casados* e *moradores* (married and settled) in Goa. Like others, he also dealt mainly in Kanara pepper. During 1617-18, he provided a loan of 22,526 Ashrafis to the Portuguese authorities for the purchase of pepper from Kanara.(25)

Jerónimo da Costa

He was among other big merchants who allocated cinnamon from Ceylon. As the purchases had to be made prior to the arrival of the ships, the Portuguese officials needed funds in order to keep the merchandises ready for the ships. In 1621, the Portuguese shortage of cash was met by this businessman who arranged about 76,000 Ashrafis.(26)

Dom Jerónimo de Azevedo

Most probably a fidalgo resident in Goa, financed the Portuguese activities in trade during most part of the sixteenth and the early seventeenth centuries. In 1621, like others, he too provided a loan of 77,580 Ashrafis to the *Fazenda Real* (the royal treasury at Goa) when the authorities required for some necessary expenditures.(27) But to his surprise his complaints were unattended for long time for his debt.(28)

Francisco de Melo

Not only were the Portuguese residents, *castiços* and *mestiços* involved in loaning money and goods to the nominees of the of Portugal, but some of the Portuguese officials also took active part in financing the government in the East. Francisco de Melo was a *provedor da fazenda* real (overseer of the goods) at Goa, was one of the officials who provided goods on loan to the Portuguese state. He supplied about 603 quintals of pepper from his personal account to be dispatched on the annual ships in 1622.(22)

Dom Diogo Coutinho

He was another merchant financier who directed 29,694 Ashrafis to the royal treasury in 1624 for the purchase of goods and to meet the necessary expenditures.(31)

Gaspar Fernandes and António de Pinto da Costa

They can be named among the rice traders. Though helped the government in the procurement of this commodity whenever it was needed, the only information about their participation I could find out is in 1632 when his money was given back which was about 6,000 Pardaos.(32)

Rui Dias da Cunha

He often assisted the Portuguese authorities in providing pepper on credit that had been purchased by his own money. In 1627, the only year for which I got the information, supplied about 5,821 quintals of pepper, bought from Kanara and Malabar for the Portugal-bound ships. (33)

João Serrão da Cunha

He was a cinnamon trader and resident of Goa. Along the years he accompanied the Portuguese maritime activities besides in 1635 he allocated more than 235,000 Ashrafis apart from cinnamon, which he gave on credit.(34)

Jerónimo Lucena Tavora

He too dealt in cinnamon and during 1646-47 furnished the cargo ships with 2,095 quintals of cinnamon on credit on a promise that he could be paid back only after the arrival of the annual ships from Portugal.(35)

António Correia

In 1651, he gave more than 750 quintals of pepper of Kanara on credit to the Portuguese government in India.(37)

Indian Merchant Financiers

Indian merchants and bankers were not less important than the above-mentioned Portuguese financiers in financing the *Estado da India*. After a century of commercial contacts with the dealers of the Indian merchandises, the Portuguese had created sufficient confidence among them. The king of Portugal despite his distaste for the local merchants especially the non-Christian's participation in the oriental merchandises, came to realise that it was quite impossible to obtain the necessary commodities for his annual cargo ships on his own cash in a moment when due to the risk, the participation of the European financier started decreasing and the brutal inquisition led the New Christians and Jews run away from the Portuguese provinces. Therefore, he had to issue various orders for their good treatment.(38) The following were the merchant bankers who dealt with the Portuguese in the difficult years in India and Indian Ocean.

Govinda and Pandya Chatim

Though the exact genealogy of these two merchants could not be traced out except for Goinda e Pondia, in the Portuguese sources, they were settlers of Goa, owning several business houses. But it is certain that they dealt in pepper and supplied, occasionally, on credit to the Portuguese. For instance in 1607 they sold pepper worth 1,50,000 Ashrafis.(39) Though they had to complain several times to the King of Portugal for the return of this amount and finally they got back along with its interest of about 47,000 Ashrafis in 1613.(40) Somehow, Govinda was paid 1,27,000 Ashrafis and Pandya claimed 70,000 Ashrafis.(41)

Jasrath Parekh and Goraji Bania

Presumably Gujarati merchants having business houses in Goa. They used to exchange commodities like textiles with pepper and other spices. But they provided textiles to the Portuguese. During 1615-16, they met the Portuguese demand for textiles on credit.(42)

Narsu Sinai

After the refusal of Pascoal Rodrigues in 1628 for the further supplying of Kanara pepper, Narsu Sinai signed a contract for the provisioning of Kanara pepper over a period of five years. During the tenure of his contract, Narsu Sinai provided all the volume collected through his agents from the various parts of Kanara and supplied them for cash as well as on credit. In 1635, he gave a loan of 7,500 Ashrafis to his agent to buy pepper and give that to the Portuguese factor at Goa.(43)

Timappa Nayak

After the completion of Narsu Sinai's contract, he was assigned the contract to supply pepper.(44) He too, like others, had relation in both the terms, credit and cash. At the beginning of his contract during the late years of forty's, furnished the Portuguese ships with 1,310 quintals of pepper on credit.(45)

Sancara da Gama

He was brother of Timappa Nayak, and appears to had been converted to Christianity and also dealt in pepper trade. After his brothers' contract was over, he carried on with the supply of pepper to the Portuguese. In 1641, he gave 375 quintals of pepper on credit(46) and in 1642, allocated funds for the purchase of pepper from some other region (47) as he himself could not do.

Vitula Nayaka (Vithal Nayaka)

A rice and saltpetre trader during 1629-59, at Barcelore and dealt with the Portuguese for long time. In 1629, as per the sources, besides other items, furnished rice and some cash on credit for the provisioning of the fortresses and factories.(48) Again in 1652 and 1656, he provided the Portuguese government with, 5,000 quintals of saltpetre for the preparation of gunpowder to fight the 'interlopers' during this period.(49)

Rama Queny

Another merchant of rice from Mangalore. In 1635, he loaned 12,000 Ashrafis to the Portuguese authorities for the purchase of commodities from different regions as he himself could not do so.(50)

Pallu Nayaka, Vishnu das Sinai

It is believed that they were partners in business and lent money on interest to the Portuguese government. Vishnu das Sinai was brother of Nagorca Sinai. They loaned about 9,000 Ashrafis to the Portuguese authorities in Goa for the purchase of saltpetre.(51)

Bengali Muslims

Even the Muslims were also not left apart. Bengali Muslims, whose name, and origin is not found but they dealt in saltpetre of Bengal with the Portuguese during the fourth decade of the century. In 1640 they extended their support with saltpetre worth

18,000 Ashrafis and demanded elephants in return.(52) It is, somehow, known that they neither received the money nor the elephant even after their period was over for which they lodged a complaint to the King of Portugal.(53)

Anonymous Bankers

In 1617, it is reported that a certain banker gave 5,000 Ashrafis to the *conselho da fazenda* on an interest of 13.5%.(54) In 1626, the king expressed his gratitude to the Hindus, whose identity is not found, for providing the Portuguese authorities a loan of 32,000 Ashrafis.(55) In 1643, one other financier, gave 28,500 Ashrafis to the state on interest.(56)

Baniyas of Hormuz

Not only did the Indian merchants provided cash on loan for the purchase of Indian commodities but also Baniyas settled in the fort-city of Hormuz. In the early seventeenth century these Baniyas gave a certain, unspecified, amount to the Captain of the fort of Hormuz.(57) It was only in 1616 when they complained to the King that it came to the knowledge. Somehow, it was not before 1661 that their dues were repaid.(58)

Casa da Misericordia (House of Charity)

This was an important institution from which the Portuguese official often took loans to defray the expenditures of the *Estado da India* and for the purchase of spices. During the government of Fernão de Albuquerque (1619-1622), money was twice borrowed from *Misericordia* at Goa. The first time, the viceroy took about 200,000 *Cruzados* (about 270,000 Ashrafis) which was spent in purchasing pepper and other spices.(59) Till the period of Conde de Linhares (1629-1635) this amount was not given back.(60) Another big amount taken during his period was about 197,000 Ashrafis which was to be used in founding the artillery.(61)

The *misericordia* attached to the Church of Saint Francis Xavier at Cochin was another place from where the authorities drew money for necessities. In the year 1616, about 19,000 Ashrafis were borrowed on interest from this place.(62) Although instructions were also issued to borrow money from their in 1623,(63) it is not certain whether they actually did. In 1630, 15,000 Ashrafis were again borrowed from this institution for the purchase of rice in the vicinity of Cochin.(64) The last information that could be derived is for 1651. The Portuguese factor at Cochin borrowed from there about 15,000 Ashrafis for the purchase of cinnamon from Ceylon.(65)

Other Sources of Finance

Apart from the sources mentioned above, there were various others, which were exploited for the sake of the trade. Income of the *Estado da India* from different bureaus such as customs, minting of coins, issuance of *Cartazes* and so on, were utilised for the continuation of the trade.

(i) Revenue of the State

It is quite difficult to say any thing precisely about the exact revenue of the state from all the sources because of unsystematic or fragmentary nature of the documents available, a vague idea could be drawn out of it about the total income. The exact revenue, as far as our information goes, of the whole Goa area, consisting of Ilhas -Bardez and Salssete- was in 1600, around 406,299 Ashrafis; in 1616-17, 550,107 Ashrafis in 1635, 668,359 Ashrafis; around 1680, 359,579 Ashrafis. For the whole of Portuguese India-from East Africa to Malacca, the receipt were around 1600, 1,185,202 Ashrafis; in 1635, 1,185,264; around 1680, 731,828 Ashrafis. The listed expenses of the whole state in these three years were: 785,592 Ashrafis; 1,185,264 Ashrafis and 454,663 Ashrafis.(66) Thus, one gains a glimpse of the income and the expenditure of the whole estates of the Portuguese Asia.

(ii) The Customs Duties

The *Alfandega,* or the customs house, was one of the most reliable sources of income for the Portuguese government in India. On all the import and export of goods, the Portuguese authorities imposed taxes. By a letter of 1619, a fixed rate of customs duty on almost all the commodities are given.(67) The account book of customs was made ready by the end of every week and it was presented to the chief accounts officer.(68) Customs duty derived on each commodity was imposed in the following manner:

While importing pepper in Goa, 23 *Barganis* were paid on each Khandi and half *Bargani* to the *Dangui*(69) (probably some post) and clerk each. Customs duties differed to the quality and value of cloths by area. For example, textile imported from Balaghat and entering in the land of Salsete would pay two and a half pagoda on each 100 pagoda worth of cloths and 2 *Larins* for stamping and evaluation by the Dangui. All the cloths brought from the side of Bicholim and Ponda on boats, would pay on each 100 *Pagodes* three and a half and two *Larins* to the clerk and Dangui. Besides this, all other commodities yielded about two to twelve

Leals depending upon the category.(70) Thus, from *Alfandega* a sizable sum was driven which could be used in the purchase of commodities and other expenditures of the state.

(iii) Income from Minting and Issuance of Cartazes

Soon after the capture of Goa in 1510 by Albuquerque, the necessity of minting coins for the purchase of Indian commodities was understood.(71) At the end of the same year, a *Casa da Moeda* (or mint house) was founded by Albuquerque there and began striking coins. Initially these coins were named *Manuel, Esperas,* half *Esperas* and *Leals* respectively.(72) The *Manuel* or *Cruzado* was of gold, and was meant to replace *Pagodas* or *Huns* which were widely circulated before the arrival of the Portuguese. Along with the Manuel, there was a meio Manuel (half Manuel) in gold, and there was also *Esperas* and *meia-Esperas* issued in silver.(73) In 1519, the issue of these coins was suspended on order of the then governor of Goa. Thereafter, only in 1549, were gold and silver coins again minted. At that time, a new coin was also introduced in India. It was named as *São Tomé*. Later, among the silver coins *Tangas* and half *Tangas* and gold coins, *Ashrafis,* of 300 *réis,* were issued during the reign of Dom Sebastian (1557- 1578).(74)

All these coins were in circulation with a slight change in weight and value in the seventeenth century. In the meantime, copper coins called *Bazarucos* had already been introduced.(75) As the workload increased on the Goa mint house, in 1611, at Bassein and Daman, two more mint houses were opened for the issuance of copper coins. Later one *Tutenaga* coins were also struck from these mints. Thereafter, a mint was established at Chaul but was not much in use.(76)

The Portuguese used to make much profit by minting of coins. For instance, out of one quintal of copper, which valued in the beginning of the sixteenth century at 18.5 *Ashrafis* a quintal, the government fetched 32 *Ashrafis* if minted into coins.(77) Then during the period of viceroy Martim Afonso de Sousa, (1542-45) for the first time it rose to an exorbitant rate of 48 *Ashrafis* when the purchase price of copper was only 24 to 25 *Ashrafis* a quintal.(78) It went on oscillating in the seventeenth century. The rate of copper per quintal in the early seventeenth century was about 61 *Ashrafis*.(79) As just noted, in the sixteenth century, the profit value of each quintal was about 100%. It grew to between 100 and 120 percent in the early seventeenth century.(80) But because of much fluctuation in its price and devaluation of copper coinage, it was not much accepted by the local merchants because they feared big losses and preferred to accept only the gold or silver coins. On the gold and silver coins too the Portuguese *casa da moeda* derived a profit of 80 to 100 percent.(81) Thus, it is quite obvious that minting of coins in India yielded reasonable income to the treasury of Goa.

Issuance of *cartazes* was another prime source of income of the Portuguese *Estado da India*. As it has been seen in previous chapters, the merchants and rulers interested in coastal and transoceanic trade were obliged to get a *cartaz* for their ships to sail. The Portuguese charged a substantial amount on each *cartaz* from the ship owner.

However, it brought much more money to the Portuguese exchequer. They received half of the income from this sources and half from the customs houses as was the case in the sixteenth century.(82) In the seventeenth century, the number of *cartazes* issued also increased.(83) In this way it can be noted that the income from the *cartazes* or due to the *cartazes* also added to the income of the Portuguese in the east.

Trading Commodities and the Profit derived on them

In this section an attempt has been made to highlight the purchase prices of the commodities in Asia and their sale at the *casa da India*, with the profits reaped on them.

(i) Pepper Price in India

There were a lot of fluctuations in the purchase prices of pepper in the southwest of India due to the competitions during the period of this study. As it has been already discussed in the chapter three that during the first decade of the seventeenth century it was between 10.5 and 12.4 *Ashrafis* per quintal; during the second decade, it rose between 12.5 to 19 *Ashrafis* per quintal; while in the third and the fourth decades, it was around 24.5 or a little less. The maximum price paid by the Portuguese during the first half of this century was some thing between 28 and 35 *Ashrafis* a quintal.(84)

(ii) Freight Charges from India to Portugal

It is noted in the available sources that during the first three decades, the expenditure on the transport per quintal of pepper from India to Portugal was about 35 to 40 percent. But during the last decades of the first half of seventeenth century it rose to between 45 to 60%.(85) Thus when a quintal of pepper, with an average purchase rate of 12-13 *Ashrafis*, after reaching Portugal cost between 18 and 20 *Ashrafis*, and with the rate of twenty *Ashrafis* average price, it presumably cost between 28 and 30 *Ashrafis* at Lisbon.

(iii) Sale Price of Pepper at Lisbon

During the last decade of the sixteenth century, at Lisbon, pepper was sold between 75.5 *Ashrafis* and 79.5 *Ashrafis* per quintal to a few big merchant contractors-Konrod Rott, Rovellasca and Adnré Ximenes.(86) This price continued more or less till the fourth decade of the seventeenth century.(87) For the sixth and the early years of the seventh decades, details are not found. However, on the basis of the documents available for the period just mentioned, it can be calculated that in the early years the profit reaped by the Portuguese was on the order of 250 to 300 percent and at least never less than 250%. But as the situation of the Portuguese commerce deteriorated through the glutted circumstances of the European market, sale prices went down heavily, particularly for the Portuguese pepper. At the same time, as has been seen, the purchase prices in the Indian sub-continent were increasing. Thus, it can be assumed that the profit gained by Portugal was far less than in the early decades of the century. The total export of pepper from Goa to Lisbon per year was between 9,000 and 10,000 quintals with 18 *Ashrafis* come to 162,000 along with freight charges, which derives a profit of 553,500 *Ashrafis* per year, or something more or less.

Cinnamon

Cinnamon was another profitable items of the Portuguese monopoly trade during the seventeenth century. Cinnamon's purchase price during the second and the third decades oscillated between 9 and 11.5 *Ashrafis* per quintal, (88) during the fourth decade it went up to between 12 and 25 *Ashrafis*.(89)

(i) Freight Charges

On the cinnamon also, like pepper, their freight charges were about 35 to 42 percent on each quintal.(90) Thus the cinnamon cost in Ceylon around 10 and *Ashrafis* per quintal, valued between 16 and 18 *Ashrafis* at Lisbon or a maximum of 25 *Ashrafis* per quintal.

(ii) Sale Prices at Lisbon

According to a valuable sources, the sale price of cinnamon during the third and the fourth decades is gathered about 98 to 137 *Ashrafis* per quintal.(91) Nevertheless, if this is assumed to be the standard rate, then the profit will not amount to less than between 400 and 500 percent which was still higher than the profit derived from pepper. Since this was comparatively less in demand than pepper, its volume was also less. It averaged about 2,500 to 3,000 quintals per year. Thus, a rough picture of profit can be drawn at some thing around 241,500 *Ashrafis* per year at the rate of 98.5 *Ashrafis*.

The foregoing discussion may enable one to understand that the Portuguese king and his men exploited various means to finance the Asian trade during the seventeenth century. After using his own resources to finance the trade, he welcomed the private merchants, both from Portugal and the other European countries. In India the Portuguese authorities were thereafter instructed to seek help from the Portuguese settlers as well as from the local business class people. Baniyas settled in Hormuz also did not fail to extend their aid. Finally, the treasury of Goa under the authority of the ministers of the council of finance extended maximum support to the crown. Nevertheless, the profit reaped by the Portuguese had also a considerable impact on its economy. The international turmoils affected adversary the profit of the Portuguese crown on its Indian goods but it did survive.

Notes

Finances and Financiers of the Portuguese Trade

1. See Boyajian, *Portuguese Bankers at the Court of Spain*, (passim). The book provides a clear picture of the participation of the Portuguese merchant bankers in the official as well as unofficial trade. Also see *India*, cx. 12, doc. 19.
2. See Chapter 3
3. See Chapter 4
4. See Chapter 3
5. See Chapter 3.
6. ANTT, *Corpo Cronologico*, 1-3-20; Mathew, *Portuguese Trade...*, pp. 157-158.
7. F. Falcão, *Livro em que se..*, pp. 55-75; BSGL, Res. Maço 4, No. 88, docs. 1-25; Virginia Rau, *Um grande mercador...*, No. 24, pp. 4-5.
8. BSGL, Res. Maço 4, No. 88, docs. 18/1-3.
9. *India*, cx. 9, doc. 113.
10. AHU, cod. 37, fls. 3, 8.
11. *India*, cx. 12, doc. 1
12. *India*, cx. 11, doc. 31.

13. Mathew, *Portuguese Trade...*, pp. 179.
14. Mathew, *Portuguese Trade...*, pp. 158-62; Virginia Rau, *Um grande mercador...*, No. 24, pp. 4-10.
15. Lach, *Asia in the Making...*, vol. I, part I, pp. 131-142.
16. BSGL, Res. Maço 4, No. 88, doc. 21/2.
17. *India*, cx. 8, doc. 116.
18. B.Ajuda, *Jesuitas..*, No. 46-XIII-30; *India*, cx. 8, doc. 38.
19. See Chapter 2.
20. ANTT, *Corpo Cronologico*, 1-3-20; *LML*, cod. 31, fl. 263.
21. Pearson, 'Indigenous Dominance, in *Mare Luso-Indicum* pp. 61-73.
22. *India*, cx. 2, doc. 87.
23. *India*, cx. 2, doc. 87.
24. *India*, cx. 9, doc. 177; cx. 12, (Passim); B.Ajuda, *Jesuitas..*, No. 46-XIII-30; fls. 21-24; 32-33; *LML*, cod. 16, fls. 183-84; cod. 17, fls. 20-20v; cod. 23, fl. 301; cod. 26, fl. 264; cod. 28, fl. 370; cod. 30, fls. 186-186v, 294- 294v; cod. 52, fl. 182; cod. 55, fls. 182, 380v.
25. *Ibid.*
26. *India*, cx. 9, doc. 177; *LML*, cod. 13a, p. 176.
27. *India*, cx. 9, docs. 20, 85; *LML*, cod. 23, fl. 285; *ACF*, cod. 1162. fls. 238-238v.
28. *India*, cod. 32, fls. 180v-182.
29. *Ibid.*
30. *India*, cx. 9, doc. 177; *LML*, cod. 13a, fls. 176-79; *ACF*, cod. 1161. fls. 133v-134.
31. *Ibid.*
32. *LML*, cod. 30, fls. 230-230v.
33. *LML*, cod. 24, fls. 57-57v, 58v, 369; *ACF*, cod. 1161. fls. 1-1v.
34. AHU, cod. 40, fls. 146v-47.
35. *LML*, cod. 55, fl. 216; cod. 57, fl. 195. *ACF*, cod. 1166, fls. 34v-35.
36. *ACF*, cod. 1161, fls. 4v, 24v.
37. *ACF*, cod. 1161, fl. 63.
38. *LML*, cod. 31, fl. 263.
39. *India*, cx. 3, doc. 40.
40. *India*, cx. 3, doc. 400.
41. *India*, cx. 3, doc. 40.
42. *India*, cx. 4, doc. 50.
43. *ACF*, cod. 1162, fls. 182-83.
44. *ACF*, cod. 1162, fls. 198, 204, 206v-7, 212, 215; *LML*, cod. 33, fl. 254-254v.

45. *ACF*, cod. 1162, fls. 198, 204; 206v-7, 212, 215; *LML*, cod. 33, fl. 254-254v.
46. *ACF*, cod. 1163, fls. 130-30v, 150-50v, 153, 155-56v, 160-60v,
47. *ACF*, cod. 1163, fls. 130-30v, 150-50v, 153, 155-56v, 160-60v, 202, 219, 226.
48. *ACF*, cod. 1162, fls. 88-89v.
49. *ACF*, cod. 1166, fl. 111v.
50. *ACF*, cod. 1162, fl. 170.
51. *ACF*, cod. 1162, fl. 212.
52. *ACF*, cod. 1163, fl. 116v.
53. *ACF*, cod. 1163, fl. 116v.
54. *India*, cx. 4, doc. 186.
55. *LML*, cod. 23, fls. 209, 211.
56. *India*, cx. 15, doc. 28.
57. *LML*, cod. 9, fls. 188, 189, 30-306v.
58. *LML*, cod. 9, fls. 188, 189, 30-306v.
59. *LML*, cod. 18, fls. 20-20v; cod. 19, fls. 54-54v; cod. 20, fl. 215; *India*, cx. 9, doc. 98.
60. *LML*, cod. 18, fls. 20-20v; cod. 19, fls. 54-54v; cod. 20, fl. 215; *India*, cx. 9, doc. 98.
61. *India*, cx. 8, doc. 98.
62. *LML*, cod. 17, p. 29.
63. *LML*, cod. 17, p. 29.
64. *ACF*, cod. 1162, fl. 124.
65. *ACF*, cod. 1165, fls. 69v-70.
66. *India*, cx. 6, Account of August 19, 1618; AHU, *Rendas de Goa*, Res. (passim); F. Falcão, *Livro em que se..*, pp. 75-78.
67. *ACF*, cod. 1160, fls. 147-151.
68. *ACF*, cod. 1160, fls. 147-151.
69. In the document it is mentioned-O *DDangui*- most probably it is a post. His duty was to help the custom officers providing the neces sary information regarding evaluation of the goods etc.
70. *ACF*, cod. 1160, fls. 147-151.
71. Barros, *Dácada*, II, part I, p. 558-59; *APO-CR*, Fasciculo II, p. 179; Fasc. V, p. 6.
72. *Comentàrios de Affonso de Albuquerque*, parte II, Capt. XXV; J. Gerson da Cunha, *Contribuição...*, pp. 18-20.
73. *Ibid*.
74. Da Cunha, *Contribuições...*, pp. 20-27.
75. Da Cunha, *Contribuições...*, pp. 22-74 See Appendix V.

76. *LML*, cod. 11, fls. 548-49; Ferrão Vaz, *Dinheiro Luso-Indiano..*, p. 133; T. Aragão, *Descripção geral e História..*, vol. I, (passim)
77. Cartas, tomo I, p. 413; APO-CR, Fasciculo II, V, parte I, pp. 8-9; *ACF*, cod. 1161, fls. 138-138v; cod. 1162, fl. 21; cod. 1167, fls. 178v-179, 250v.
78. Da Cunha, *Contribuições...*, pp. 46.
79. *India*, cod. 35, fls. 55-56v, 83v-84, 138-140, 142-145.
80. Refer to F. Note nos. 77, 78.
81. *ACF*, cod. 1160, fls. 65-65v; cod. 1161, fls. 170-71; cod. 1166, fl. 42; *India*, cx. 10, docs. 13, 22.
82. Cartas, tomo I, p. 133, 251, 409; AHU, cod. 1043, fls. 54-104.
83. AHU, cod. 1043, fls. 54-104.
84. See Chapter 3, tables 3.3 - 3.5.
85. *Ibid.*; *LML*, cod. 13a. fls. 164-79.
86. See Chapter 5; BSGL, Res. Maço 4, No. 88, doc. 6/6; F. Falcão, *Livro em que se..*, pp. 75-80.
87. See Chapter 3; *India*, cx. 13, docs. 31.
88. See Chapter 5; *India*, cx. 2, doc. 82; cx. 8, doc. 192.
89. See Chapter 5; *India*, cx. 8, doc. 101; cx. 12, doc. 140; *ACF*, cod. 1162, fl. 123; cod. 1163, fl. 5; cod. 1165, fls. 62, 84, 87; cod. 1166, fls. 34-35.
90. *ACF*, cod. 1163, fl. 5.
91. *India*, cx. 8, doc. 192.

Plate 9 An Indo-Portuguese Tailor.

CHAPTER - 9

Impact of the Portuguese Trade and Conclusion

Portuguese trade during the seventeenth century brought several changes in the world economy in general and in the Indian economy in particular. The commercial revolution of the sixteenth century had introduced multi-dimensional changes in the pattern of the world's trade and commerce.(1) The most important international enterpots like Alexandria, Aleppo, Beirut, on the Asian sub-continent; Venice and other ports in Europe suffered immensely, if they were not completely ruined.(2) All the trade normally conducted through these ports was diverted via Cape of Good Hope and centralised at Lisbon, a port hardly known to the world before the discovery of the new sea route to India. All the distributive traders of Europe who once depended mostly on the merchants of Venice for their supply of spices and pepper, inevitably turned their faces towards Lisbon reasonably because the Portuguese left no choice.(3) The Germans and the Italians settled their trading posts and warehouses in Lisbon. Many trading factories were opened in the north and north-east of Europe such as in Antwerp, Hamburg, Levant and Geneva, by their agents for the distribution of the commodities in the European countries.(4) Throughout the sixteenth century, Lisbon remained one of the most important trading centres of the world- in spite of a certain revival of the Arab-Mediterranean spice trade.(5)

By the end of the sixteenth century, this situation took a new turn. The incorporation of Portugal into Spanish crown doomed the port of Lisbon. Because of the conflicting Spanish-Dutch relationships, king Philip II of Spain (I of Portugal) severed the Portuguese trading links with the Dutch and virtually invited the Dutch to encroach with ever-greater boldness on the Portuguese overseas preserves that Philip sought to keep as his monopoly. Though Lisbon remained as commercial headquarters in the seventeenth century, most European merchants feared sending their ships to this port and avoided any direct transactions.(6)

The Dutch and the English participation in the eastern commerce glutted the European market with Asian goods and thus the aforesaid German and Italian merchants sent their galleys to the English and the Dutch ports instead of sending them to Lisbon. Of course, the city could not remain on top under those circumstances. Likewise, the same international commercial rivalries brought calamity to the Portuguese eastern colonies at the sources of the spices themselves. Inversely, among the Indian peoples, it resulted growth of towns and the economy of the merchant class generally, increased the production of the merchandises and so on. Keeping these developments in mind, I shall now consider the impact of the Portuguese trade on the coastal western India amidst the international rivalries.

Impact of the Portuguese Trade on the Western Coast of India

The Portuguese amidst international rivalries in the seventeenth century had a deep-rooted effect on the Indian economy. The unstable relations with the Dutch and the English as well as with the Indian rulers, together with the new competition in the spice markets led to considerable increases in the prices of goods, once which brought affluence to the purely merchant classes, both the Portuguese traders and the Indians. The quest for prosperity brought the merchants and their agents to the port towns on the western coast of India from the far interiors. This migration helped the towns and the Portuguese colonies. The gain of gold and silver coins for the purchase of their goods brought monetisation to sectors of the Indian economy hitherto dependent on barter. The rise in prices and the growth in the production of the Indian trading commodities are two main by-products of the rivalry. In the following passages, these points will be considered in detail.

(a) Development of Towns

The Portuguese trade contributed a great deal to the development of the western coastal towns of India. In the sixteenth century, Goa developed faster than the other towns along the west coast to the south of Surat and become thickly populated, with a number of establishments. All Portuguese ships loaded with the commodities from all parts of India and farther east were brought here for the re-inspection of their cargoes qua weight and qualities aboard and then dispatched to Portugal. For these activities many people were employed; hence, the prospects of employment attracted people from the interior who settled there. The activity also affected other ports in the region. Since loading and unloading of goods destined for Goa also affected all the regional ports, other people from their hinterlands also made use of their opportunities and were drawn in similar fashion. For the sake of convenience in their trade, local merchants also established their warehouse and made commercial headquarters in almost all the port towns. Thus, the number of person especially merchants and workers, presumably, went on increasing until the Dutch stormed the towns at the end of the sixth decade.

Among all the towns on the western coast, Diu, Cambay, Surat, Bassein, Chaul, Goa in the north, and Onor, Barcelore, Mangalore, Cannanore, Calicut, Cranganore, Cochin and Quilon, in the south, there was flourishing trade with other parts of the world. Usually, there were Muslims, Hindus, Armenians, Arabs, Christians and various nationals residing in these port towns under the Portuguese. Normally, the houses of Muslims and the Hindus merchants were made of white stones, bricks roofed with lime clay or tiles in the Portuguese fashion. Their houses were intended to be the best in the town, other than those of the Portuguese residents in the fort areas.(7)

Several other institutions grew up in the Portuguese settlements of coastal western India, designed to serve the needs of both the European population, the Portuguese and the indigenous residents, who went on increasing day by day. Almost all the Portuguese colonies and towns had hospitals attached to them for taking care of the infirm. The hospitals were provided with food, medicines and all other necessary things, by the Portuguese government.(8) Slaves were employed for the menial works from the very beginning of the sixteenth century.(9) Later, when the public works become unbearable for the factory officers, municipalities were brought into existence. The *câmara* municipal of Goa was followed by similar municipalities for Cochin, Diu, Daman, and Bassein, among the developed city governments in the Portuguese settlements.

In addition to the hospitals, a new institution broadly dedicated to care of poor, sick, orphans, widows and the handicapped, was established in all these Portuguese towns and known as *casa da misericórdia*. Much attention was paid to the proper care of these houses by the state government.(10) Each city had once church in the beginning of the sixteenth century. But their numbers in each town increased in the seventeenth century, now to accommodate both the Portuguese and the New Christians. Monasteries of various religious orders also were founded in the cities, adding to their development. Such monasteries were found in Goa, Cochin, Daman and Diu.(11) Later on, other religious groups like those of the Augustinians and Jesuits established their houses in these towns.

The Portuguese government also took steps in educating the children of town residents by opening schools. Such schools were found in the early sixteenth century in Cochin, Quilon and Cranganore.(12) In the villages, such duties were discharged by the Jesuit missionaries. The missionary people used to move around from village to village for propagation of Christianity as well as for teaching the children. It is worth mentioning here that the efforts made by the Jesuits for educating the village folks were painstaking and had a far-reaching impact on the formation of a Christian society. It was a work greatly appreciated.

The special favours and privileges given by the Portuguese to the converted Christians plus the possibilities of employment in the factories and the towns attracted numerous people to become Christians and inspired them to settle in the urban areas. In this way the Christian population increased heavily during the sixteenth and the seventeenth centuries.(13)

Besides other activities already mentioned, shipbuilding in the dockyards of the western coast, especially at Bassein, Goa and Cochin, also provided much employment to the skilled and non-skilled workers. Formerly this work was performed at Cochin, Cannanore or Calicut but soon after the Portuguese occupation of Bassein, Ships were constructed at these cites only. Since timber was easily available at Bassein, and also at Goa, it was convenient to carry on such work there. Almost every biennium, two or more ships were commissioned. (14) Repairing of ships was done at Goa, except in rare case when it was done at Cochin or Diu. A large number of persons were needed for such maintenance.

(b) Rise of Colonies

Soon after the arrival of Alvares Cabral in 1500, the need was felt to establish a permanent Portuguese factory and colony. This was mainly determined because some of the necessary export commodities needed to be purchased in advance of the fleets from Portugal. Later, in due course a number of Portuguese factories were created and the Portuguese settled around them. Soon it was realised that the number of persons required for the Portuguese

Indian trade could not be provided by such a small nation as Portugal. Therefore, the king and the governors of the Portuguese India, Affonso de Albuquerque, both encouraged the unmarried Portuguese mare residents to marry the local Indian women in order to increase the population of those living within the sphere of Portuguese culture.(15) The intent was far reaching; to have many armed men to fight the enemies of the Portuguese government. Special preference was given to the Muslim and Brahmins ladies, as they were fair colour and could mix easily with the Portuguese race.(16) Such encouragements, helped in bringing many of Portuguese men to settle in India, and those in turn helped the government form new colonies.(17)

During the sixteenth century, as the trade and commerce flourished, the number of the Portuguese *casados* (married) increased. In the Portuguese colonies, there were three types of residents, the *reinóis*, one *castiços* or the Portuguese, second, the *mestiços* or the Eurasians, and lastly, the New Christians- converted from Hinduism, Muslims, or Jews- to Christianity. Thousand of such families were found in the different Portuguese colonies.(18) In the later part of the sixteenth century, when the conversion was enforced by the government orders, the number of the Portuguese colonial residents increased considerably. Many of these Portuguese *casados* and settlers in colonies, took a very active part in various aspects of the Portuguese Indian trade.

In the later sixteenth and in the seventeenth centuries a new policy was observed. The Portuguese government encouraged the practice of bringing of orphans to India having married them later.(19) They also encouraged the Hindu Brahmins and Baniyas to marry their daughters with them and give maximum dowries, (20) though the exact number of such types of married settlers is not found. But it should be remembered that there were quite a good number of them who helped the Portuguese government out by employing their wealth. Incidentally, the teenagers who had no family in India were sought after by the Portuguese Jesuit Missionaries and other religious groups like Santa *Mónica* for recruitment. They also increased the ranks of soldiery and proved of much help for the Portuguese trade and commerce. (21)

Since the Portuguese headquarters was transferred to Goa from Cochin during 1529-30, the majority of the Portuguese population in India, preferred Goa or its surroundings for their residence. This was the most convenient place for trading activities.

Hence Goa rose to prominence for the whole sixteenth and the seventeenth centuries. Not were the only *casados* included in the colonies but the great number of Portuguese official also resided there. Although no clear picture of the Portuguese *casados* and New Christians are found, it may certainly be assumed that it might have been far greater than that of other colonies on the western coast of India. During the seventeenth century more than 500 Portuguese officers, both high and petty, lived there.(22) Normally all these officers had one to three slaves each who could be easily turned to soldiers whenever needed.(23) Goa had been divided into three main subdivisions, Panjim, Salssete, Bardez, and many other small municipalities for the sake of convenience. All these areas from north to south had been resided in by the Portuguese, local converts and the "married settlers".(24)

In the northern territories, Diu was once an affluent colony of the Portuguese. During the seventeenth century, this territory under Portuguese control had developed considerably because of its trade. Probably, more settlers resided there during this period than in the sixteenth century. There were more than 350 soldiers garrisoned in this land to look after the safety of the fort and the residents.(25) More than fifty-nine *reinóis* Portuguese married with Indian women, were resided in this colony.26) Each family had at least one slave. Sometimes this number reached two to five. Apart from these residents, there were more than fifty-two officers and office-holders who also lived in this area. Among these officers, all including captain to small soldiers were counted. Thus, all these constituted more 200 soldiers in this colony.(29)

Bassein had been one of the biggest Portuguese settlements and colonies on the western coast of India. In 1635, there were about 400 Portuguese *casados* and more than 600 New Christians families residing in the Portuguese fortress. They formed a *sizeable* colony in this period. Each *casado* possessed on an average three slaves.(30) Thus the total number of slaves can be calculated around 1,200. Other than garrison soldiers, there were more than 2,000 slaves employed for the service of the Portuguese government. Normally, they were used as watchman for the tobacco fields and other important places under the Portuguese control.(31) There were about forty Portuguese officers in the colony.(32) Thus, the number of the Portuguese settlers in Bassein was more than any other Portuguese settlements save Goa.

Chaul had 200 settlers of Portuguese engaged in local trade. Each of these Portuguese families had one to two slaves in their services.(33) There were 500 Portuguese *casados* lived there with their children. There were 37 officers for maintenance of the fortress and the factory as well as to look after the welfare of the colony.(34)

Cambolim, a little south of Goa, had been recently founded by viceroy Conde de Linhares in 1629, had three *castiços* settlers for dealing in trade. More than twelve casados and 150 native Christians soldiers constituted this colony.(35)

Barcelore, in the region of Kanara had twenty-nine Portuguese officers resident in the fortress.(36) About 35 *casados* Portuguese families along with 35 soldiers lived in this colony during the third and fourth decades of the seventeenth century.(37)

Mangalore was another Portuguese colony in the seventeenth century. Here, the number of the Portuguese settlers was about the same as those of Barcelore but officers were certainly fewer in number.(38)

Malabar had been somewhat neglected during the Hapsburg period (1580-1640) in comparison to the Kanara regions. But its importance as a pepper producing area had not been forgotten completely. Some of the old *casados* were encouraged to continue trading from this region, as has been seen in the previous chapters.

Among the Malabar states, Cannanore was one of the important colonies of the Portuguese during the period under review. Originally, there were forty families along with their children, more than hundred *casados* and eleven officials resided in this region.(39) Cochin had been one of the oldest and most prosperous regions under the Portuguese on the Malabar Coast since the very beginning of the sixteenth century. During the early seventeenth century, there were fifty-eight Portuguese families other than soldiers who were residing in Cochin.(40) But the number of the Portuguese residents in this colony increased in the seventeenth century. In all there were more than 1,065 residents in the fourths decade of this century. Among those, about three hundred were white Portuguese, five hundred casados, 200 Indian converts and about 65 officials were residents in this area.(41) The increase in number can be assumed only because of the flourishing trade during the early part of the seventeenth century. During the late sixth and the early seventeenth decades, when this region was stormed by the Dutch, some of the residents, including those who were not included in the colony, fled to safer places. Thus when the Dutch occupied this land in 1663, must have found completely deserted.

Further south was the region of Quilon. This was founded in 1505. The exact number of the Portuguese residents during the sixteenth century is not clear but it would had been certainly reasonable.(42) In the seventeenth century, at least till the fifth decade, the Portuguese colony in this area had estimated at more than 190 families residing including the officers but excluding the soldiers.(43)

Thus, this short discussion reveals the existence of a number of colonies that had attained affluence through trade. Of course these colonies also existed in the sixteenth century, the number of the residents surely increased in the seventeenth century. All these said colonies and settlements did functioned well at least till 1658, when the Dutch began their forceful attacks on the territories of Malabar. Finally prosperity came to an end in 1663, when the territories of Cochin and Cannanore were occupied simultaneously.

Impact on the Portuguese Merchants Settled in India

The greatest benefactors from the Portuguese India trade were the Portuguese private merchants, both *castiços* and *mestiços* settled there. Local Christians also enjoyed the privileges granted to them by the Portuguese authorities. As has been seen earlier, the majority of these merchants had played a very important role in the Portuguese trade. All of them, at some or other time, had been in the Portuguese government services, and after voluntary retirements, involved themselves in the Asian trade. So long as the Portuguese trade flourished, they became rich and settled their business houses in any of the ports of their choice. They became so rich that they could even finance and dictate terms to the Portuguese government whenever it was required.

Impact on the Local Merchant Class

It was not only the Portuguese merchants gained riches from the trade, but also the Indian merchants who provided the commodities. Among these merchants who dealt with the Portuguese, some were quite in a position to supply the whole of the crown's demand.(44) Among these merchants majority of them were Hindu either from Gujarat, Maharashtra, Kanara or Malabar. Very few of them were Muslims.

The Indian merchants, as result of their transactions, became very prosperous. There were some merchants in Goa and Diu who led a very luxurious life. Their personnel treasure amounted between 100,000 to 400,000 *Ashrafis* in cash.(45) Among these, many helped the Portuguese crown in buying the commodities, as have been seen in the previous chapters

Impact on the Production

The international political situation and commercial rivalry had far-reaching effects on the production of the merchandises. Increasing demands pressured the producers and contractors to increase the production and therefore, the supply accordingly increased. For instance textiles, saltpetre, and rice were among the commodities other than spices and pepper, which increased to a considerable volume. Some of them were very as follows:

(i) Textiles

The production of Indian textiles during this period of rivalry has been found remarkable. During the sixteenth century, very small amount of Indian textiles were exported to Portugal.(46) But during the early decades it swelled to a heavy volume.(47) The reason has already been discussed in the chapter four, i.e. the hostility between the Portuguese and the Dutch. Because the Dutch had previously supplied the major Portuguese needs for the textiles, it became a considerable problem to obtain supply after the outbreak of war between the two nations. Demands had to be met from other place and India itself a great textiles producer was at hand. The Portuguese, as noted earlier, had bound to carry this item back home. Nevertheless, when the English and the Dutch entered in the scene, they faced the same difficulty as the Portuguese did, namely, to get their supplies from the Indonesian archipelago in the absence of a proper commodity for exchange there, or sufficient gold or silver. Thus, they also were drawn towards Gujarat where textiles were produced in abundance. However, the producers were squeezed to boost their production in order to meet the demand from all these Europeans.

The Portuguese of course, continued to need textiles not only for consumption at home but also in the exchange for slaves from African regions who were badly needed on the ships during the Portuguese-Dutch and English wars.(48) The increase in the volume of cloths has been demonstrated by the tables.(49)

(ii) Saltpetre

The second most important commodity, which grew to heavy volumes during the seventeenth century, was saltpetre. It was mainly used for the production of gunpowder. As gunpowder was needed to fight the enemies, and the war continued unabated, the demand for saltpetre rose considerably for the production of gunpowder. In order to meet the needs of the Portuguese, the local merchants, both the Portuguese and the Indians, forced the producers to provide more by utilising more manpower and machines.(50) In this business, both the contractors and the producers gained considerable profits. The requirements of the Portuguese went on increasing, while simultaneously, the production also increased.(51)

(iii) Rice

As the fight went on, the consumption of rice increased for the provisioning of the soldiers. The multi-phased supply of this item certainly increased the production. Earlier, the Portuguese used to obtain their requirements from the local areas. But after war broke out in Muscat, Ceylon, Malacca and other places, the local supply presently stopped, except that from Goa. It was never before that this item of essential use rose to such state of importance over what it was in the sixteenth century. The circumstances forced the authorities to meet the requirements from elsewhere. Thus, the cultivators and the merchants had to increase the production either by intensive farming or by bringing more land under cultivation. This might have occurred presumably which led the volume of production-increased considerably.(52)

(iv) Tobacco

It is believed that tobacco cultivation was introduced in India by the Portuguese sometimes during the sixteenth century.(53) Mentions of considerable cultivations are found only in the seventeenth century documentation. The Portuguese had a considerable trade in this commodity, produced mainly in Bassein, Daman and some parts of Goa.(54) This assertion is based mainly on the Portuguese auction of the tobacco rents to the local contractors. For even though the contract was normally for three years, it still yielded an annual income of 12,000 Ashrafis from each of the cultivated areas.(55) The contract and the payment of rent of tobacco inclines one to believe that tobacco was certainly cultivated to a reasonable volume.

(v) Pepper, Cinnamon and Other Spices

In reality, the volume of the Portuguese trade in pepper, cinnamon and various sort of spices decreased gradually during this period as has been seen in the previous chapters. In fact going through the documental evidences it can be assumed that it was the Portuguese official trade that declined on the contrary, the unofficial and private trade did not stop. Making use of war and disturbed political situations, many merchants involved themselves in other commodities and unofficial trade. On the other hand, the Portuguese-Dutch-English struggle for the acquisition of the Asian trade, increased both the demands and their supply to a considerable extent. However, the exact picture of the increase in production can be brought to light only after the simultaneous study of the quantitative details of the Dutch and the English trade during the first half of the seventeenth century, since the data regarding the production by the peasants are not found.

Increase in Prices

It was the low priced commodities in India, and the high rate of profit on them gained by the Portuguese at home, among various other reasons, had brought the two powerful rivals from the North-west of Europe. As soon as they entered into the competition of the mentioned commodities, their prices rose exorbitantly from 100 to 350 percent comparing with that of the sixteenth century rate. In the sixteenth century, there were forced contracts exclusively favourable to the Portuguese. Even so, there were numerous complaints from the cultivators and the merchants to the King of Portugal against the excesses of the Portuguese officers, especially for the low price paid by them. But it seems that the Portuguese rulers never bothered about this. Therefore, by the beginning of the seventeenth century, the appearance of the Dutch and the English came as a boon for these suppressed merchants, as the newcomers were prepared to pay more than what they used to get. This situation reached such a pass that occasionally, the Portuguese ships returned home without the required Indian commodities. Thus, forced by the circumstances, they were obliged to increase the purchase rates of their commodities. For instance, in the third decade, the cost of per quintal saltpetre was two and a half Ashrafis but during the fifth and the sixth decades it rose to twelve Ashrafis per quintal almost 300 percent. Similarly, the cost of per quintal rice fluctuated between one and a half and two and a half Ashrafis. Cinnamon rose from six to twenty five Ashrafis per quintal and the same way pepper rose between twelve and thirty-five Ashrafis during the first half of the seventeenth century, the period of conflicts. Thus, it can be concluded that international situation and the rivalries for trade during this period had a far-reaching effect on the prices of the commodities. This rise in prices did affect the Portuguese trade but it increased the profit of the suppressed merchant class.

Monetisation of Economy

Portuguese governors and factors had experienced many difficulties during the early sixteenth century due to their lack of medium of exchange in general and the suitable coins in India, in particular. For this reason, they created mint houses and requested their kings to send quantities of silver and gold both in bullion and in coins. However, many of gold and silver coins, such as *Ducats, Cruzados, Ashrafis,* and *Tankas* came into circulation. Later, copper coins-*Bazarucos, Reis,* etc., were also introduced into the market. In the seventeenth century a regular flow of gold and silver coins in *Cruzados* predominated. These coins brought from Portugal were converted into local currencies according to the needs of the merchants.

During the first half of the seventeenth century, as has been shown in the previous chapter, more than two million *Ashrafis* in *Cruzados* were brought to India every year for the purchase of the Indian spices and to meet the other expenditures of the state. More than 40,75,201 *Ashrafis* were issued from the Goa treasury during the period under review. Of course, there were several instances when the Portuguese authorities provided commodities instead of cash for the purchase of pepper, saltpetre, textiles and elephants. But such types of cases were few. Normally all these transactions were made in cash due to the risk of losses. Above all, these are the information based on the documents available, but not the exact one which were, presumably, much higher as much of the documents are not available or destroyed. In brief, coins were in rapid circulation during this period. Besides, the brisk flow of silver and gold bullions sent by the big New Christian Merchants for its use into Asian trade, mostly in textiles and diamonds flooded the Indian market with gold and silver coins. Thus, it can be, however, assumed that the Portuguese on the western coast of India in this century brought increased monetisation in the economy of the coastal western India.

Therefore, it can be asserted that the Portuguese trade in the seventeenth century had multifarious impacts on the Indian economic and commercial system. In India, Portuguese commerce in general brought riches and prosperity to the Portuguese settled there as well as to many Indian merchants. They had the most chances of making more profit via the Portuguese-Dutch struggle for mastery in the Indian Ocean. Urban life and the flow of more people from the villages to the towns were boosted by the Portuguese trade. Colonies of the Portuguese as well as Eurasians took root in India and developed daily in size. Above all, the international rivalries and the Portuguese trade increased the production rate heavily; some commodities like textiles, saltpetre, and rice had become the commodities of much necessity for the Portuguese. In this many more areas were brought under cultivation and production of goods and the merchants had better chances of making much profit. The traditional trade in spices was in decline gradually for the Portuguese but the production of commodities increased in proportion to the increasing demands. The flow of Portuguese wealth for the purchase of Indian goods, certainly leads one to believe that the Portuguese trade accelerated the monetisation of the Indian economy, which in a later period helped the mercantilism in other part of the world. In other word, it sowed the seeds for the later industrialisation.

Conclusion

It has been believed by several historians that the *carreira da India* trade and the Portuguese power was already on decline by the second half of the sixteenth century.(56) It is slightly difficult to agree on this point after having analysed the sources available for the seventeenth century. I am convinced that these historians have looked at the declining pepper and spice cargoes that belonged to the crown and a few privileged contractors and have ignored the much richer cargoes of Indian textiles and furnishing, indigo, lacquers, pearls and the diamonds. The volume of *carreira* trade proved to be the easy way to prove. Volume of trade, I always feel less secure, especially given variety of goods and the undetermined nature of their packing. However, during the late sixteenth century, the average export of spices has been accounted between 10,000 and 11,000 quintals.(57) But in the early decades it fluctuated between 9,000 and 11,000 quintals.(58)

Textiles trade on the contrary had risen from negligible volume to a considerable one during the first three decades. Other commodities like rice, saltpetre and precious stones rose to their climax during the period when the Portuguese power and lucrative trade declined. One may argue about the share of the Portuguese official trade in the precious stones? The answer is that the New Christians who used to finance the whole Portuguese commercial set-up, in order to avoid the risk and customs diverted their attention from heavy volume of textiles and spices, the less profitable to them, towards the light weight and more profitable goods in which the state gained almost no custom duty. This was the item easily concealable and occupied less space on the ships. One may not deny the Portuguese trade and their commercial settlements on decline during the first half of the seventeenth century even after their unsuccessful attempt to keep it going. Presumably enough, the commencement of the Portuguese fragmented relations with the Indian states also took place during the first decade of the seventeenth century but it is also to be remembered that only at this period was the most fearful enemy of the Portuguese government on the Indian soil and the sea, the Kunjali Marakkar, was hanged to death at Goa.

The Portuguese traded in more than fifty to sixty items of Indian goods. More than eighty types of textiles were carried home. This also can be assumed a period of shift of powers from kingships to merchant capitalism. At times the merchants provided money on loan to the Portuguese government and often served as ambassadors for the negotiations between the Portuguese authorities and the Indian rulers. However, if this period, on the one side, marked the weakening of the Portuguese sea power and decreasing volume of trade in the Indian Ocean, on the other, this was a transitional period from dependent merchant class to merchant capitalism. The Portuguese government, in order to keep the trade, continued even under such disturbed political conditions, tried to shift the responsibility onto the Portuguese Commercial Company. Eventually it failed due to the lack of co-operation among the hierarchy in Portugal, obstructionism of the officials at Goa and indifference within the directorate. Even in such circumstances, saltpetre, as an item of exclusive use in defence, increased considerably. So did rice, which was indirectly an item of defence, being used for the provisioning of soldiers and populations surrounded by enemies.

From the very beginning of the sixteenth century, the Portuguese trade was dependent on the finance of the private merchant bankers, both the Portuguese and the foreigners, belonging to different religion such as the Catholics, New Christians and the Jews. When the overseas commerce was attacked by various European nations during the late sixteenth and the seventeenth centuries, the referred bankers simply avoided into heavier things and preferred the light weighted and more profitable ones. The New Christian's ever increasing interest in the Brazilian trade instead of India trade also had an impact on the *Carreira da India* trade. Even the most important thing is still to be examined by some historian, the impact of inquisition on the Indian trade. Late sixteenth century had played havoc with the New Christians, Jews and other communities in all the Portuguese settlements including Portugal. Most of the business houses, either burnt, or moved away to far distant lands beyond the Portuguese reach. Thus avoided the Portuguese relations. Naturally after this event which history will never forget, the Portuguese government had felt the lack of funds. Even in such circumstances the more important cause for the Phillips of Portugal was to preserve his fights with the Dutch than to save the Portuguese maritime trade!

If an analysis of the situation is made, it will be found that it was not that the Portuguese commerce declined but only the official trade. The trade which had been started from the very beginning of the sixteenth century depending on the bankers money, still continued but in different merchandises and different manners. Besides the Portuguese maritime officials, out of greed, joined hands even with the enemies of their nation and traded in spite of all restrictions and prohibitary orders. Apart from this as Moreland has pointed out, there were "grave errors of policy and administration, but the central fact is that the strength of Portugal had been overtaxed by the enterprises carried on simultaneously in Asia, Africa, and Brazil. To all appearance, then the Empire stood firm for a time but its foundations were cracked and it was in no condition to resist a determined invader".(59)

Causes for the Downfall of the Portuguese Commerce and their Power

In a few paragraphs, I shall try to discuss in brief the causes, which might have led the decline of the Portuguese maritime power and their trade in the East.

In the early sixteenth century, the first Portuguese viceroy, Dom Francisco de Almeida, wrote his oft-quoted letter to the King Manuel I, "Let it be known for certain that as long as you may be powerful at sea you will hold India as yours and if you do not possess this power little will avail you a fortress on shore".(60) This was partially true, but Almeida did not realise the importance of a fortress and the cordial relations with the natives. His policy was later completed by Dom Affonso de Albuquerque, who stressed more on building fortresses and having good relations with Indian states. However, in one sense, Almeida was quite far-sighted to realise the need for a strong naval power in the early sixteenth century, though he could have meant it only in the context of the Indian merchan's and rulers who were always awaiting opportunities to overthrow them from the Indian side. Portuguese naval power to all intent invincible in that context and it largely enabled them to control the Indian Ocean and the Arabian seas. But when they came to face the challenge from two very prepared maritime nations, their strength proved to be insufficient. Here, in following passages, I shall focus in brief the causes that led to weaken their navy during the period under review which could have been much more stronger.

Without entering into details of the fights that Portuguese had to confront in several points, has been majored as one of the determining factors in the weakening of the Portuguese commerce, which was base of every thing. In the beginning of the sixteenth century their competitors were the Asian who hardly reached to Europe and concentrated their attentions only in Asia. The competitors of Europe glutted the whole European market, which decreased the demand and reduced the area of distribution for the Portuguese commodities brought from the Orient.

The increasing expenditure on war and the decreasing official trade, hampered the movements of *Carreira da India* trade. Exorbitant investments on war materials, reduction of investments in spices, burning of ships, loans on high rate of interest and the price rise had reduced the Portuguese position to minor defenders of their colonies.

Corruption in the Portuguese administrative system was another leading factor for the dismemberment but not inactivating the Portuguese movements in the East. The Portuguese administration from the Eastern archipelago to the African countries, as has been pointed out by several historians, was characterised by corruption and mal-practices.(61) All the important offices like treasury, the courts of justice and the marine department had been found in the grip of corruption during the seventeenth century. As early as in 1616, complaints were lodged with the king of Portugal about the disorderly management at the port of Goa. Even the persons in charge of the loading and unloading were found in the forgery and smuggling.(62) There are clear indications that some of the rich Lisbon based New Christians who had lived or still had there family contacts, had trade links between India and European markets avoiding the port of Lisbon in order to avoid the customs. Manuel de Paz , Francisco Tinoco de Carvalho, Fernão Jorge da Silveira, Pero Gonçalves Brandão, and other major Goan merchants each shipped up to 50,000 pieces of cloths and dozens of *bizalhos* of diamonds as well as quintals of other goods each year.(63) The port of Angola was important to the New Christians, not only as slave trade centre but also in an illicit trade that diverted cotton textiles from India ships to smaller vessels in the south Atlantic for delivery in Buenos Aires or in Brazilians or Caribbean ports. We know that many ships landed in Angola (or St. Helena, or in Brazil) on the return voyages to Lisbon, to take water and provisions. Sometimes they remained several months waiting storms, a process called *invernar* (wintering). The crown forbade wintering on several occasions, but it continued. In the meantime they transferred their cargoes on different ships to take to Brazil or other destinations. Thus when the ships reached finally to Lisbon, they were vacant of merchandises. (64) Niels Steensgaard has observed that many of the carracks arrived in Lisbon with much less cargo than they were capable of carrying.(65) Administrative officers were interested more in making their fortunes through liberty granted to them than in the trade for the crown.(66) They went on increasing their volume on board according to their own will. Many a times the officials had their merchandises on the ships and in the name of crown, none. (67) The treasury was often found empty. For years no accounts were presented to the authorities.(68) Moreover, the balance of the church accounts were not kept in order and much money was found missing.(69) Strict orders were issued by the king but who really bothered? The whole set-up was based on hierarchy and the officers did not do their duty. What to expect from such a set-up? All of them contributed to weaken themselves and finally loss of rich enterprise.

Notes

Impact of the Portuguese Trade and Conclusion

1. Azevedo, *Épocas de Portugal...*, p. 89; Mathew, *Portuguese Trade...*, pp. 200.
2. Mathew, *Portuguese Trade...*, pp. 200-206.
3. Before the discovery of the sea route to India via Cape of Good Hope by the Portuguese, pepper was sold between 70 and 90 Ducats. But after, it was sold at the rate of 22 to 25 Ducats per quintal at Lisbon. Mathew, *Portuguese Trade...*, pp. 157-70, 185-90; Lach, *Asia in the Mak ing...*, vol. I, part I, pp. 145.

4. Mathew, *Portuguese Trade...*, pp. 157-70; Lach, *Asia in the Making...*, vol. I, part I, pp. 131-43.
5. Lane, *'Venice and History..'*, pp. 10-20.
6. Lach, *Asia in the Making...*, vol. I, part I, pp. 131-43.
7. *APO-BP*, tomo IV, vol. II, part I, pp. 106-360.
8. *APO-BP*, tomo IV, vol. II, part I, pp. 106-360; *LML*, cod. 18, fls. 288; cod. 21, fls. 235-37, 331-33; cod. 22, fl. 93; cod. 24, fl. 175; cod. 34, fl. 184.
9. *Cartas*, tomo IV, pp. 288, 303-304.
10. *LML*, cod. 17, fl. 247; cod. 18, fl. 255; cod. 19, fls. 13, 18v, 30v, 84v; cod. 20, fl. 11; cod. 21, fl.s 15, 183; cod. 22, fl. 89, 92; cod. 24, fl. 199; cod. 36, fl. 270; cod. 38, fl. 417; cod. 52, fl. 66; cod. 60, fl. 135; *India*, cx. 9, doc. 170; cx. 15, doc.
11. *Ibid.*
12. *SPHI*, pp. 27, 39.
13. *LML*, cod. 20, fl. 357; cod. 26, fl. 630.
14. *India*, cod. 31, fl. 67v-68; cod. 34, fls. 9-10.
15. Mathew, *Portuguese Trade...*, pp. 215-216.
16. *Ibid.*
17. Mathew, *Portuguese Trade...*, pp. 215-218.
18. *Ibid.*
19. *LML*, cod. 48, fl. 318; cod. 54, fls. 51, 109-11, 123, 207-208
20. *Ibid.*
21. *LML*, cod. 13, fls. 73, 255; cod. 14, fl. 108v; cod. 37, fl. 289; cod. 41, fls. 49-49v; cod. 60, fl. 91.
22. *APO-BP*, tomo IV, vol. II, part I, pp. 206-305.
23. *Ibid.*
24. *Ibid.*
25. *APO-BP*, tomo IV, vol. II, part I, pp. 106.
26. *APO-BP*, tomo IV, vol. II, part I, pp. 114-116.
27. *Ibid.*
28. *APO-BP*, tomo IV, vol. II, part I, pp. 130.
29. *APO-BP*, tomo IV, vol. II, part I, pp. 130.
30. *APO-BP*, tomo IV, vol. II, part I, pp. 176-78.
31. *APO-BP*, tomo IV, vol. II, part I, pp. 170-80.
32. *Ibid.*
33. *APO-BP*, tomo IV, vol. II, part I, pp. 197-200.
34. *Ibid.*
35. *APO-BP*, tomo IV, vol. II, part I, pp. 312-14..

36. *APO-BP*, tomo IV, vol. II, part I, pp. 215-16..
37. *Ibid.*
38. *APO-BP*, tomo IV, vol. II, part I, pp. 319-320.
39. *APO-BP*, tomo IV, vol. II, part I, pp. 323-324.
40. Mathew, *Portuguese Trade...*, pp. 216
41. *APO-BP*, tomo IV, vol. II, part I, pp. 338-340.
42. Mathew, *Portuguese Trade...*, pp. 218.
43. *APO-BP*, tomo IV, vol. II, part I, pp. 356-357.
44. Mathew, *Portuguese Trade...*, pp. 29-77; See Chapter 8; Also see Boyajian, *Portuguese Bankers at the Court of Spain*, (passim).
45. *India*, cx. 18, doc. 99.
46. Mathew, *Portuguese Trade...*, pp. 143.
47. See Appendix IV.
48. *India*, cx. 4, doc. 159.
49. See Appendix IV
50. *ACF*, cod. 1161, fl. 166.
51. See Chapter 6
52. See Chapter 5
53. Panikkar, *Malabar and the Portuguese...*, p. 206.
54. See Chapter 5
55. *Ibid.*
56. Panikkar, *A History of Kerala,...*, p. 143-145.
57. See Table 1.1
58. See Chapter 3
59. Moreland, *From Akbar to Aurangzeb..*, p. 10.
60. *APO-BP*, tomo IV, vol. II, part I, pp. LXXII-LXXV.
61. *LML*, cod. 29, fls. 42-42v, 64; cod. 44, fls. 95, 264; Panikkar, *A History of Kerala,...*, p. 171-765; Panikkar, *Malabar and the Portuguese...*, (See the last chapter)
62. *LML*, cod. 9, fl. 128; *India*, cx. 1, doc. 78.
63. *India*, cx. 1, doc. 78; cx. 9, doc. 73; cx. 12, doc. 19.
64. Angola, cx. 1, docs. 14, 22, 27.
65. Niels Steensgaard, *Carracks, Caravans...*, (passim)
66. B. Aj. *Jesuitas na Asia*, No. 46-XIII-30, fls. 34-35, *India*, cx. 8, doc 38.
67. *Ibid.*
68. *LML*, cod. 29, fls. 42-43, 64; cod. 44, fl. 93; cod. 52, fl. 266.
69. *LML*, cod. 29. fl. 184.

Appendix - I

Specimen of a Cartaz - Issued to Nizam Shah's Ships (1)

Fernão de Albuquerque ette faço saber aos que este virem que tendo en repeito a amizade que Nizamoxa Ellrey do Decão tem com este estado, e pollo contrato das pazes que com elle este feito lhe serem concedidos sete cartazes para sete naos suas poderem navegar, cinco para Ormuz hum para Mecca, e outra para Malacca e da sua parte me ser ora pedido o presente, hey por bem desta dar licença e seguro a este sua nao por nome Unexe (?) (2) que carrega seiscentos candis de que vay pela Nacoda(3) Sidi Belela (4) de hidade de trinta e seis annos e leva para defenção quatorze peças da artilharia de ferro, quarenta espinguardas, setenta e cinco lanças, com panelas de polvoura e cinquenta bombas de fogos para nesta monção do março seguinte possa partir de porto de Chaul pera Ormuz e tornará ao mesmo porto nao levando nem trazendo couza algua defeza a saber, rumes, turcos, abexins, aço, breu, cobre, chumbo, latao, ferro, pimenta, canela de ceilão nem de mato, bombas machos, salitre, emxofre, tudo mais contendo e declarando no regimento do S.M. nem levaré Portugueses, nem trará cavalos sem minha licença e poderé trazer escravos e escravas de sua nação somente, e avendo suspeito, ou informação que alguns delles são christãos, ou folhos de christãos, se farão com elles o exame declarado no concilio provincial que neste cidade se cellebreu e antes que a dita nao parta do dito porto seré vista e buscada pollo alcaide mor delle onde deixaré dado fiança na feitoria de sua majestade a vir de tornaviagem direitamente ao dito porto de que lançaré certidão de huma e outra cousa nas costas deste, cartaz

1. HAG, Codex nº 1043 (Mss.), *Consultas do serviço de partes*, pp. 59-59v.
2. Probably INXA an Arabic name means the will
3. Means Captain
4. It is read as Sidi Belal

que valeré por huma viagem somente a hida e vinda e seré sellado com o sinete das armas reaes da coroa de Portugal. Noteficoo assy ao capitão de Chaul, ao feitor e alcaide mor daquela fortaleza, aos capitães mores, e mais capitães das armas de S. M. e aos mais officiaes e pessoas, e que pertencer para que assy o cumprão e quardão e fação inteiramente cumprir e guardar como se neste conthem sem dúvida nem embargo algum. Salvador Gonçalves o fez em Goa do (5) Janeiro de 1621. O secretário António Rodrigues de Guevaras o fez escrever.

---

5. No date is given

Plate 10 Portuguese Coins: Cruzados

APPENDIX - Ia

Summary of the Cartaz

Fernão de Albuquerque, the Governor, taking into account the friendship between Nizam Shah the ruler of Deccan (Ahmadnagar) and the Portuguese and also in virtue of the terms of the treaty of peace and friendship seven *Cartazes* for his ships were issued. Out of which five were destined to Hormuz, one to Mecca for pilgrimage, and the other to Malacca. These ships were due to leave the port of Chaul during the month of March, 1621. There were certain items, specified in the Cartaz, forbidden to carry on the ships. But a few pieces of arms and ammunitions for defence were allowed to be carried. The name of the captain ship is mentioned as Unexe (1) and the name of Nakoda(2) was Sidi Belela, (3) of thirty six year old. The Cartaz was issued in the month of January 1621 at Goa.

---

1. Probably INXA an Arabic name means the will
2. Means Captain
3. It is read as Sidi Belal

Appendix - II

Map of a Cargo Ship Showing space Occupied by Pepper

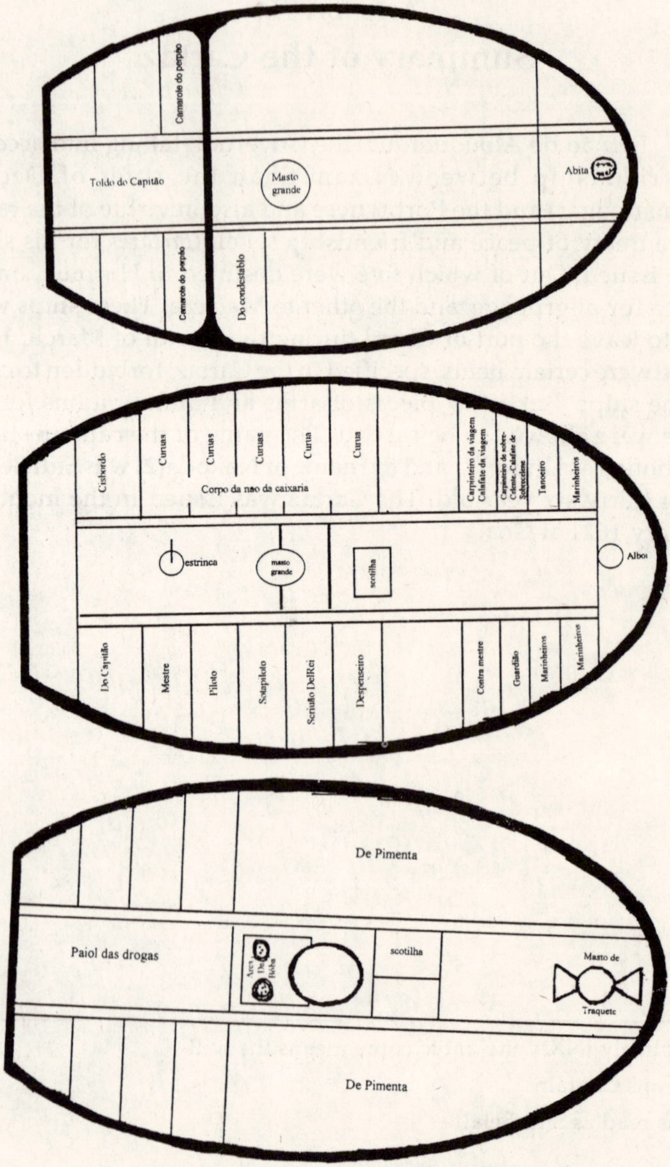

APPENDIX - III

Pepper Trade from Goa to Lisbon showing the Area of its Origin, in Quintals 1601-1663

1 YEAR	2 KANARA	3 CRANGA-NORE	4 COCHIN	5 QUILON	6 MALACCA	7 TOTAL
1601-7	-	-	-	-	-	25,590
1608-10	-	-	-	-	-	46,360
1611	7,025	483	-	-	2,001	9,508
1612	4,237	518	-	585	2,583	8,002
1613	6,402	-	-	-	-	6,402
1614	2,950	-	7,722	-	-	10,355
1615	11,741	-	2,126	1,374	-	15,841
1616	4,374	-	1,341	-	-	5,715
1617	9,602	-	491	-	1,498	11,591
1618	10,078	-	814	-	-	10,892
1619	5,916	-	83	-	-	5,999
1620	3,266	-	4,320	-	-	7,586
1621	5,478	-	394	-	-	5,872
1622	2,980	-	6,178	-	-	9,158
1623-24	17,577	-	3,794	-	-	21,373
1625	2,920	-	3,528	3,522	-	9,970
1626	5,150	-	9,680	-	-	14,830
1627-28	2,957	-	2,864	-	-	5,821
1628-29	1,790	-	3,715	-	-	5,505
1629-30	1,877	-	3,321	4,686	-	10,884
1630-31	-	-	-	-	-	9,061
1631	-	-	1,855	3,663	-	5,518
1632-33	9,686	-	-	-	-	9,686

1	2	3	4	5	6	7
YEAR	KANARA	CRANGA-NORE	COCHIN	QUILON	MALACCA	TOTAL
1635	5,133	-	1,418	3,492	-	10,043
1636	2,628	1,000	3,100	-	-	6,725
1637	-	-	-	-	-	4,284
1638	1,000	-	-	-	-	1,000
1639	-	-	-	-	-	-
1640	1,623	-	2,000	-	-	2,623
1641	-	-	-	-	-	-
1642	0,490	-	2,500	-	-	2,990
1643	-	-	-	-	-	8,000
1644	-	-	-	-	-	-
1645	-	-	2,000	-	-	2,000
1646	-	-	2,808	-	-	2,808
1647	-	-	-	-	-	-
1648	-	-	-	-	-	1,125
1649	1,125	79,769 Bags	-	-	-	-
1650	-	-	-	-	-	-
1651	0,750	-	5,000	-	-	5,750
1652	0,938	-	2,220	-	-	3,158
1653	-	-	-	-	-	-
1654	-	-	1,402	0,952	-	2,354
1655	-	-	0,842	-	-	0,840
1656	-	-	1,209	1,123	-	2,332

1657-1663 ***Portuguese engagements in war with the Dutch and Local powers and their loss of Ceylon, Quilon, Cranganore and Cochin to the Dutch.***

Reference: See Chapter 3

(-) means not available

APPENDIX - IV

Pepper Trade from Goa to Lisbon at a Glance in Quintals 1601 - 1663

YEARS	TOTAL VOLUME	FROM MALABAR	FROM KANARA	AVERAGE PER YEAR
1601-1610	71,950	-	-	7,195
1611-1620	90,563	29.5 %	70.5 %	9,056
1621-1630	91,810	55.5 %	44.5 %	9,181
1631-1640	41,017	42.5 %	57.5 %	8,203/4,101
1641-1650	8,923	82.00%	18.00%	0,892
1651-1663	14,434	88.5 %	11.5 %	2,405/1,110

Over all grand total between 1601-1656-63, was 3,18,697

Over all average in 63 yers 5,058.5 quintals

Average in 56 years 5,691

Average for the years of exports only (fifty years), 6,373 quintals.

Appendix - V a

Table of Equivalent of Coins in the XVI and XVII Centuries

The following coins were in circulation in the sixteenth and the seventeenth centuries. There were fluctuations in the value of coins during the seventeenth century due to some infliction and import of bullion by other Europeans. This has been shown in **Appendix V-B**

All the coins- silver, gold or copper have been reduced into a nominal réis.

NAME OF THE COINS	REIS
Ashrafi (xerafins)	380.00
Berganis	28.02
Cas (copper)	1.37
Cruzados	390.00
Dinheiro	4.88
Dobre (castillian coin)	400.00
Ducat	390.00
Horas (oras)	360.00
Livre (coin of frandos or Flanders)	1170.00
Madrafaxão (Muzaffar Shahi-of Gujarat)	1440.00
Metical (Chinese Coin)	420.00
Panam	20.53
Pardao	320.00
Raja (of Quilon)	40.00
Real (390 reis = 1 Ashrafi)	
Soldo	58.56
Sultani	420.00
Tanga (Tanka)	60.00
Tanka (silver)	72.00
Tanga Branca	115.02
Tare	1.37
Varel	160.00
Veneziano	420.00
Vintem	18.00

Refrence: SPHI, op. cit, pp. 61-64; Aragão, Moedas... pp. 464-471.

Appendix - V b

Indo-Portuguese Coins and their Relative Value in the World Market

NAME OF THE COINs	VALUE	SOURCES
Ashrafi (Xs.)	300.00 Reis or 5 Tanka	*LMG*, 13a, pp. 164-79
Ashrafi	3.89 Fanaos	*India*, cx. 3, doc. 1
Bazarucos	25.00 Vintem or 450.00 reis	*ACF*, 1162, p. 21
Cruzado	400.00 reis	AHU, Cod. 39, p. 31v.
Cruzado (Onor)	1.50 Xs.	*India*, cx. 3, doc. 185
Cruzado (Portugl)	2.00 Xs.	*LMG*, 13a, pp. 164-179; *India*, cx. 9, doc.177,186
9 Fanões (kayamkulam)	2.00 Xs.	*India*, Cx. 3, doc. 174
Marc (Gold in Goa)	197.00 Xs. and 28.00 reis	*ACF*, 1161, p. 5
Mahmudi (Diu).	1.50 Xs	*APO-BP*, tomo IV, vol. II, part 1
Pagoda (Gold)	4.00 Cruzados	*ACF*, 1161, p. 41
Pagoda (Gold in Ceylon)	10.00 Xs.	*ACF*, 1164, p. 226v.
Pagoda (Onor)	16.00 Tankas	*ACF*, 1163, pp. 160-61
Pagoda (Onor)	12.00 Tankas	*India*, cx. 3, doc. 185
Pagoda (Onor)	2.00 Xs.	*Simancas*, 1571, p. 305
Pardao	6.00 Fanões	*India*, cx. 8, doc. 38
Pardao	1.55 Xs.	*Ibid.*
1.25	Pardao 1.00 Cruzado	*Ibid.*
Pardao (Quilon)	8.00 Tanka	*India*, cx. 3, doc. 174
Pataca (Onor)	8.00 Tanka	*ACF*, 1161, p. 42
Pataca	1.22 Xs.	*Ibid.*
Pataca (Cochin)	1.60 Tanka	*India*, cx. 9, doc. 26
Pataca	1.00 Pardao	*India*, cx. 8, doc. 38
Real 8.00	Tanka	AHU, *cod.* 33, p. 148
Sao Tomé	3.40 Xs.	*ACF*, 1161, p. 1
Sao Tomé	15.00 Tanka and 1.00 Vintem	*ACF*, 1161, p. 82v.
Sao Tomé	16.00 Tanka	*ACF*, 1162, p. 182v.
Sao Tomé (Gold)	5.00 Xs.	*ACF*, 1168, pp. 51, 150
Sao Tomé (silver)	5.00 Xs.	*ACF*, 1161, p. 82v.
Sao Tomé	5.50 Xs.	*ACF*, 1166, p. 128
Tanka	60.00 Reis	*Ibid.*
Vintem	1.00 Xs.	*ACF*, 1162, p. 21

APPENDIX - VI

Table of Weights and Measures used in the Seventeeth Century

WEIGHTS	EQUIVALENT (Kilograms)
Almeno	1.20
Arratel (Old weight)	0.36
Arratel (New weight)	0.41
Bhar	116.30
Candil	220.32
Faraçola	6.31
Fardo	209.84
Mão	11.10
Mark	0.20
204 Mitkals	1.00
312.32 0itavas	1.00
39.04 Ounces	1.00
Quintal (old)	52.450
Quintal (New)	54.450
16 Ounces	1 Arratel
32 Arratels	1 Arroba
4 Arrobas	1 quintal
1 Quintal=2048 Ounces	128 Arratels

MEASURES

Name		Measurements
Cori	=	20 Pcs
Covados	=	64 cms.
Pipa	=	27 Almudes
Bar	=	20 Cori

Sources: *Dic. Morais*, Vol. I; *India*, cx.3, docs. 35, 174; cx. 5, doc. 83; cx. 8, doc. 38; cx. 9, doc. 17; Cx. 17, Doc. 7; AHU, *cod*. 38, pp. 12.12v; *cod*. 35, 37; cod. 37, pp. 42-43; *ACF* 1164, p. 175v; *cod*. 163 (passim); *LMG*, cod. 13a, pp. 174-179; *AGS*, cod. 1571, 302-308; *SMHI*, pp. 45-55:

Appendix - VII

List of Textiles Exported from Goa to Lisbon During 1600-1663

ALCATIFA: Carpet, It was produced in various kinds: silk, wool and cotton. They were of very good quality and an expensive stuff. Normally bought for royal use. Surat, Ahmedabad and Agra were the major carpet producing centres in India from where the Portuguese got their supply. Occasionally they procured good quality carpets from Persia for the royal use. All the carpets bought from the different areas were brought to Goa for the export to Portugal.

ALGODÃO, MOLHO DE, Cotton thread balls, It had been the major product of Gujarat and Balaghat.

ALMOFADINHO: Cotton and silken Pillows, This was procured mostly from Cambay, Surat and regions of Balaghat.

ALAQUEQUA: A Precious Stone and a kind of cloth. Origin not mentioned.

ARGANIZES/ORGANIZES: Cotton Fabric. Thin and coarse both in blue and white colours. A Product of Bijapur, Golconda and Balaghat.

BALACHACHOS : Unidentified cloth.

BALAGHATI:A cotton fabric. It was produced in blue and white colours. Usually it was coarse in quality. Mostly taken to Angola and coast of S. G. Minas for the exchange with slaves. It was procured from Balaghat.

BAMES: Unidentified cloth, but it was collected from the regions of Gujarat.

BANCAIS: Unidentified.

BEATILHAS: Golconda Muslin. Fine textile esteemed much in the European Countries. Procured from the areas of Balaghat and Burhanpur. It was found in the coastal Massulipattam and Pullicut (Paleacate is mentioned in the document) as well.

BEIRAME: A Printed Cotton Cloth. Chintz. It was fine cloth for daily use and produced mostly in Cambay. (Gujarat)

BEIRAMINHO: Chintz. An inferior quality cotton textile from Gujarat.

BENGALINHO : Unidentified. Probably a product of Bengal.

BERTANGIL: Calico. It was blue and black colour cotton cloth. A product of Daman. It was mostly used for the exchange of South-East Asian and African goods.

BIÇA/BISSA: Unidentified. It was produced in Gujarat.

BAFETA:BAFTA: Calico of different qualities in blue, red and gaze cloth from Burhanpur and Macchiwara.

BORALHO: Unidentified.

BOTALHO: Unidentified.

BORNEO : A cotton fabric.

CACHA: Probably Cacha of today. Seems to be corrupt form of *Gamcha*. Almost 128 cms. long and 64 cms. broad. *(dois covados compridos e um covado largo)*

CANEQUIN: A thin cotton fabric produced in Daman. It was much in demand in western European countries. A Good quality Calico.

CASCASIS:Unidentified.

CASSA:A cotton textile. It was a very thin and white in colour. It was produced in Bengal.

CAELA: A silk textile from Bengal. Not much known and exported.

CHANDES : A cotton Fabric from Gujarat and Balaghat.

CAJROTI: Cajrauti. A cotton textile from Daman.

CHITA: Chintz. Printed cotton fabric of Massulipattam in the kingdom of Golconda, Daman and Diu. But the one from Massulipattam had been in great demand by the Portuguese and later by the Dutch for their exported consignments.

CHUNDERIS:A very thin cotton printed fabric. Mostly used as scarf by the women to cover their heads. It is commonly known as *CHUNNI AND CHUNDERI* in India.

CEOLEO: A Chinese cloth. Detail not available.

CUNTUNIAS/COTONIAS :A silk scarf, or a big handkerchief. It was produced mostly in Bengal and Surat.

COLCHAS : BED. It was of two types one of cotton and other of cotton with silk covers. Surat had been known for its production.

DAMASCO : Silk fabric with printed designs.

DAMASQUILHOS: A product of Bengal and was expensive quality.

DARYABADI: A Cotton textile from Daryabad (In the North India) known as Daryabadi.

DARYAPURI: A printed cotton fabric known as DARYAPURI (A Chintz)

DESPICES/DESPIZES: Unidentified.

DOTINS/DHOTINS: DHOTI. Probably loin cloth. A six metre cotton, and silk fabric used by men.

FIADOS: Means threaded or weaved. Most probably a cotton piece of cloth.

FOFOLIE/FOFOLIS: An inferior quality linen made in Balaghat.

FUFULIS: Unidentified

GANAPOR: Unidentified, but it was linen cloth.

GANDARES: Linen and silk cloth, with blue strips. It was produced, both in Golconda and in Cambay.

GASEASEI: Unidentified.

GOLDARES: Unidentified.

GORGÃO/GORGORÃO: A textile made with mixed threads of wool and silk. An expensive variety.

GUINE GROSSO/:GUINE CLOTH. There were two kinds of cloths *ROUPAS PRETAS*: in this variety one thin and the other coarse having two colours, blue and black. Bulk of this textile was produced in the regions of Balaghat and Golconda and exported to the African countries for the use of slaves or for its exchange. Normally, in Portuguese sources this has been mentioned as *ROUPAS PRETAS*, the Black Cloth or the cloth for the Africans (Blacks). Since this was purposely made for the exchange in the forts of the Mina, Sofala, Mozambique and Angola, why, probably, it was named as *Roupas Pretas*.

GUINGÃO: Cotton and silk textiles of Balaghat and Cambay.

GUDURIAS/GODORIAS: Bed covers made of silk.

HAMAUS: Silk textiles. Origin not found. from Gujarat, Pulicut and Golconda.

JURINS/JOINS: Unidentified textile.

LADRILHO: Chintz. It was a printed cloth

LOUÇA: Means pottery but there was also cloth of this name.

MANTAGENS GRANDE: Cambay cloth in big size. Perhaps it was a broader in breadth and length. It is also possible that it used to come in bales.

MANTAGENS PEQUENO: Cambay cloth in small size. Probably piece cloth.

MERBOLANOS/MALEMOLE: MALMAL, A very thin cotton cloth of Bengal. It used to come from Dacca and other surrounding regions.

MAURIS: It was a Cambay product.

MEMUDI: Mehmudi. An expensive textile from Gujarat produced in the name of the Sultan Mehmud Begra.

PACHORIS/PACHARIS: A Cotton textile produced in Balaghat. Golconda, and Bijapur.

PANOS : Textile pieces made of linen, cotton, woollen, and silken threads.

PERCALÇOS/PERCALE: Cambric-Muslin, Cotton textile, white and thin. It was very tightly woven.

RENDA: Literally it mean knitted or hand made by Qureishe. A netlike ornamental fabric. (LACE work).

RENGO: Spun cotton to weave Muslin.

ROUPAS SORTEADAS: Cloths in Lot.

SAGARIS/SAGURIS: Unidentified cloth.

SACOS: Bags / Gunny Bags.

SLAMPURI: It is named on the name of a city called Salempur but its how about not traceable.

SANDOL BAGIS: Unidentified cloth.

SARIS/SARIÇA: Sarassa, or Pleasant Printed cotton fabric

SARASSA (Chintz) from Gujarat.

SARJA : Silk and Woollen textiles.

SARSALA: Unidentified cloth.

SATIN/SATIM: Satin / Velvet. It was incorporated with silk, gold or silver threads. It was very expensive cloth. Mostly they were from Persia, Gujarat and Bengal.

SATIM FALSO AMARELO: Imitation of satin in yellow colour.

SEDA, BARQUASSE DA/:Silk Cloth. Plain silk cloth in different (ROUPAS DA SEDA) colours.

SEMEANOS/SEMIANOS: Semiano (a Chintz) produced mostly in Samana, in the neighbourhood of Delhi and Sirhind.

TAFECIRA DOS SINDEA: Stripped Cloth from Sindh.

TAFICIRA/TAFESIRA

TAFETA: Silk Fabric. It was a silken textile generally illustrated with various colours and used for the curtains of doors, windows, and for the cover of chairs. It could be used for the clothes also. It was an exclusive use of aristocrats.

TENDA: Cotton cloth. It was produced in Balaghat, Bijapur and Golconda.

TENDAROS/TANDAROS: Unidentified cloth.

TAPETE: Carpet. It was small size rather inferior quality stuff.

TAUQUAS/TOAQUAS: Though real variety not known but it seems that it was brought from China.

TOALHA: Towel.

VELUDE/VELLUDO: Velvet. As mentioned above. Mostly brought from Persia. An inferior quality was also produced in Gujarat and Bengal.

ZUARTE: Cotton textile from Camay and Surat.

Appendix - VIII

Volume of Textiles Export during the Seventeeth Century in Bails 1607-1658

Year	Alcatifa	Algodáo	Almofadinho	Arganizes	Balachachos
1607-9	: In all there were 30 big boxes, 70 Half boxes, 83 Bales, 59 half Bales, 13 *Mafemedes* (exact word in English is not known) 3 *Canastras* e 4 *Quartos*.				
1614	-	-	-	20	-
1615	20	820 balls	9	-	-
1616	7	-	-	6,970	1,760
1617	a	a	a	a	a
1718	In all there were 109 big boxes, 403 small boxes, 423 bales, 17 small bales were exported on two ships.				
1719	In all there were 70 big boxes and 7 bales were exported among which there 2,200 pieces in 8 varieties of textiles among these bundles.				
1723	In all 100 big boxes of fine cloths were exported.				
1630	60	-	-	4,800	-
1635	In all 36 big boxes, 13 boxes and 23 bales were exported.				
1636	Only 12 *Fardos* (bales) were exported- all *Roupas Pretas* (black cloths).				
1643	In all 40,000 pieces of cloth exported from Diu to Mozambique				
1649	169 *alcatifas* (carpets) 30,188 kgs.. cloths				
1657	In all 1,440 pieces of cloths were exported to Portugal.				
1658	In all 80,000 pieces of cloths were exported from Diu to Mozambique.				

a - *Trade was conducted but details are not available.*

Appendix - VIII Contd.

YEAR	BALAGHATI	BAMES	BANCAIS	BEATILHA	BEIRAME	BEIRAMIHO
1614	50	-	-	-	-	20
1615	304	-	-	10,362	5,464	-
1616	-	7,540	3,070	25,350	9,700	2,710
1617	a	a	a	a	a	a
1643	-	-	-	8,650	-	-
1649	-	-	-	6,864	-	-

a - Trade was conducted but details not found.

\- Means volume not available.

APPENDIX - VIII Contd.

YEAR	BENGALINHO	BERTANGIS	BIÇA	BOFETA BORALHO	BORNEO	BAFTA
1614	-	-	-	5	-	-
1615	-	70	-	2	-	-
1616	50	2,520	-	160	100	30
1630	-	10,000	-	-	-	-
1649	-	-	-	4,360	-	-

- Means volume not available.

APPENDIX - VIII Contd.

YEAR	CACHA	CANEQUIN	CASCASIS	CHANDES	CEO-LEO	CASSA DE BENGAL
1615	1,757	10,019	-	-	-	620
1616	2,750	53,810	1,640	19,460	2	-
1630	18,200	79,880	-	7,760	-	-
1633	-	-	-	2,290	-	-
1634	-	-	-	800	-	-

- Means volume not available.

APPENDIX - VIII Contd.

YEAR	CAELA	COCHINILHA	COLCHA	COTONIA DAMASCO	DESPICES	CUTUNIA
1613	-	-	-	-	69	-
1615	92	160	47	40	11	-
1616	-	-	841	10,060	-	2,000
1619	-	-	-	-	-	2,680
1630	-	-	9,188	-	-	-
1649	-	-	158	-	-	

- Means volume not available.

APPENDIX - VIII Contd.

YEAR	DARYABADI	DARYAPURI	DOTINS	FIADOS	FUFULIS	GANAPOR
1616	-	-	8,330	76,120	29,100	800 kgs.
1630	-	-	43,920	-	-	-
1649	2,000	600	-	-	-	-

- Means volume not available.

Appendix - VIII Contd.

YEAR	GANDARES	GORGÃO	ROUPAS PRETAS	GUDURIAS	JOIN	HAMAUS	LADRILHO
1615	-	200	-	-	8,440	-	-
1616	4,200	-	-	400	180	-	8,320
1617	-	-	5,000	-	-	-	-
1619	4,000	-	77,000Kg	-	-	-	18,920 pcs.
1630	-	-	2,160	-	1,580	-	-
1633	4,750	-	-	-	-	-	-
1634	2,840	-	-	-	-	-	-
1635	8,500	-	-	-	-	-	-
1649	-	585	10,132	-	-	280	-

- Means volume not available.

Appendix - VIII Contd.

YEAR	MANTAGENS	MAURIS	PACHORIS	PANOS	PERCALES	MEHMUDI
1615	-	-	-	1,877	-	-
1616	3,520	-	2,770	3,790	-	-
1619	3,620	-	-	-	-	-
1649	-	3,675	-	580	32,590	200

- Means volume not available.

Appendix - VIII Contd.

YEAR	RENGOS	ROUPAS DE ALGODÃO	ROUPAS DA SEDA	SACOS	SAGARIS	SALAMPURI
1615	-	8	163	1,960	-	-
1616	120	18,460	-	-	1,050	-
1619	-	18,920	-	-	-	-
1623	-	100 Boxes	-	-	-	-
1630	-	40,540	520	-	-	-
1649	-	-	-	-	-	1,277
1657	-	1,440	-	-	-	-

- Means volume not available.

APPENDIX - VIII Contd.

YEAR	SIAVENI DORNAEL	SARISA	SARSALAS	SATIN FALSO	SEDA	SEMEANOS
1613	-	-	-	-	44kgs..	-
1615	--	-	53		1,955kgs. 1,953Bundles	20
1616	-	100	1,900	-	5,035kgs..	2,400
1649	3,510	-	-	-	18,966kgs..	-

- Means volume not available.

APPENDIX - VIII Contd.

YEAR	TAFECIRA	TAFETA	TANDAROS	TAPETE	VELUDE
1615	110	432	105	-	5
1616	280	-	-	70	-
1630	11,600	180	-	-	-

- Means volume not available.

Appendix - IX

Export of Textiles from Goa to Lisbon at a Glance

YEAR	TOTAL EXPORT IN PIECES	SILK/COTTON ROLLS	SOURCES
1613	151 pcs./3 Gunny Bags.	44 kgs..silk	*India* cx. 2, doc. 93
1614	95 pcs.	-	*India* cx. 2, doc. 147
1615	42,332 pcs. /24 carpets	1,955 kgs.silk 1,132 rolls silk 820 rolls cot.	*India* cx. 3 doc. 152
1616	239,803 pcs./77 carpets 200 bales,/72 big boxes 35 boxes,/9 half boxes/126 pcs.	5,035 kgs.. silk 2,400 rolls silk 76,120 kgs. cot.	*India* cx. 4 docs.25,50 93, 104, 135, 177, 186
1617	5,500 pcs.	-	*India* cx. 4, doc. 137
1618	108 big boxes/403 small boxes 423 bales /17 half bales	-	*Ibid*
1619	70 boxes/7 bales/31,620 pcs. Cloth /77,000 kgs.. Guine Grosso	-	*India* cx. 6, doc. 55
1623	100 big boxes	-	*LML*, 17, pp. 164-179
1630	265,423 pcs. / 60 carpets	-	*LMG*, 13b, pp. 164-79
1633	7,046 pcs.	-	*India* cx. 10, docs. 122, 206
1634	3,800 pcs.	-	*India* cx. 13
1635	8,300 pcs.	-	*India* cx. 13 doc. 66, *LML*, 32, pp. 172-72v.
1643	40,000 pcs. for Mozambique	-	*India*, cx. 15, doc. 87, cx. 17, doc. 49.
1649	40,001 pcs./146 carpets	-	*India*, cx. 20, doc. 126
1657	1,440 pcs.	-	*India*, cx. 23, doc. 85
1658	80,000 pcs. (Diu-Mozambique)	-	*ACF*, 1167, pp. 197; *India*, cx. 17, doc. 49.

- Means data not available.

APPENDIX - X

Purchase Price of Textiles in India

YEAR	NAME OF THE TEXTILE	PRICE /CORI IN XS.	PRICE P/P IN Xs./TANKA	SOURCES
1614	Arganizes	26.50	1.32	*India*, cx. 2 doc. 147
	Balagate	25.00	1.25	
	Satin	53.33	2.66	
	Beiraminho	36.50	1.82	
	Bafta	100.00	5.00	
	Cabaia	40.00	2.00	
1615	Cochinilha	8.00	2.00	*India*, cx. 3, doc. 1
	Damasquilho	122.50	12.50	
	Bags	3.00	.75 T	
	Velvet	50.00 Xs.		
1616	Bames	14.00	3.50 T.	*India*, cx. 4 doc. 50
	Biças	10.00	2.50 T.	
	Chandes	12.00	3.00 T.	
	Despices	10.00	2.50 T.	
	Dotin	25.00	2.25	
	Gandares	6.00	1.50	
	Mantagens Large	10.00	2.50	
	Mantagens small	6.00	1.50	
1633	Gandares	10.00	2.50	*India*, cx. 13,
	Gandares silk	15.00	3.75	docs. 122, 206.
	Chandes	20.00	1.00 xs.	doc. 66
1635	Gandares silk	30.00	1.50 xs.	
	Gandares Linens	23.50	1.60 xs.	
1637	Bames white	20.00	1.00 xs.	
	Botalho	26.50	1.32 xs.	
	Canequin	20.25	1,1.50 xs.	
	Calico-coarse	60.00	3.00 xs.	
	Chandes super	30.00	1.50 xs.	
	Chandes Infer.	23.50	1.17 to	
		26.50	1.32 xs.	
	Chandes silk	33-36	1-2.00 xs.	
	Chandes linen	26-30	1-1.50 xs.	
	Mantazen large	20-24	1-1.50 xs.	
	Mantazen small	13.50	3.50 T.	

APPENDIX - XI

Rice Trade at a Glance
1628 - 1661

YEAR	FROM VARIOUS PARTS TO	VOLUME IN QUINTALS
1629-1655	Ceylon	43,356
1629-1661	Goa	42,513
1628-1640	Malacca	22,319
1633-1657	Mozambique	16,620
1629-1652	Muscat	97,576
Over all total purchase and consumption -		2,22,392
Over all average out of 21 years exports		10,587

Purchase of Rice with its Geographical Origin 1626-1661

AREA	PURCHASE IN QUINTALS	PERCENTAGE
Goa	70,586	31.74 %
Kanara	1,10,974	50.00 %
Malabar	3,756	1.68 %
Northern ports	20,444	9.19 %
Unidentified	16,628	7.47 %

APPENDIX - XII

List of Commodities sent for the Exchange of Saltpetre To the Nayaka of Madurai

NAME OF THE COMMODITIES	Xs.	T(a	R(b)
5 Quintals 1.02 of Clove with the R/ of 220 Xs	1,184	3	50
2 Bahar 2.10 of Ivory with the R/O 430 Xs.	0,922	0	40
60 Quintals of Leads with the R/O 20 Xs.	1,200	0	00
53 Quintals 3.14 of Sulphur with the R/O 20 Xs.	1,107	1	00
SILK			
1 Ps. of Velvet grey colour 21 covados with the R/O 4.5 Xs	.0,094	2	30
1 Velvet of China, 21.5 covados, with the R/O 4.5 Xs.	0.094	3	45
2 Ps. of Velvet Golden from Agra, each of 20.5 covados at the R/O 5 xs.	0,205	0	00
1 ps. of Tabi	0,032	0	00
1 ps. of Damasco blue and yellow	0,034	0	00
2 ps. of white Damasco 34 Xs. p/p	0,068	0	00
2 ps. of Damsco of Lacara 40 xs. Each	0,080	0	00
1 ps. of Damasco Carmesian	0,030	0	00
1 ps. of Damasco of 34 covados	0,064	0	00
180.25 Covados of Cochineal (of Mexico insect dyed) 4 Fardos, 11 Xs. per Covado	1,982	3	45
GOLD CHAIN			
1 Necklace of Gold of Lajo de Pontas which weighed 5 Mark. 2 Onc. 3 Oitavas with the rate of 224 xs. per Mark. (Marco)	1,186	0	30
1 Necklace of Gold of Laja which weighed 6 Mark and 3 Oitava and 1/2 with the rate of 235 Xs. per Mark.	1,422	4	15
1 Big necklace which weighed 4 Mark. 5 Ounce 1 oitavas 48 graos with the rate of 230 Xs. per Mark.	1,069	3	40
1 Necklace of which weighed 3 Mark 7 Ounce 24 Graos with the rate of 243 xs. per Mark.	0,942	4	27
1 Chaneiro with one Pendulon along with other two more pendulom, weighed 4 Mark 1 ounce 1 oitava and 48 Graos with the rate of 243 Xs. per Mark	1,008	2	13
1 Necklace of Braga style weighed, 3 Mark1 ounce and 7 oitava and 24 graos at the rate of 230 Xs. per Mark.	0,745	0	35

1 Small necklace which weighed 1 Mark 1 ounce and 1 oitava and 24 graos at the ate of 230 xs.	0,263	2	43
1 Cordão which weighed 1 Mark 4 ounces1 oitava and 30 grãos at the rate of 218 xs. per mark.	0,331	4	00
1 Necklace of the Gold of Laja del cochado weighed 3 mark 4 oitavas 18 graos at the rate of 230 xs.	0,705	1	22
GOLD IN POWDER			
11 Pães of gold of China which in all weighed 17 mark 4 ounces 18 grãos at the rate of 234 xs. And a half	4,126	3	18
Total expenditure on all the commodities	18,805	2	10

Sources : AHU., *India*, cx. 11 Doc. 44, dated 1635

a : Tanka. **b** Reis, (It was na identical coin.)

APPENDIX - XIII

Saltpetre Export at a Glance 1616-1663

YEAR	VOLUME IN kgs.	VOLUME IN QUINTAL
1616	420	8
1621-1630	1,10,350	2,105
1631-1640	6,63,100	12,737
1641-1650	5,23,65	69,984
1651-1660	5,69.239	10,852
1661-1663	22,920	436
Over all total	18,94,693	36,124
Average for 20 years	94,735	1,806
Over all average for 43 Years	44,063	840

Bibliography

The material for this work has been collected, mainly, from a couple of archival repositories in Europe and in India. The Arquivo Histórico Ultramarino, Lisbon, the Arquivo Nacional da Torre do Tombo, Lisbon, Portugal, Arquivo General de Simancas, Spain, Historical Archives of Goa at Panjim were some of the major source of information besides many libraries in all these places. The entire work is based chiefly on 15,000 documents in manuscripts (consisting of about 18,000-20,000 pages) or original papers. A brief detail about the archives, libraries and the series utilised in has been furnished here below:

1. Manuscript Sources

Portugal

Arquivo Historico Ultramarino, Lisboa

This archives is the major source of information for the quantitative data of this study on the Portuguese trade in the seventeenth century. The documents are preserved mainly in *Caixas* (boxes), consisting of loose manuscript papers in files. Each file contains from 1 to 200 fólios, *Maços* (bundles of documents) and *Códices* (codex-bound volumes)- Following are the series of documents which were consulted for this work:

Documentos soltos relativos a India (Loose papers)

There are about 40 *caixas* in this series which cover the period from 1509 to 1833, but only twenty eight *caixas* were used for this study since the period was limited to 1663. Each *caixas* had between 109 and 259 files, and each file has from 1 to 10 documents covering ten to 200 pages of manuscripts. Years and other details of the each *caixas* consulted by me are as follows:

Section Sala da India	S. N. of Caixas	Period	No. of Documents (in files)
do	Caixa 1	1509-1611	109
do	Caixa 2	1612-1614	149
do	Caixa 3	1615	190
do	Caixa 4	1616-1617	208
do	Caixa 5	1618	201
do	Caixa 6	1619-1621	149
do	Caixa 7	1622-1623	171
do	Caixa 8	1624-1625	232
do	Caixa 9	1626-1629	233
do	Caixa 10	1630-1634	217
do	Caixa 11	1635	225
do	Caixa 12	1636-1637	153
do	Caixa 13	1638-1639	191
do	Caixa 14	1640-1643	184
do	Caixa 15	1643	132
do	Caixa 16	1644	173
do	Caixa 17	1644-1645	180
do	Caixa 18	1645-1646	200
do	Caixa 19	1646-1647	116
do	Caixa 20	1648-1650	199
do	Caixa 21	1650-1652	168
do	Caixa 22	1653-1654	145
do	Caixa 23	1655-1656	125
do	Caixa 24	1656-1660	173
do	Caixa 25	1661-1663	254
do	Caixa 26	1664-1665	229
do	Caixa 27	1668	192
do	Caixa 28	1669-1671	247

Besides these *Caixas*, there are about 350 *Códices* under various heads covering the period from 1657 to 1848. It contains documents regarding various subjects such as treaties between the Portuguese and the Indian rulers, instructions from the king of Portugal to his servants in the East, provision, and various matters regarding the income and expenditure of the state of India. All these papers were received and kept by the *Conselho do Estado da India*

(Council of the Indian States) at Lisbon. There are about thirty-seven *códices* under various heads that I have utilised in the preparation of this work as they were dealing about the period of this study.

No. of the Códice	Year	Fols. and Doc.
Códice 31/1042	1617-1618	280
Códice 32/1043	1620-1621	448
Códice 33/1044	1621-1622	365
Códice 34/1045	1622	268
Códice 35/1046	1623-1624	504
Códice 35a	1624	302
Códice 35b	1624	116
Códice 36/1049	1635	296
Códice 37/1050	1627	279
Códice 38/1051	1629	350
Códice 39/1052	1631/1632	326
Códice 40/1053	1634-1635	466
Códice 41/1054	1635-1636	506
Códice 42	1636-1637	566
Códice 43/1056	1637-1639	562
Códice 44/1057	1640-1643	638
Códice 45	1653-1656	766
Códice 46	1656-1669	920

Registo de Cartas

No. of the Códice	Year	Fols. and Doc.
Códice 208	1643-1678	784

Forais da India (1630-1670)

No. of the Códice	Year	Fols. and Doc.
Códice 218	1630	680
Códice 219	1621	120
Códice 220	1646	104
Códice 221	1618-1628	600
Códice 222	1614	500

Cartas Régias

No. of the Códice	Year	Fols. and Doc.
Códice 275	1624-1667	900
Códice 276	1668-1708	
Códice 278	1643-1652	884

Livro das Consultas de Documentos vindos da India

No. of the Códice	Year	Fols. and Doc.
Códice 432	1629-1651	
Códice 435	1651	234
Códice 443	Séc. XVII	294
Códice 281	1588-1596	600
Códice 282	1601-1604	400
Códice 283	1607-1609	380
Códice 284	1614	450
Códice 285	1624-1629	624
Códice 286	1630-1636	500
Códice 476		
Códice 1164		

Arquivo Nacional Da Toree Do Tombo, Lisbon

The second most important repository for the collection of valuable sources is the National Archives of Lisbon (Arquivo Nacional da Torre do Tombo). Here, nothing could be found better than the *Livro das Monções* or *Documentos Remettido da India* by an economic historian. There are 62 vols. (Códices) of this series consisting of folios 200 to 800 in each *códice*. Besides this, there were many other series found useful for this present work. The following are the details of each series consulted for extracting necessary documents.

Livro das Monções **or** ***Documentos Remettido da India***

This series has mainly the correspondence between the king of Portugal and the Viceroys and Governors of Portuguese India regarding trade and economic matters.

No. of the Códice	Year
Códice 1	1565
Códice 2	1607-1608
Códice 3	1609-1610
Códice 4	1610-1611
Códice 5	1612
Códice 6	1612-1613
Códice 7	1613-1614
Códice 8	1614-1615
Códice 9	1616
Códice 10	1616-1617
Códice 11	1618-1619
Códice 12	1619
Códice 13	1620
Códice 14	1624
Códice 15	1620-1622
Códice 16	1622
Códice 17	1622-1645
Códice 18	1645-1623
Códice 19	1623-1624
Códice 20	1624
Códice 21	1624
Códice 22	1625-1626
Códice 23	1626
Códice 24	1626-1627

Códice 25	1627-1628
Códice 26	1628-1629
Códice 27	1630
Códice 28	1631
Códice 29	1631-1632
Códice 30	1632-1633
Códice 31	1634-1634
Códice 32	1635
Códice 33	1634-1636
Códice 34	1635-1636
Códice 35	1635-1636
Códice 36	1636
Códice 37	1636-1637
Códice 38	1636-1637
Códice 39	1637
Códice 40	1637-1638
Códice 41	1638
Códice 42	1637-1638
Códice 43	1638
Códice 44	1638-1639
Códice 45	1638-1639
Códice 46	1639-1641
Códice 47	1640-1641
Códice 48	1640-1644
Códice 49	1641-1642
Códice 50	1641-1644
Códice 51	1642-1643
Códice 52	1643
Códice 53	1643
Códice 54	1644
Códice 55	1645-1646
Códice 56	1645-1653
Códice 57	1645-1648
Códice 58	1647-1649
Códice 59	1648-1649
Códice 60	1649-1650
Códice 61	1650-1651
Códice 62	1651-1660

Cartas dos vicereis da India e outras pessoas para El-Rei, e Alguns Alvarás

Códice	B267

Registo da Correspondência de El-Rei D. João 4º para diversas Autoridades do Reino

Livro - 1	1645-1681

Chancelarias Reais de Dom Manuel I

Códice	38

Corpo Cronológico

It contains, mainly, the correspondence between the Viceroys of India and the king of Portugal, and the Papers of the Portuguese exchequer. The collection dates from 1611 to 1699 in 525 Maços (82,902 documents).

Maço	1-3-20

BIBLIOTECA DE ACADEMIA DAS CIENCIAS, Lisboa

Série Vermelho

Códices 559, 312[a]

Biblioteca Da Ajuda, Lisboa

Jesuitas na Ásia

There are several hundreds of codices in this series throwing light on the pepper, and cinnamon trade. It provides a bulk of information about the foundation of the Portuguese India Company on the pattern of the other European companies. It also provides information regarding the position of the Portuguese state in India. The following are the series and documents consulted for the present work:

No. of Códice	Period
46-xiii-30	XVII century (1603-1664)
49-v-8	do
49-x-28	do
49-xii-38	do
49-xiii-12	do
50-v-37	do
51-vi-2	do
51-vii-12	do
51-vii-13	do
51-vii-30	do
51-vii-32	do
51-x-2	do
51-vii-13	do
51-vii-30	do
51-vii-32	do
51-x-2	do

Biblioteca da Sociedade de Geografia De Lisboa

Casa da India

This is one of the best series and for the first time brought into light. This series of documents are kept in Maços (bundles). They are kept in the *Reservado* section.

Maços 3 & 4, deal with the income and expenditure of the fortresses and factories in India in the early seventeenth century. They were written around 1615-1618.

146 - Reservado, maço Nº 4, docs. 88. are known as **Papeis de Bartolomeu Caldeira, Tesourero de Especiaria 1587-1624 (de Casa da India).**

There are seventy-seven (77) files of manuscript documents in this series which have been collected and numbered by Luciano Cordeiro (Mss. **colleccionado e numerado por Luciano Cordeiro)** Besides, the following documents are also made use of by me from this library.

146, Res. Maço no. 4, Doc. Nº 101, *Casa da India* - Contas relativas a pimenta nos anos de 1560-a-1564 (Mss. 9 fols.)

Spain

Archivo General De Simancas
Secretarias Provinciales
Libro 1479, Codex 1571 (2784)

England

Archives in the Library of King's college
University of London
Sir Joseph Lynch Bart Collection,
Mss. *Codex* 14, Vol. I

This codex is known as *Codex Lynch.* In fact this is the true account of the Portuguese political as well as economic status during 1627-1634 written by Captain-in-chief of the Indian Voyage in 1611, and Governor of Portugal, 1633, Dom António de Atayde (Conde de Castro). It is a bound volume entitled, *Companhia das Indias* and composed of original papers and contemporary copies covering the entire history of the *Portuguese East India Company.* This volume is a gift to the King's College Library (Archives section) by Sir Joseph Lynch Bart.

India

Historical Archives of Goa, Panaji
Livro das Monções ou Moções do Reino

This is one of the biggest collections of the Goa Archives. It contains correspondence between the Portuguese Viceroys and the kings of Portugal regarding the political as well as the economic affairs. There are about 456 *códices* in this series, dating from mid sixteenth century to the early twentieth century (1560-1914). Only 28 vols., out of the total, have been found useful for the present work as they deal with period of this study. The detail regarding the codices I have made use of for my thesis are as follows:

No. of the Códice	Year
Códice 1	1605-1607
Códice 2a	1583-1585
Códice 2b	1595-1601
Códice 3a	1585-1589
Códice 5	1595-1590
Códice 6-A	1604-1606
Códice 6-B	1605
Códice 7	1601-1603
Códice 8	1601-1602
Códice 9, 10 and 11	1604-1609
Códice 12	1613-1617
Códice 13-A	1611-1630
Códice 13-B	1629-1630
Códice 14	1630-1631
Códice 15	1631-1632
Códice 16-A	1632
Códice 16-B	1632
Códice 17	1632-1633
Códice 18	1633
Códice 19-A	1633-1634
Códice 19-B	1634-1635
Códice 19-C	1634-1635
Códice 19-D	1634-1635
Códice 20	1634
Códice 21-A	1640
Códice 21-B	1640-1641
Códice 22-B	1620-1653
Códice 23-A	1653-1654
Códice 23-B	1653-1654
Códice 24	1615-1654
Códice 25	1654-1656
Códice 26-A	1656-1658
Códice 26-B	1657-1660
Códice 28-A	1661-1663
Códice 28-B	1662-1663

Assentos do Conselho da Fazenda

This is one of the most useful series an economic historian comes across in the Goa Archives. This mainly deals with the financial affairs of the states of India. All the expenditures of the state had to be sanctioned by the Ministers of the Council of the Finance. In reality, this is a collection of the minutes of the Council of Finance of Goa. Local trade and income are the major subjects. The details regarding this series are as follows:

No. of the Códice	Year
Códice 1159	1613-1621
Códice 1160	1618-1625
Códice 1161	1627-1631
Códice 1162	1631-1637
Códice 1163	1637-1643
Códice 1164	1643-1647
Códice 1165	1647-1649
Códice 1166	1652-1666
Códice 1167	1653-1660
Códice 1168	1660-1660

Besides these two series, there are various others also which has been used in the present work. They are as follows:

Cartas e Ordens

No. of the Códice	Series	Year
Códice 779	*Livro das Cartas e Ordens* (Secretari geral)	1609-1706
Códice 2595	*Livro das Cartas e Ordens* (Fazenda)	1624
Códice 2596	*Livro das Cartas e Ordens* (Fazenda)	1642-1667

Cartas Patentes e Alvarás

Códices 4469- 4513	1596-1664

Consultas do serviços de Partes

No. of the Códice	Year
Códice 1041	1614-1649
Códice 1042	1629-1679
Códice 1043	1618-1652

Regimentos e Instruções

No. of the Códice	Year
Códice 1418	1564-1631
Códice 1419	1596-1640
Códice 1420	1616-1640

Regimentos das Fortalezas da India

No. of the Códice	Year
Códice 3025	1545-1630
Códice 3030	1565-1605
Códice 4460	1564-1690

Printed Sources (Primary)

ALBUQUERQUE, Afonso de, *Cartas de Afonso de Albuquerque*. 7 Vols., ed. Raymundo António de Bulhão Pato, Acad. Ciên., Lisboa, 1884-1935.

ALBUQUERQUE, Braz Afonso de, *Commentários do Grande Afonso Dalbuquerque*, 2 vols. ed. Joaquim Verissimo Serrão, INCM, Lisboa, 1973.

BALDAEUS, Philippus, <A True and Exact Description of the Most Celebrated East India Coast of Malabar and Coromandel> in *A Collection of Voyages and Travels...*, comps. Awn sham Churchill and John Churchill, 4 vols., London, 1704

BARBOSA, Duarte, *The Book of Duarte Barbosa, an Account of the Countries Bordering on the Indian Ocean and their Inhabitants*, Transt. & ed. Mansel Longworth Dames, 2 vols., Hakluyt Society, London, 1918-1921.

BARROS, João de, e Couto, Diogo do, Da Ásia de..., Décadas Primeira a Duodécima 24 vols., Livraria Sam Carlos, Lisboa, 1973.

BIKER, J.F.J., (ed.) Collecção *de tratados e concertos de pazes que o Estado da Índia Portuguesa fez com os reis e senhores em que teve relações nas partes da Ásia e África Oriental desde o princípio da conquista até ao fim do Século XVI*, vols. 1-13, Lisboa, 1881.

BOCARRO, António, *Década 13ª da História da Índia*, 2 vols. ed. Rodrigo José de Lima Felner, Lisboa, 1876.

BRAGANÇA PEREIRA, A. B. de (ed.) *Arquivo Português Oriental*, 11 vols., Tip. Rangel, Bastorá, Goa, 1936-1940

CORREIA, Gaspar, *Lendas da Índia*, publicação por Rodrigo José de Lima Felner, 4 vols. , Coimbra, 1922.

COSTA, Francisco da, <Relatório sobre o trato da pimenta>, feito por Francisco da Costa, escrivão da feitoria de Cochim, (cód. 1571, Sécretarias provinciales, Archivo General de Simancas, Espanha,) in António da Silva Rego, ed. *Documentação Ultramarina Portuguesa*, vol. 1, CEHU, Lisboa, 1963, pp. 295-379,

CUNHA RIVARA, J.H. da, (ed.) *Arquivo Português Oriental*, 6 vols. em 9 partes, Nova Goa, 1857-1876.

DANVERS, Frederick. C., (ed.) *Letters Received by the East India Company from it's Servants in the East*, 6 vols., London, 1896.

DELLA VALLE, Pietro, *The Travel of Pietro della Valle in India*, 2 vols., London, 1892.

FALCÁO , Luís de Figueiredo, *Livro em que se contém toda a fazenda e real património dos reinos de Portugal, Índia e ilhas adjacentes e outras particularidades*, Lisboa, 1859.

FARIA E SOUSA, Manuel de, *Ásia Portuguesa*, 6 vols., Porto, 1947.

FELNER, José de Lima, *Subsídios para a História da Índia*, Lisboa, 1868.

FERNAM MENDEZ PINTO, *Peregrinaçam de Fernam Mendez Pinto* (nova edição, conforme a de 1614), 2 vols., Porto, 1962.

FOSTER, William, (ed.) *The Embassy of Sir Thomas Roe to India*, 1615-19, London, 1929.

- (ed.) *The English Factories in India* 1616-1669, 13 vols., Oxford, 1906-1927.

GROTIUS, Hugo, *The Freedom of the Sea (Mare Libervm) or the Right which belongs to the Dutch to take part in the East Índia Trade*, Oxford, 1916.

JOURDAIN, J., Journal of John Jourdain, *Describing the Experiences in India.*, ed. W. Foster, Hakluyt Society, Series , vol., XVI, London.

LINSCHOTEN, Jan. H. Van, *The Voyages of John Huyghen Van Linschoten to the East Indies*, 2 vols., London, 1895

LUZ, Francisco P. Mendes da, <Livro das cidades e fortalezas, que a coroa de Portugal tem nas partes da Índia, e das capitanias e mais cargos que nelas ha, e da importância delles>, in *Stvdia*, nº 6, CEHU, Lisboa, 1960.

LUZ, Francisco P. Mendes da, *O Conselho da Índia*, Lisboa, MCML.

MATOS, Luis de (Introdução), *Imagens do Oriente no Século VI* (Reprodução do códice Português da Biblioteca Casanatense), INCM, Lisboa, 1985.

ORTA, Garcia d', *Coloquios dos simples e drogas e cousas medicinais da Índia*, Ed. por Conde de Ficalho, 2 vols., Imp. Nac., Lisboa, 1891-1895.

PAIVA, Costa e Herculano, Alexandre, *Roteiro de Viagem de Vasco da Gama, MCCCXCV*, Lisboa, 1861.

REGO, António da Silva, (ed) *Documentos sobre os Portugueses em Moçambique e na África Central*, vols. I-VI, CEHU, Lisboa, 1962.

SEN, Surender Nath, *The Indian Travels of Thevenot and Carreri*, vol. I, New Delhi, 1949.

SOUSA, Alfredo Botelho de, *Subsídios para a História Militar Marítima da Índia*, vol. 1, (1585-1605), Lisboa, 1930.

TAVERNIER, Jean-Baptiste, *Travels in Índia*, trad. e ed. V. Ball Crook, 2 vols., London and New York, 1889.

TOMÉ PIRES, *The Suma Oriental of Tomé Pires*, 2 vols., London, 1944.

VARTHEMA, Ludovico di, *Travels of Ludoviço di Varthema in Egypt, Syria, Arabia Deserta and Arabia Felix, in Persia, Índia, and Ethiopia*, Hakluyt Society, London, 1863.

- *The Dutch in Malabar - Selection of the Madras Government*, No. 13, Madras, 1911.

- < Monumenta Historiae Índiae>, in *Journal of Bombay Historical Society* (JBHS) vol. , N°s. I & 2, Bombay, 1929 (March and September).

Published Sources

ARAGÃO, A. C. Teixeira de, *Descrição geral e história das moedas cunhadas em nome dos reis, regentes e governadores de Portugal*, 3 vols., Lisboa, 1874-1880.

AZEVEDO, João Lúcio de, *Épocas de Portugal Económico*, Lisboa, (IVª edição.)

BOXER, Charles R.; <O General do mar! António Telles, o seu combate naval contra os Hollandeses na barra de Goa em 1630>, in *BIVG*, nº 37, Goa, 1938.

BOXER, Charles R., *The Portuguese Seaborne Empire*, London, 1977.

BOYAJIAN, James C., *Portuguese Bankers at the Court of Spain*, 1626-1650, New Jersey, U.S.A., 1983.

BRAUDEL, Fernand, *O Mundo Mediterrâneo e o Mundo Mediterrânico*, 2 vols., Lisboa, 1983.

CAMPOS, J.J.A., *History of the Portuguese in Bengal*, Delhi, 1979.

COMMISSARIAT, M. S., *A History of Gujarat*, 2 vols., New Delhi, 1983.

COSTA, C. A. Delduque da, <Os portugueses e os reis da Índia> in *BIVG*, nºs. 18, e 20, Goa, 1933.

CUNHA, J. Gerson da., *Contribuições para o Estudo da Numismática Indo-Portuguesa*, Lisboa, 1955.

DANVERS, Frederick Charles, *The Portuguese in Índia*, 2 vols., London, 1894.

DIFFE, Bailey W., and Winius, George D., *Foundation of the Portuguese Empire*, 1415-1580, Oxford, 1977.

DISNEY, Anthony R., *Twilight of the Pepper Empire- Portuguese Trade in South-West India in the Early Seventeenth Century*, Harvard, 1978.

ELPHINISTONE, Mountstuart, *The Rise of the British Power in the East*, London, 1887.

GODINHO, Vitorino Magalhães, *Os descobrimentos e a economia Mundial*, 4 vols., Lisboa, 1981.

HAMILTON, C. J., *The Trade Relations between England and India (1600-1896)*, Delhi, 1975.

HARRISON, J. B., *New Cambridge Modern History*, vols. I-IV, Cambridge, London, 1929.

JOSHI, P. M. (ed.), *History of Medieval Decan*, 2 vols., Hyderabad, 1943.

KAIL, O. C., *The Dutch in India*, New Delhi, 1981.

KUSUMAN, K.K., *A History of Trade and Commerce Travancore*, Mittal Publications, Delhi, 1987

KYD, N. Alexander, *History of Konkan*, London, 1899.

LACH, F. D., *Ásia in the Making of Europe*, 2 vols., in two parts, Chicago, 1971.

LANE, Fredric C., <Venice and History, The Mediterranean spice trade: Its revival in the sixteenth century> in *American Historical Review*, XLV, 1940. pp. 581-590 Foreword by Fernand Braudel, Baltimore, 1966.

LOBATO, Alexandre, *Relações Luso-Maratha*, Lisboa, 1965.

MACLAGAN, Sir Edward, *Os Jesuitas e o Grão Mogol*, Porto, 1964.

MATHEW, K. S., *The Portuguese Trade with India in the Sixteenth Century*, New Delhi, 1983.

MAURO, Frédéric, *L'Atlantique Portugais et les esclaves, (1570-1670)*, Lisboa, 1956.

MELINK-ROELOFSZ, *Asian Trade and European Influence between 1500 and about 1630*, The Hague, 1962.

MORELAND, W. H., *From Akbar to Aurangzeb*, New Delhi, 1972

- *India at the Death of Akbar*, Delhi 1923.

NAMBIAR, O. K., *The Kunjalis Admirals of Calicut*, Delhi, 1963.

NAQVI, Hamida K., *Urban Centres and Industries in Upper India*, 1550-1803, Delhi, 1968.

NAYEEM, M. A. (ed.), *External Relations of the Bijapur Kingdom*, 1489 1686, Hyderabad, 1976.

PANIKKAR, K. M., *Asia and the Western Dominance, 1498-1945*, London, 1960.

- *Malabar and the Portuguese*, Bombay 1929.

PEARSON, M. N., <Indigenous Dominance in Colonial Economy-The Goa Rendas 1600-1670,> in *Mare Luso-indicum*, Geneva, Librarie Droz, 1973, pp. 61-73.

- *Merchants and Rulers in Gujarat, The Response to the Portuguese in the Sixteenth Century*, New Delhi, 1976.

PISSURLENKAR, P.S.S., <Fragmentos Históricos> in *BIVG*, nº 47, Goa 1940.

- <Portuguese e Maratha> in *BIVG*, nºs 1-6, Goa, 1926-1929.

- <Tentativas dos Portugueses para a ocupação do Concão>, *separata dos Anais*, Lisboa, 1955.

RADAWAN, A. B., *The Dutch in Western India, 1600-1632*, Calcutta, 1976.

RAMA SWAMI, Vijaya, <Weavers in Medieval South India>, *in Indian Historical Review*, vol. VI, Nºs 1-2, New Delhi, 1982.

RIBEIRO, V., *Fatalidade Histórica da ilha de Ceilão*, Lisboa, 1971.

SASTRI, Nilakanta, *A History of South India*, Delhi, 1976.

SERJEANT, R.B., *The Portuguese Off the South Arabian Coast*, Oxford, 1963.

SEWEL, R., *A Forgotten Empire*, London, 1900.

SHASTRI, B.S., <A Note on Portuguese Shivaji Relation> in *Chhatrapati Shivaji Coronation Tercentenary Commemoration Volume*, Bombay, 1974-1975.

SILVA MORAIS, A. da, *Dicionário da Língua Portuguesa*, 2 vols., Rio de Janeiro, 1891.

SILVA, José Gentil da, <Contratos da trazida de drogas no Século XVI> subsídio e documentos, in *Revista da Faculdade de Letras*, tomo XV-2ª série, Nºs 1-2, Universidade de Lisboa, 1949, pp. 5-28.

STEENSGAARD, Niels, *Carracks, Caravans and Companies: The Structural Crisis in the European-Asian Trade in the 17th Century*, Copenhagen, 1973.

TRIPATHI, R.P., *The Rise and Fall of the Mughal Empire*, Allahabad, 1969.

VAZ, J. Ferrão, *Dinheiro Luso-Indiano*, Braga, 1980.

VIRGINIA RAU, <Um Grande mercador-banqueiro Italiano em Portugal> separata de *Estudos Italianos em Portugal*, nº 24, 1965.

WHITEWAY, R. S., *The Rise of Portuguese Power in India*, New Delhi, 1979.

WINIUS, G. D., *The Fatal History of Portuguese Ceylon, Transition to Dutch Rule*, Harvard, 1971.

ZINADÍM, História dos Portugueses no Malabar (ms. arabe do Século XVI, traduzido por David Lopes), Imprensa Nacional, Lisboa, 1898.

Bibliography for Further Reading

ADIL, Luis, e Lima A. de, *Bartolomeu Dias: Descobridor do Cabo da Boa Esperança*, Typ. C. Militar, Lisboa, 1909.

AHMAD, Afzal, <Commodity Composition of the Portuguese Trade in the 1st Half of the 17th Century, 1603-1630> *Historians at the Sea*, Seminar at the Xavier Centre for Historical Research, Panjim, Goa, February, 1981.

- <Goa Based Portuguese Export Trade in the Early 17th Century 1611-1626> *Indian History Congress*, 41st Session, Bombay, 1980 (pp. 349- 356)

- <Merchant Class in Konkan and the Portuguese Trade in the 17th Century, 1600-1662.> *All India Seminar, Department of History*, University of Poona, May, 1984.

- <Portuguese Sources for the Study of Socio-Economic Condition of Gujarat in the 17th Century>. *Urban History Seminar*, Department of History, University of Baroda, India, March, 1980.

- <Some Aspects of the Organisation of the Portuguese Trade in the 1st Half of the 17th Century>. *Indian History Congress (IHC)*, 40th Session, Waltair, India, December, 1979.

- <Socio-Economic Changes on the Western Coast of India in the 17th Century.> *All India Seminar, Friends at Archives Group*, National Archives of India, New Delhi, July, 1981.

-"Indian Textiles and the Portuguese Trade in the Seventeenth Century (1600-1663)", in ***STVDIA***, N° 48, Lisboa, 1989.

-"Desenvolvimento Económico-Comercial na Costa Ocidental da Índia (1600- 1663)" in *Encontro sobre Portugal e a Índia*, Fundação Oriente, Livros Horizonte, Lisboa, 2000.

ALBUQUERQUE, F. M. de, *Albuquerques*, G. Imperial, Lisbonne, 1967.

- *O Nosso Grande Apóstolo*, Tip. Rangel, Bastora, 1907.

- *O Senado de Goa: Memória Histórico-Archeológica*, Imp. Nac., Nova Goa, 1909.

ALMEIDA, Furtado de, *História de Portugal*, Imp. da Univ. de Coimbra, tomos I- VI, 1922-1929.

ALMEIDA, Furtado de, *Portugal e as Colónias Portuguesas*, Brasil. Ed., Coimbra, 1927.

ANDRADE, I. F. de, *Vida de Dom João de Castro*, Of. Craesbeckiana, Lisboa, 1651.

ANDRADE, J. I. de, *Cartas escriptas da Índia e da China nos anos de 1815-1835*, 2 vols., Imp. Nac., Lisboa 1847,.
-*Diário da Viagem de Vasco da Gama*, 2 vols. (com manuscrito original), Liv. Civil., Porto, 1945

ATHEIM, Franz, *A Ásia a caminho da Europa*, Liv. do Brasil, Lisboa.

AUBOYER, Jeanine, *A Vida quotadiana na Índia Antiga: Desde o Século a.c. até ao Século V d.c.*, Livros do Brasil, Lisboa, 1960.

AYALLA, Frederico Diniz, *Vasco da Gama-Quando Partiu?* Alenquer, 1898.

AZEVEDO, A.E. d'Almeida, *As Comunidades de Goa*, Lisboa, 1890.

BAIÁO, António, *Affonso de Albuquerque*, Liv. Ferin, Lisboa, 1913.

BALSEMÁO, E.A.S.N.P.de, *Os Portuguezes no Oriente*, Imp. Nac., Nova Goa, 1881.

BARBUDA, Cláudio L.M. de, *Instruções com que El-Rei D. José I mandou passar ao Estado da Índia, o Governador e Cap. general e o Arcebispo Primaz do Oriente em 1774*, Tip. Nac., Panjim, 1841.

BASTO, A. de Magalhães, *Fernão Lopes: Suas Cronicas Perdidas e a Cronica Geral do Reino*, Liv. Progredure, Porto, 1943

BEAZLEY, C. Ramond, *O Infante D. Henrique ẹ o Início dos Descobrimentos Modernos*, Liv. Civ., Porto, 1945.

BEIRÁO, António, *Segundo Cerco de Dio*, Imp. da Univ. de Coimbra, 1927.

BEN-BATUTA, *Viagens extensas e dilatadas do celebre Arabe, Abu-Abdullah.*, tomos 1 e 2, Lagoa, 1840-55.

BORCA, José, *Estado da Índia*, AGU, Lisboa, 1965.

BORDALO, Francisco Maria, *Ensaios sobre a Estatistica das Possessões Portuguezas no Ultramar*, serie, Livro V, Estado da Índia. Parte I[a] (única).

BOSSA, José, *Ao Cabo de um Ano de Caminho*, Imp. Nac., Goa, 1947.

BRAGANÇA PEREIRA, A.B. de, *Goa Portuguesa*. Imp. Nac., Goa, 1952.

- *Etnografia da Índia Portuguesa, A Civilização da Índia*, 2 vols., Tip. Rangel, Bastorá, 1940.

- *O Sistema das Castas (Ensaios Histórico-Sociológicos)*, Imp. Nac., Nova Goa, 1920.

BRION, Hypácio de, *A Índia Portugueza*, Typ. C. Militar, Lisboa, 1908.

BRITO, F. Mendes, *O Infante D. Henrique, 1394-1460*, Liv. Portugália, Lisboa, 1942.

BROCHADO, Costa, *Affonso de Albuquerque*, Portugália Ed., 1943.

BROCHADO, Costa, *Descobrimento do Atlântico*, 1958.

CABRAL, P.A., *Os sete unicos documentos de 1500, conservados em Lisboa referentes a viagem de Pedro Alvares Cabral*, Agen. Geral das Colonias, Lisboa, 1940.

CABREIRA, António, *Vasco da Gama sobre a Terra e sobre o Mar*, Typ. Inglesa, Lisboa, 1924.

CADAMOSTO, Luís de, *Viagens*, Portugália, Lisboa.

CAETANO, Marcelo, *Tradition principes et methodes de la colonisation Portugaise*, AGU, Lisboa, 1951.

CAMINHA, Pero Vaz de, *Carta a El-Rei Dom Manuel sobre o achamento do Brasil*, (1 de Maio de 1500), Imp. Nac., Lisboa, 1974.

CAMPOS, Moreira, *D. Francisco da Almeida, 1º Vice-Rei da Índia*, Ed. de Marinha, Lisboa, 1947.

CAMPOS, Viriato, *Viagem de Diogo Cão e de Bartolomeu Dias*, Perciaria, A.M Perciaria, Lisboa, 1966.

CARVALHO, A. de, *Índia Misteriosa: Povos e costumes Indus*. Tip. Atlántida, Coimbra, 1948.

CARVALHO, J.V.G. de, *Leis de Manue, Primeiro Legislador da Índia*, Imp. Nac., Nova Goa, 1859.

CASA, Alfred David, *Vasco da Gama*, Bíb. da Infância, nº. XVI, Typ. C.A. Rodrigues, Lisboa, 1916.

CASTRO, D.J. de, *Obras completas de D. João de Castro*. (ed. crítica), Luís de Mendonça de Albuquerque e A. Cortesão, Acad. Int. de Cult. Port., Lisboa, 1968-1971.

CHUMOVSKY, T.A., *Três roteiros desconhecidos de Ahmed Ibn-Majid*. ed. Acad. Ciên. da URSS, Moscow, 1957.

COELHO, C.Z. Pinto, *Apontamentos para o Estudo da História da relação de Goa*, Coimbra, 1900.

CORREIA, C. Germano da Silva, *Os Franceses na Colonização Portuguesa da Índia*, CEHU, Lisboa, 1959, (Sep. *Stvdia* No. 4)

CORREIA, F. António, *Consequência Economicas dos Descobrimentos*, Acad. Ciên. de Lisboa, Lisboa, 1937.

CORTE-REAL, M. Henrique, *Na Rota da Índia*, M.E.N., Lisboa, 1969.

CORTESÁO, Armando, *A Política do Sigilo nos Descobrimentos*, 1960.

- *Os Portugueses no Descobrimento dos Estados Unidos*, Seara Nova, Lisboa, 1949.
- *A Expansão de Pedro Álvares Cabral*, Aillaud & Bertrand, Lisboa, 1922.
- *O Mistério de Vasco da Gama*, JIU, Coimbra, 1973.
- *Primeira Embaixada Europeia à China "O Boticário e Embaixador", Tome Pires e a sua "Suma Oriental"* Caderno da Seara Nova, Lisboa, 1945.
- *Teoria Geral dos Descobrimentos Portugueses :Geografia e a Economia da Restauração*, Seara Nova, Lisboa, 1940.

CORVO, J. de Andrade, *Roteiro de Lisboa-Goa por Dom João de Castro*, Acad. Ciên., Lisboa, 1882.

COSTA, A. Fontoura da, *As Portas da Índia em 1484*, Imp. da Armada, Lisboa, 1936.

- *A Sciência Nautica dos Portugueses na Epoca dos Descobrimentos*, 1958.

COSTA, A. Manuel da, *Literatura Goesa; Apontamentos Bio-Bibliográficos para a sua História*, AGU, Lisboa.

COSTA, Brochado, *Historiógrafos dos Descobrimentos*, 1960.

COSTA, C.R. da, *Les communautés des villages à Goa*, Imp. Nac., Lisbonne, 1892.

COSTA, C.R.B.S. da, *Vade-mecum Notorial*, Tip. Literária, Margão 1923.

COSTA, Cristóvão da, *Tratado das Drogas e Medicinas das Índias Orientais*, J.I.U., Lisboa,1964.

COSTA, M. Fernandes, *As navegações Atlânticas no Século* XV, Bib. Breve, Lisboa, 1979.

COSTA, M. Gomes da, *Descobrimentos e Conquistas, Afonso de Albuquerque (1509-1515)*, Lisboa, 1929.

- *Descobrimentos e Conquistas, A Viagem de Vasco da Gama (1497-1499)*, Lisboa, 1929.

- *Descobrimentos e Conquistas. O Início do Ultramar Português (1415-1495)*, S.G. do Exército, Lisboa, 1927.

COSTA, Roberto Bruto da, *A Hidra do "Nativismo": Para História Política da Índia Portuguesa*, Typ. Bragança, Nova Goa, 1920.

COSTA, S., *Goa na História da Civilização*, Imp. Nac., Goa, 1947.

COUTO, Diogo de, *Malaca conquistada pelo Albuquerque Poema Heróico*, Off. J. A. Bulhõens, Lisboa, 1779. (3ª ed.)

COUTO, Monsenhor G., *História da Antiga Casa da Índia em Lisboa*, 1932.

CUNHA RIVARA, *Brados- A favor das comunidades das aldeias do Estado da Índia*, Imp. Nac., Nova. Goa 1870.

CUNHA, A.M. da (ed.) *Congresso na Índia Portuguesa; Subsídios para a sua História, Casa Luso-Francesa*, vols. I-IX, Nova Goa, (Congresso), 1925-1933.

CUNHA, Amadeu, *Nas Vésperas da Descoberta 1481-1486*, AGC, Lisboa, 1939.

CUNHA, J. Gerson da, *Notes on the History and Antiquities of Chaul and Bassein*, Thacker Printing, Bombay, 1876.

D'AYALLA, Fredrico Diniz, *Goa Antiga e Moderna*, Typ. Jornal do Commércio, Lisboa, 1888.

DADSHAH, Bhaganlal R., *Aryan Theory of Divine Incarnations, Memoires to Internal Congress of Orientalists*, N.P. Office, Lisbon, 1892.

DYMOCK, William, *A History of the Principal Drugs of Vegetable Origins met within British India*. vols. I-III, London, 1890-1893.

EHRIHARDT, Marion, *Um Opúsculo Alemão do Século XVI sobre a História Portuguesa do Oriente*, Borsenverein des Deutschen, Frankfurtanman, 1964.

FARIA, A. de P. de, *Christophe Colomb et les Ecrivains Gaditans*, Ernest Leroux, Paris, 1891.

FARIA, F.L. de, *Um Impresso de 1531 sobre as Empresas dos Portugueses no Oriente*. Lisboa, 1966.

FARIAS, António J. de, *Avreola dos Indios & Nobiliarchia Brahmana: Tratado Histórico. Geneologico, Panogírico, Político & Moral*, Imp. A.A. Fialho, Bombaim, 1892.

FEIO, Mariano, *As Castas Hindus de Goa, Estudos de Antropologia Cultural*, JIU, Lisboa, 1979.

FERNANDES, Braz A., *A Guide to the Ruins of Bassein*, B.H.S, Bombay, 1911.

FERNANDES, Valentim, *O manuscrito "Valentim Fernandes"*, APH, Lisboa, 1940.

FERO, J. de Sousa e, *A Índia: Impressões e Sugestoes*, Tip. Cooperativa Militar, Lisboa, 1911.

FERREIRA, C.E.J.F., *Manual Jurídico dos Cidadãos Indo-Portugueses*, Tip. Rangel, Bastorá, 1909.

FERREIRA, M. António, *Os que fizeram Portugal*. Tip. Rangel, Bastora, 1942.

FERTERO, Agostinho, *Portugal- O Factor principal da civilização moderna*, Tip. Silvas, Lisboa.

FICALHO, Conde de, *Garcia de Orta e o seu Tempo*, Imp. Nac., Lisboa, 1886

- *Memória sobre a Malagueta*, AGU. Lisboa, 1945.

FIGUEIREDO, Candido de, *A Penalidade na Índia segundo o Codigo de Manu*, Imp. Nac. Lisboa, 1892.

FIGUEIREDO, João de, *Relações entre Metrópole e a Índia*, Ed. Anglo-Lusitano, Nova Goa, 1934.

FONSÉCA, Faustino da, *A Descoberta do Brasil*, Liv. Central de Gomes de Carvalho, Lisboa, 1908.

FONSÉCA, L. Adão da, *O Essencial sobre Bartolomeu Dias*, Imp. Nac., Lisboa, 1987.

FONSÉCA, Quirino da, *A Obra Colonial de Afonso D'Albuquerque*, Typ da Coop. Militar, Lisboa, 1910.

- *Os Navios do Infante D. Henrique*, 1958.

GALVÃO, António, *Tratado dos Descobrimentos*, Liv. Civil., Porto, 1944.

GANDAVO, Pero de M. de, *História da Província Santa Cruz a que vulgarmente chamam Brasil*, Acad. Sciên., Lisboa, 1858.

GARCIA, Ismael, *As Comunidades de Goa*, Tip. Rangel, Bastorá, 1907.

GODINHO, P. Manuel, *Relações do Novo Caminho da Índia para Portugal*, Imp. Nac., Lisboa, 1974.

GODINHO, Vitorino Magalhães, *A Expansão Quatrocentista Portuguesa Problemas das origens e da linha de evolucão*, Imp. Cont. de Edições, Lisboa, 1944.

- *Documentos sobre a Expansão Portuguesa*, Ed. Gleba, Lisboa, vol. II, 1945-1956.

- *História Económica e Social da Expansão Portuguesa*, Terra Ed., Lisboa, 1947.

GÓIS, Damião de, *Chronica d'El-Rei D. Manuel. Escriptório*, vols. I-X, Lisboa, 1909-1912.

- *Opúsculos Históricos*, Liv. Civilização, Porto, 1945.

GONÇALVES, C., *O Estado da Índia, Passado e Presente*, SGL, Lisboa, 1947.

- *O Império Português no Séc. XIX, Contribuição para uma História Geral*, Minerva, V.N. de Famalicão, 1942.

GONÇALVES, José J., *Sintese Bibliogrãfica de Goa*, AGC. Lisboa, 1966-1967.

GONÇALVES, J·lio, *Capitão Renato Baptista: O Seu Centenário 1855-1955*, Tip. G. & Rodrigues, Lisboa, 1955, (sep. BSGL, Out-Dez)

- *Da Crise do Arabismo: As Chamadas " Crises do Suez e da Síria", Esboço de Síntese Histórica, Casa Portuguesa*, Lisboa, 1957 (sep. *BSGL*, Abril-Junho)

- *Da Finalidade do Descobrimentos. (Filosofia da História Marítima da Índia,)* Typ. LCGG, Lisboa, 1949.

- *Affonso de Albuquerque*, Imp. Moderna, Porto, 1907.

- *Marco Paolo e os Portugueses: Duas fases de Geografia do Oriente*, G. e Rodrigues, Lisboa, 1955, (sep. BSGL Junho-Set.).

- *Os Portugueses e o Mar das Índias da Índia antiga e Sua História*, Liv. Luso-Espanhola, Lisboa, 1947.

- *Seis Fortalezas, Feitórias da Índia- Introdução a uma História do Dominio Português no Oriente*, Tip. Liga dos Combatentes da Grande Guerra, Lisboa, 1943.

- *Sobre uma Hermeneutica dos Descobrimentos: Notas Criticas(Filosofia da História Marítima Portuguesa)*, LCGG, Lisboa, 1954.

- *Valentim Fernandes, Rodrigues de Santinella, and The Recognition of the Antilles as "Opposite Índia"*, C. Portuguesa, Lisboa, 1957 (sep. *BSGL*, Julho-Set).

GONÇALVES, L. M. J. F., *Ensaio Histórico de Portugal*, Tip. Ultramar, Margão, 1864.

GRACIAS, A.C.G. da Silva, *Os Lusos Descendentes da Índia*, Rangel, Bastora, 1920.

GRACIAS, Amâncio, *Portugal na Índia*, Ed. Col. Div. Cultural, nº 8, Goa, 1946.

GRACIAS, J.A. Ismael, *Carta Constitucional da monarchia Portugueza e seus actos addicionais*, Imp. Nac., Nova Goa, 1895.

- *Legislação para a administração das confrarias 1878-1886*, Imp. Nac., Nova Goa, 1886.

- *Leis Orgânicas da Administração Civil e Financeira das províncias Ultramarinas*, Imp. Nac., Nova Goa, 1914.

- *Regimento do Conselho de Governo do Estado da Índia*, Imp. Nac., Nova Goa, 1934.

GRACIAS, J.B. Amâncio, *Affonso de Albuquerque*, Imp. Nac., Nova Goa, 1911.

- *Origens do Christianismo na Índia*, Typ. Univ., Lisboa, 1903.

GUERREIRO, Amora D., *Panorama Económico dos Descobrimentos Henriquinos*, 1961.

GUIMARÃES, A. J. Gonçalves. *Chronica do Principe Dom Joam*. Imp. da Univ. Coimbra 1905.

HALL, D.G.E., *A History of South East Asia*, Macmillan, London, 1956.

HARMAND, Jules, *Domination et colonisation*, Ernest Flammarion, Paris, 1910.

JESUS, Montalto de, *O Oriente Modernizado, Horoscópio Internacional*, Lisboa, 1912.

JORGE, Evagrio, *Goas awakening*, Reminiscences of the 1946.

KAYE, John W., The *Administration of the East India Company. A History of Indian Progress*, London, 1853.

KINKAID, C. A., e Parasnis, *Rao Bahadur, History of the Maratha People*, Oxford, 1931.

- *The Invasion of Indian from Central Asia*, Rechar Bently & Sons, London.

LANGHANS, F.P. de Almeida, *Armorial do Ultramar Português*, vols.1-2, Agen. Geral Ult., Lisboa, 1966.

LAPA, Rodrigues, *Quadros da História Trágico-Marítima*, Imp. L. da Silva, Lisboa, 1951.

LAVAL, F. Pyrard de, *Viagem de Francisco Pyrard de Laval*, Liv. Civilização, Porto, 1944.

LAWRENCE, Leo, *Nehru sizes Goa*, Pageant Press, New York, 1963.

LEITÃO, Comt. Humberto, *Dois Roteiros do Séc. XVI de Manuel Monteiro e Gaspar Ferreira Rumão, Atribuídos a João Baptista Lavanha*, C.E.H.U., Lisboa, 1963.

LIMA, Américo P. de, *A Botica de Bordo de Fernão de Magalhães*, Porto, 1942. (sep. dos *Anais* de Fac. de Farmácia do Porto)

LOBATO, Alexandre, *Estado da Índia*, AGU., Lisboa, 1955.
- *Fundação do Estado da Índia em 1505*, AGU, Lisboa, 1955.
- *Índia: Relações Luso-Maratas, 1658-1737*, CEHU, Lisboa, 1965.
- *Notas sobre O Estado Portuguesa da Índia*, AGU, Lisboa, 1954.

LOBO, F. M. da Costa, *A ação diplomática dos Portugueses nos Séculos XV e XVI, destinada a realização de descobertas e conquistas*, S. N. Typ., Lisboa, 1937.
- *A Secção marítima dos Portugueses*, Imp. Nac., Lisboa, 1929.

LOPES, David, (ed.) *Chronica dos reis de Bisnaga*, (ms. inédito do Séc. XVI, Soc. de Geog. de Lisboa, Imp. Nac., Lisboa, 1897.
- Extractos da História da Conquista de Yaman pelos Othomanos.
- *História dos Portugueses no Malabar, ou Tuhfat-ul-Mujahedin. por Zain-ud-Din* (ms. do Séc. XVI), Imp. Nac., Lisboa, 1898.

LUÍZ, D. França S., *Portugueses em África, Ásia, América e Oceania*, Typ. Borges, Lisboa. vols. I-VI, 1848-1850.

LUPI, Eduardo do Couto, *A Empresa Portuguesa do Oriente, Conquista e Sustentação do Senhorio do Mar, (Séc. XVI)* AGU, Lisboa, 1943.

MACHADO, A. Reis, (ed.) *Collecção de opúsculos reimpressos-relativos a História dos navegações, viagens, e conquistas dos Portugueses*, Acad. Sciên., Lisboa, 1844.
- *História das causas que o muy esforçado capt. D. Cristovão da Gama fes nos reynos do Preste João, com quatrocentos Portugueses que consigo levou*, Acad. Sciên., Lisboa.
- *Livro em que dá relação do que viu e ouviu no Oriente, Duarte Barbosa*, AGC, Lisboa, 1946.

MACHADO, A.B., *Memória para a História del-Rey D. Sebastião*, tomos 1-3. Off. Joseph A. de Sylva, Lisboa, 1736-1747.

MACHADO, F. Falcão, *Os Descobrimentos no Reinado do D. João II, 1481-1495*, Off. Atlântica, Coimbra, 1929.

MAHEM, Conde de, *Goa Nossa Terra*, Liv. Popular, Lisboa, 1940.

MAJUMDAR, R. C., *An advanced History of India*, Macmillan, London, 1956.

MANOEL, J. de Canoso, *Missões dos Jesuitas no Oriente nos Séc. XVI e XV*, Imp. Nac., Lisboa, 1894.

MARKHAN, Clements R., *A General Sketch of the History of Persia*, Longman Green, London, 1874.

MARTINS, Bertos, *Tempo de Falar (Diário da Invasão de Goa)*, Casa Portuguesa, Lisboa, 1961.

MARTINS, J. F. Ferreira, *Fernão D'Albuquerque, Ed. Cosmos, Lisboa, 1938.*

- *História da Misericórdia de Goa (1520-1620)*, 3 vols., Imp. Nac., Nova Goa, 1910-1914.

MARTINS, Oliveira, *O Brasil e as Colonias Portuguesas*, Guimarães, Lisboa, 1953.

- *Sistema dos Mitos Religiosos*, Guimarães Ed., Lisboa, 1953.

MASCARENHA, António, *Essays for Diplomats on the Case of Goa*, Ed. Paulista, Lisboa, 1959.

MASCARENHAS, Constâncio, *O Descobrimento do Caminho Marítimo da Índia*, Tip. Rangel, Bastorá, 1949.

MAURICIO, Domingo, *A "Carta do Preste João" dos Indus e seu reflexo nas Descobertas do Infante D. Henrique*, Brotéria, Lisboa, 1960.

MAXMULLER, F. Max, *The Six Systems of Indian Philophy*, Longman-Green, London, 1919.

MELLO, Rudolfo de, *Goa as Union Territory*, A.C. Fernandes, Panjim, 1965.

MELO, M.J.H., *Portugal, o Ultramar e o futuro*, Gráfica Imperial, Lisboa, 1962.

MENDES, A. Lopes, *A Índia Portugueza*, 2 vols., Imp. Nac., Lisboa, 1886.

MENDONÇA, A. P. Lopes de, *Damião de Góes e a Inquisição de Portugal*, Acad. Sciên., Lisboa, 1859.

MENDONÇA, H. Lopes de, *Navegaçaõ dos Portugueses*, Imp. Nac., Lisboa, 1929.

- *Caracter e Influência da Obra do Infante*, Liv. Ferrin, Lisboa, 1894.

MONTEIRO, J.M. de Souza, *Diccionário Geographico das provincias e posseções Portuguezas no Ultramar etc.* Typ. Lisbonense, Lisboa, 1850.

MORAIS, A Faria de, *Índia -Terra Nostra,* Ed. Santelmo, Lisboa, 1954.

MORAIS, T.F. de, *China e Portugal,* Typ. LCGG, Lisboa, 1943.

MORAVIA, Alberto, *Uma Visão da Índia,* Arcadia, Lisboa.

NOGUEIRA, A. F., *A Índia Portugueza em 1887,* Typ. C. A. Rodrigues, Lisboa, 1890.

- *O Descobrimento da América e o Tratado de Tordesilhas.*

OLIVEIRA, Armando, *Os navios de Vasco da Gama,* JIU, Coimbra, 1973.

PATO, Bulhão, *Portuguezes na Índia,* Imp. Nac., Lisboa, 1883.

PEDROSO, S. Souza, *Resumo Histórico acerca da Antiga Índia Portugueza,* Acad. Sciên., Lisboa.

PEDROZO, Z. Consiglieri, *Influência dos Descobrimentos dos Portuguezes na História da Civilização,* Off. Typ., Lisboa, 1898.

PEREIRA, A. Gonçalves, *Índia Portuguesa.* AGU, Lisboa, 1954.

PEREIRA, André Gonçalves, *O Ultramar Português no plano mundial,* SGL, Lisboa, 1959.

PEREIRA, J.P.J. dos Santos, *Chatrias,* Tip. Índia-Portuguesa, Orlim, 1899.

PERES, Damião, *Américo Vespucci e a expedicão de 1501-1502 (resposta de Marconde de Sousa)* Portucalense, Porto, 1940.

- *O descobrimento do Brasil por Pedro Álvares Cabral.* Comp. Ed. do Minho, Barcelos, 1949.

- *Uma Prioridade Portuguesa Contestada mas Incontestável: A Circum navegação da África Austral por Bartolomeu Dias,* APH, Lisboa, 1960.

PERESTELO, M. M., *Roteiro da África do Sul e Sueste desde Cabo da Boa Esperança até ao das Corrente (1576),* AGC, Lisboa, 1939.

PERGALLO, P., *Carta de El-Rei D. Manuel ao Rei catholico- narrandolhe as viagens Portuguesas a Índia desde 1500-1505,* Acad. das Sciên., Lisboa, 1892.

PERREIRA, J., *Roteiro Portuguez de Viagem de Lisboa à Índia nos Séculos XVI e XV.* Imp. Nac., Lisboa, 1898.

PIERIS, P. E., *Portugal in Ceylon, 1505-1658,* Colombo Daily News Press, 1948.

PIMENTA, Énio, *Glimpses into Goas' Heritage, A Memorandum to the Prime Minister Bureau of Goanology,* Xaverian Press, Goa, 1963.

PIMENTEL, Luís S., *Prática da Arte de Navegar*, AGU, Lisboa, 1960.

PINTO, F. de Paula Leite, *Les découvertes Portugaises*, Coimbra, 1936.

PISSURLENKAR, P.S.S., *Goa pre-portuguesa através dos escritores lusitanos dos Séculos XVI e XVII*, Rangel, Bastorá, Goa 1962

- *A antiga Índia e o mundo externo*, Liv. Coelho, Goa, 1922.
- *A Portuguese Record on Rustamji Manekji- The Parsi Broker of Surat*, Sadanand press, Nova Goa, 1933.
- *Aspectos da civilização da Índia Antiga*, Liv. Coelho, Goa, 1925.
- *Os Portugueses nas Literaturas Indianas dos Séc. XVI, XV*, Lisboa,1955
- *Os primeiros livros Maratas impressos em Goa*, Rangel, Bastorá, 1956.

PRESTAGE, Edgar, *The Portuguese Voyages of Discovery, A Lecture by...* at the King's College London, Ang.-Port. Soc., London, 1939.

- *Viagens Portuguesas de Descobrimento*, Liv. Portugßlia, Lisboa, 1940.

PRESTAGE, Edgar/ P. D', Castelo, *Registo de Freguesia de S. Cruz de Azevedo, desde 1536-1628*, Imp. Univ. de Coimbra, 1913.

PRIOLKAR, A.K., *The Goan Inquisition*. V.G. Mogho,

RAMÚSIO, G. B., *Delle Navigatione et viaggi nel qval si contien la descriptione della África, et del paese del prete lanni, con uarii viaggi, del mar rosso a Calicut, & infin all isol e Moluçhe, doue nascone les spertieri, et la navigacione attorno il mondo, Herede-di Lvcantonio Givnti*, Veneza, 1550. (1a. ed)

REGO, António da Silva, *O Oriente e o Ocidente, ensaios*, Off. S. José. Lisboa, 1939.

REIS, Eduardo, *O Noticiarista das Índias- Duarte de Barbosa*, Imp. Nac., Macau, 1948.

REIS, Lara, *Praias de Calicut; Em busca do local onde desembarcou V. da Gama, visita ao Samorim de Calicut*, P.C. Kunni Raja, Imp. Nac., Nova Goa, 1945.

RIBEIRO, Freitas/ Lagoas, Visconde de, *Grandes Viagens Portuguesas de Descobrimentos e Expansão: Antecedentes Históricos, Sinopse e Esquematização Cartográfica*, J. das Missões, Lisboa, 1951.

RIBEIRO, Luciano, *Collectanea de documentos acerca de D. Sebastião*. CEHU, Lisboa, 1960.

- *Em torno do primeiro cerco de Diu*, CEHU, Lisboa, 1964.
- *Mais documentos relativos ao primeiro cerco de Diu*, CEHU, Lisboa, 1966 .
- *O primeiro cerco de Diu*, CEHU, Lisboa, 1958 (sep. *Stvdia* N° 1)
- *Registo da Casa da Índia*, 2 vols., AGU, Lisboa, 1954.

RODRIGUES, Santana, *A Índia Portuguesa*, J. Rodrigues, Lisboa, 1926.

ROSSI, Guiseppe Carlo, *Navegações de Luís de Cadamosto*, IAC, Lisboa, (ed. Bi-Ling., Italiano-Português).

SÁ DA BANDEIRA, Marquês de, *O Trabalho Rural Africano e Administração Colonial*, Imp. Nac., Lisboa, 1873.

SÁ, Adriano de, *Pela Índia: Aspectos e Impressões*, Liv. Rodrigues, Lisboa, 1925.

SÁ, J. Maria de, *Projecto de codigo das Communidades Agricolas de Goa*, Imp. Nac., Nova Goa, 1879.

SACARDANDO, B.K.D. Sinai, *A Índia Portuguesa: Memórias Escritas A Convite do Governo Geral do Estado da Índia*, 2 vols., Imp. Nac., Nova Goa, 1923.

- *Índia Portuguesa, Anuário*, Imp. Nac., Nova Goa, ano I-VI, 1929-1939.

- *Sétimo Congresso provincial da Índia Portuguesa*. Typ. Brangança, Nova Goa, 1927.

SANCEAU, Elaine, *D. João de Castro*, Lic. Civ., Porto, 1946.

- *O Senhor da Índia, Afonso de Albuquerque*, Liv. Civil., Porto, 1943.

SANTARÉM, Visconde de, *Corpo diplomático Portuguêz, Portugal e a Hespanha*, J.P. Aillaud, Paris, 1846.

- *Prioridade dos Descobrimentos Portugueses*, Lisboa, 1958.

SANZ, Carlos, *Informacion de Reino de la China impressa en Coimbra en lengua castellano el an. 1565. Y Reproducida, con algumas variantes en alcala de Henares en 1575*, Graf. Yogues, Madrid.

- *Primea Relacion Publicado en Europa del-Reno de la China Impres (Em Coimbra) en 1555 y Reproducida en Zaragosa en 1561*, Graf. Yogues, Madrid.

- *Primer document impreso de la História de la Islas Filipinas: Relato la espedicion de legazpi que LLego a Cebu en 1565*, Estampado em Borcelana el ano 1565,. Graf. Yogues, Madrid,

SEHEFER, M. Charles, *Navigation de Vasquo da Gamma*, Ernest Laroux, Paris, 1898.

SERPA, A. Ferreira de, *Cronica de El-Rei D. Sebastião Pelo Padre Amador Rebelo*, Porto, 1925.

- *Como se Faz a História dos Descobrimentos*, Lisboa, 1936.

SHILLINGTON, V.M., e Chapman, A.B. Wallis, *The Commercial Relation of England and Portugal*, Gerg. Routledge, London.

SILVA, A.A, Baldagne da, *O Descobrimento do Brasil por Pedro* Álvares Cabral, Acad. Sciên., Lisboa, 1892.

SILVA, Agostinho da, *Antologia, Damião de Góis: Descobrimentos dos Portugueses*, Vila Nova de Famalicão, 1941.
- *A Primeira volta ao Mundo*, V. N. Famalicão, 1939.

SILVEIRA, Luís, *Peregrinação de André de Foro à terra dos Gentios*, Tip. Portugal-Brasil, Lisboa, 1945.

SORI, A.F. Marx, *Descobrimentos dos Portugueses nos Séculos XV e XVI*, Typ. Castro & Irmãos, Lisboa, 1867.

SOUSA, Amândia Oscar da Cruz e, *Duas Palavras sobre a Índia Portugueza*, Goa, 1909.

SOUSA, D.A. Caetano de, *História genealógica da casa Real Portuguesa*, tomos 1-4, Atlântida-Liv., Coimbra, 1946-1949.

SOUSA, Frei Luís, *Anais de D. João I*, 4 vols., Liv. Sá da Costa, Lisboa, 1938,

SOUSA, O Marconde de, *A Expedicão de 1501-1502 e Américo Vespucci com parecer de D. Peres, refutado pelo autor*, S. Paulo, 1949.

STEPHENS, H. Morse, *Albuquerque*, Ed. Gama, Lisboa, 1948.
- *The History of Nations: Portugal*, T. Fisher Unwin, London, 1891.

VASCONSELLOS, E.J.C.E., *As Colónias Portuguesas*. Typ. Comp. Nac., Lisboa, 1896.

VASCONSELLOS, F. de, *Armada da Carreira da Índia de 1560 a 1590. Relação de Duarte Gomes*. Casa Portuguesa, Lisboa, 1938.

VASCONSELOS, Basílio de, *Collecção de Notícias para História das Nações Ultramarinas*, Acad. Sciên., Lisboa, 1812.

VELHO, Álvaro, *Roteiro da primeira viagem de Vasco da Gama (1497-1499)*, AGU, Lisboa, 1969.

VELLOSO, Queiroz, *D. Sebastião, 1554-1578*, Imp. Nac., Lisboa, 1935.
- *O Reinado do Cardeal D. Henrique*, Imp. Nac., Lisboa, 1946.

VIANA, Mário Gonçalves, *Vasco da Gama*, ed. Eduardo Naci., Porto, 1937.
- *Afonso de Albuquerque*, Imp. Port., Porto, 1939.

WARNER-LIE, W., *Relação chronologica summária das navegações, descobrimentos e conquistas dos Portugueses*, Imp. Nac., Lisboa, 1840.

WING-TSIT CHAN / e Outros, *Filosofia del Oriente*, México, 1965.

XAVIER, Alberto, *A Índia Portuguesa, A Face da Razão e do direito*, SNI, Lisboa, 1950.

XAVIER, Filipe Nery, *Codigo dos usos e costumes dos habitantes das novas conquistas em Portuguez e Maratha*, Imp. Nac., Nova Goa, 1861.

ZAMARA, J. Clemente, *O Processo Histórico*, Liv. Renaisença, Lisboa, 1946.

ZWEIG, Stefan, *Fernão de Magalhães*, Liv. Civil., Porto, 1943.

Cartografia

ALBUQUERQUE, L.M. de, *O Livro de Marinharia de André Pires*, JIU., Lisboa, 1963.

- *Os Guias Náuticos de Munique e Évora*, JIU., Lisboa, 1965.

CARVALHO, J. B. de, *La Traduction Espagnole du "De Sitv Orbis" de Pomponivs Mela Par maitre Joan Faras Et Les notes Marginales de Duarte Pacheco Perreira*, JIU., Lisboa, 1974.

CORTESÃO, A., *Cartografia e Cartógrafos Portugueses dos Séculos XV e XVI*, 2 vols., ed. Seara Nova, Lisboa, 1935.

COUTINHO, A.G. e Bras, *A Náutica dos Descobrimentos*, 2 vols., C. Moura, AGGU., Lisboa, 1951.

DOURADO, F. Vaz, *Atlas de Fernão Vaz Dourado, Reproduc. Torre de Tombo*, Goa 1571, Pub. Liv. Civ., Porto, 1948.

-*Planta de cidade de Nova Goa de 1888*, Desenhado por José Francisco de Silva, Imp. Nac., Nova Goa, 1888.

EÇA, V. M. M. e Almeida D., *O Infante D. Henrique e a arte de Navegar dos Portuguezes*, Livraria Ferin, Lisboa, 1894.

MENDONÇA, H.L. de, *Estudos sobre Navios Portuguezes nos Séculos XV e XVI*, Acad. Sciên., Lisboa, 1892.

OLIVEIRA, J.B. de, *Os navios de Vasco da Gama*, Acad. Sciên., Lisboa, 1892.

PERES, Damião, *História dos Descobrimentos Portugueses*, ed. Portucalense, Porto, 1943.

REGO, A. da Silva, e Santos, Edwardo dos, *Atlas Missionário Português*, JIU., Lisboa, 1964.

Fontes Bibliograficas Sobre Macau

Manusripto

AHU Lisboa

Caixas de Macau

Caixas 1-60

Códices

Nº 1652, 1783, 2139

Biblioteca Da Ajuda

Jesuitas na Ásia,

Cód. 46-xiii-30, pp. 21-24, 32-33

Cód. 50-v-37, pp. 403-513

Obras Publicadas

AHMAD, Afzal, "Macau: Um Breve Estudo de Desenvolvimento Económico-Comercial nos Séculos XVI-XVIII," in ***As Relações Entre Índia Portuguesa, A Ásia do Sueste e o Extremo Oriente,*** (Actas do VI Seminário Indo-Português, Macau, 1991), Macau-Lisboa, 1993.

-"Portugal na Rota do Oriente: O Comércio Indo-Português (1498-1663)", in ***Liberdade,*** Vol.1, nº 2, Anais Científicos da Universidade Independente, Lisboa, 1998.

-"Macau nos Séculos XVII e XVIII, Algumas Correspondências do Leal Senado de "Cidade do Nome de Deos na China"", in ***Liberdade,*** *Vol.2, nº 1,* Anais Científicos da Universidade Independente, Lisboa, 2000

BALL, J. Dyer, M.R.A.S., *The Holy City; The Gem of the Oriental Earth,* The China Bapt. Soc. Canton, 1905.

BARREIROS, Leopoldo Danilo, *Instrucção-que o senado da Câmara de Macau oferece ao Exmº. Sr. D. Alexandre de Gouvêa,* Bispo de Pekim. Macau.

BIKER, J.F.J., *Memória Sobre o Estabelecimento de Macau (Embaixada Portuguesa a corte de Pekim no ano 1752),* Lisboa, 1879.

BOXER, C.R., e Braga J.M., *Algumas Notas sobre a bibliografia de Macau,* Escola Tip. Salesiana, Macau-China, 1939.

BOXER, C. R., *The Great Ship from Amacon,* ICM, (segunda Ed.) Macau, 1988.

-*Fidalgos no Extremo Oriente, Fundação Oriente*, Macau, 1990.

-*Portuguese Society in the Tropics: the Municipal Councils of Goa, Macau, Bahia e Luanda*, 1510-1800.

BRAGA, J .M., *A Igreja De S. Domingos E Os Dominicanos Em Macau*, Orfano da Imaculada Conceição, Macau, 1939.

BRAZÃO, Eduardo, *A Restauração-Relações diplomáticas de Portugal de 1640 a 1668*, Lisboa, 1939.

- *Apontamentos para a História das Relações diplomáticas de Portugal com a China: (1516-1753)*, Lisboa, 1949.

- Macau-*Cidade do Nome de Deus na China-Não há outro Mais Leal*, AGU, Lisboa

- *Subsídios para a História das Relações diplomáticas de Portugal com a China: A Emb. de Manuel de Saldanha (1667-1670)*, Macau, 1948.

- *The Anglo-Portuguese Alliance*, London, 1957.

CHANG, T'ien-Tsê, *Sino-Portuguese Trade From 1514 to 1644*, Leyden, 1969.

COATES, Austin, *Macau: Calçada da Histêria*, ICM, Macau, 1991.

FRANÇA, António Pinto da, *Portuguese Influênce in Indonesia*, Djakarta, 1970.

FRANÇA, Bento da, *Macau e os Seus Habitantes (Relações com Timor)*, Imp. Nac., Lisboa, 1897.

-*Subsídios para a História de Macau*, Imp. Nac., Lisboa, 1888.

FREITAS, J. de Aquino Guimarães e, *Memória Sobre Macau*, Coimbra, 1828.

GUNN, Geoffrey C., *Ao Encontro de Macau*, Uma Cidade-Estado portuguesa na periferia da China, 1557-1999

INSO, Capitão-Tenente J. do, *Macau, A mais antiga Colonia Europeia no Extremo-Oriente*, Tip. O.I. Conceição, Macau-China, 1930.

JESUS, C.A. Montalto de, *Macau Histórico*, Livros do Oriente, Macau, 1990.

JOBEZ, R.E., *Macau at the End of the XVIIIth Century*, Imp. Nac., 1949.

LIMA, Durval R. Pires de, *A Embaixada de Manuel de Saldanha ao Imperador K'hang Hi en 1667-1670, (Subsídio para a História de Macau)*, Lisboa, 1930.

MACHADO, Herlander, *Macau de ontem e de hoje (síntese Histórica)* Lisboa, 1981.

MANGUIN, Pierre-Yves, *Os Nguyen: Macau e Portugal*, CTMCDO-ICM, Macau, 1999

MATOS, A. Teodoro de, e Thomaz, L. F. Reis, (ed.) *As Relações Entre A Índia Portuguesa, A Ásia do Sueste e o Extremo Oriente*, (Actas do VI Seminário Indo-Portuguesa, Macau, 22 a 26 de Outubro de 1991), Macau-Lisboa, 1993.

MATTA, J. Caeiro da, *La Colonie de Macau Et la Question du Trafic de Lópium*, Lisbonne, 1940.

MESQUITELA, Gonçalo, *História de Macau*, 3 vols., Instituto Cultural de Macau, 1997

MOURA, Carlos Francisco, *Macau e o Comércio Português com a China e o Japão nos Séculos XVI e XVII*, Imp. Nac., Macau, 1937.

OLIVEIRA, A. Rodriques de, <Macau e o seu Movimento Marítimo>, in *BJNMM.*, N° XXXV, Jan. 1958, pp. 103- 114.

PEREIRA, A. Marques, *As Alfândegas Chinesas de Macau*, vol., I.

- *O Padroado Portuguez Na China*, Imp. Nac., Lisboa, 1873.

PINA, A. Abrisio de, <Macau no Século XVII> in *Portugal em África*, vol. XIV, Nov.-Dez. pp. 343-360.PIRES, Benjamin Videira, *A Viagem de comércio Macau- Manila nos Séculos XVI a XIX*, Imp. Nac., Macau, 1971.

REGO, António da Silva, *A Presença de Portugal em Macau*, AGC., Lisboa, 1946.

-*O Ultramar Português no Século (XVIII)*, 1700-1833.

REGO, Francisco de Carvalho, *Macau*, Macau, 1950.

SEBBES, Joseph, S.J., *O Diário do Padre Tomás Perreiras, S.J*, Os Jesuitas e o Tratado Sino-Russo de Nerchinsk (1689), CTMCDO-ICM, Macau, 1999

TANG, Domingo, (Chinês), *Macau, ponto de Irradição do Lusismo no Extremo-Oriente*, Soc. Nac. Tipografica, Lisboa, 1938.

TÇUZZU, S.J. Padre João Rodrigues, *História da Igreja do Japão*, (X-Colecção Notícias de Macau-XI), Noticias de Macau, 1954.

TEIXEIRA, Padre Manuel, *Macau e a Sua Diocese, no ano dos centenários da Fundação e Restauração*, Macau, 1940.

-*Macau no Século XVIII*, Tip. Mandarin, Macau, 1981.

TOMÉ PIRES, *The Suma Oriental of Tomé Pires and The Book of Francisco Rodrigues*, 2 vols., Hakluyt Society, London, 1944.

VASCONCELOS, Frazão de, *A Aclamação Delrei D. João IV em Macau*, (sep. do *Bol. da Agen.G. Col.* N° 53), Lisboa, 1929.

-*Naufrágio da Nau São Paulo ao Pé de Samatra em 1561*, 1948.